Vocabulary Workshop
New Edition

Level G

Jerome Shostak

Series Consultants

Sylvia A. Rendón, Ph.D.
Coord., Secondary Reading
Cypress-Fairbanks I.S.D.
Houston, Texas

John Heath, Ph.D.
Department of Classics
Santa Clara University
Santa Clara, California

Mel H. Farberman
Director of English
 Language Arts, K–12
Bay Shore U.F.S.D.
Bay Shore, New York

Sadlier-Oxford
A Division of William H. Sadlier, Inc.

Reviewers

The publisher wishes to thank for their comments and suggestions the following teachers and administrators, who read portions of the series prior to publication.

Anne S. Crane
Clinician, English Education
Georgia State University
Atlanta, GA

Susan W. Keogh
Curriculum Coordinator
Lake Highland Preparatory
Orlando, FL

Mary Louise Ellena-Wygonik
English Teacher
Hampton High School
Allison Park, PA

Lisa Anne Pomi
Language Arts Chairperson
Woodside High School
Woodside, CA

Arlene A. Oraby
Dept. Chair (Ret.), English 6–12
Briarcliff Public Schools
Briarcliff Manor, NY

Susan Cotter McDonough
English Department Chair
Wakefield High School
Wakefield, MA

Sr. M. Francis Regis Trojano
Sisters of St. Joseph (CSJ)
Educational Consultant
Boston, MA

Keith Yost
Director of Humanities
Tomball Ind. School District
Tomball, TX

Patricia M. Stack
English Teacher
South Park School District
South Park, PA

Joy Vander Vliet
English Teacher
Council Rock High School
Newtown, PA

Karen Christine Solheim
English Teacher
Jefferson High School
Jefferson, GA

Photo Credits

Corbis/Bettmann: 27, 90, 104, 163; Galen Rowell: 41; Robert Holmes: 57; George McCarthy: 97; Kelly-Mooney Photography: 116, 170; Joe McDonald: 123; Hulton-Deutsch Collection: 137; Free Agents Limited: 156. *Getty Images*/Stone/Kim Westerskov: 34; The Bridgeman Art Library: 83; Taxi/Chip Simons: 182. *Hans Namuth Ltd*: 64. *The Kobal Collection*: 130. *Lonely Planet Images*/Catherine Hanger: 149. *Picturequest*/Corbis: 71.

S is a registered trademark of William H. Sadlier, Inc.

Printed in the United States of America.
ISBN: 0-8215-7112-5
9/10 09 08

PREFACE

For more than five decades, VOCABULARY WORKSHOP has proven a highly successful tool for guiding systematic vocabulary growth and developing vocabulary skills. It has also been shown to be a valuable help to students preparing for standardized tests. This New Edition of VOCABULARY WORKSHOP has been prepared in recognition of important changes to these tests, with the introduction of two features designed to address the new emphasis on writing skills, including grammar, and reading skills on those tests.

A new **Vocabulary for Comprehension** section appears in each of the five Reviews. This two-page feature is modeled on the reading sections of standardized tests, and as in those tests, presents reading comprehension questions, including specific vocabulary-related ones, based on a reading passage. (For more on Vocabulary for Comprehension, see page 13.)

Following Vocabulary for Comprehension in each of the Reviews is another new feature called **Grammar in Context**. This one-page exercise is linked to the reading passage that precedes it, referring to a grammar or usage topic illustrated in the passage and then reviewing that topic with a brief explanation and practice questions. (For more on Grammar in Context, see page 16.)

The 15 Units that form the core of VOCABULARY WORKSHOP remain unchanged. Each of the Units comprises a five-part lesson consisting of **Definitions**, **Completing the Sentence**, **Synonyms and Antonyms**, **Choosing the Right Word**, and **Vocabulary in Context**. Together, these exercises provide multiple and varied exposures to the taught words, an approach that has been shown to be consistent with and supportive of research-based findings in vocabulary instruction.

Enrichment and vocabulary-building exercises also remain in the form of **Building with Classical Roots**, **Word Associations**, and **Word Families** in the Reviews, and **Analogies** and **Enriching Your Vocabulary** in the Cumulative Reviews.

In this Level of Vocabulary Workshop you will study 300 key words. The words in this Level, as well as all of the other Levels of this series, have been selected on the following bases: currency and general usefulness; frequency of appearance on recognized vocabulary lists; applicability to, and appearance on, standardized tests; and current grade-level research.

ONLINE COMPONENTS
www.vocabularyworkshop.com

At the **www.vocabularyworkshop.com** Web site you will also find **interactive vocabulary games and puzzles** that will help reinforce and enrich your understanding of the key words in this level of VOCABULARY WORKSHOP.

CONTENTS

PRONUNCIATION KEY

The pronunciation is indicated for every basic word introduced in this book. The symbols used for this purpose, as listed below, are similar to those appearing in most standard dictionaries of recent vintage. (Pronunciation keys and given pronunciations sometimes differ from dictionary to dictionary.) The author has consulted a large number of dictionaries for this purpose but has relied primarily on *Webster's Third New International Dictionary* and *The Random House Dictionary of the English Language (Unabridged)*.

There are, of course, many English words for which two (or more) pronunciations are commonly accepted. In virtually all cases where such words occur in this book, the author has sought to make things easier for the student by giving just one pronunciation. The only significant exception occurs when the pronunciation changes in accordance with a shift in the part of speech. Thus we would indicate that *project* in the verb form is pronounced prə jekt′, and in the noun form, präj′ ekt.

It is believed that these relatively simple pronunciation guides will be readily usable by the student. It should be emphasized, however, that the *best* way to learn the pronunciation of a word is to listen to and imitate an educated speaker.

Vowels							
	ā	lake	e	stress	ü	loot, new
	a	mat	ī	knife	u̇	foot, pull
	â	care	i	sit	ə	jumping, broken
	ä	bark, bottle	ō	flow	ər	bird, better
	au̇	doubt	ô	all, cord		
	ē	beat, wordy	oi	oil		

Consonants							
	ch	child, lecture	s	cellar	wh	what
	g	give	sh	shun	y	yearn
	j	gentle, bridge	th	thank	z	is
	ŋ	sing	t̶h̶	those	zh	measure

All other consonants are sounded as in the alphabet.

Stress	The accent mark *follows* the syllable receiving the major stress: en rich′

Abbreviations						
	adj.	adjective	*n.*	noun	*prep.*	preposition
	adv.	adverb	*part.*	participle	*v.*	verb
	int.	interjection	*pl.*	plural		

THE VOCABULARY OF VOCABULARY

There are some interesting and useful words that we use to describe and identify words. The exercises that follow will help you to check and strengthen your knowledge of this "vocabulary of vocabulary."

Denotation and Connotation

The **denotation** of a word is its specific dictionary meaning. Here are a few examples:

Word	Denotation
bereft	deprived of
adroit	skillful
swerve	turn

The **connotation** of a word is its **tone**—that is, the emotions or associations it normally arouses in people using, hearing, or reading it. Depending on what these feelings are, the connotation of a word may be *favorable* (*positive*) or *unfavorable* (*negative, pejorative*). A word that does not normally arouse strong feelings of any kind has a *neutral* connotation. Here are some examples of words with different connotations:

Word	Connotation
bereft	unfavorable
adroit	favorable
swerve	neutral

Exercises *In the space provided, label the connotation of each of the following words* **F** *for "favorable,"* **U** *for "unfavorable," or* **N** *for "neutral."*

_____ **1.** hackneyed   _____ **3.** affable   _____ **5.** motley

_____ **2.** heinous   _____ **4.** fortuitous   _____ **6.** amenable

Literal and Figurative Usage

When a word is used in a **literal** sense, it is being employed in its strict (or primary) dictionary meaning in a situation (or context) that "makes sense" from a purely logical or realistic point of view. For example:

> Yesterday I read an old tale about a knight who slew a *fire-breathing* dragon.

In this sentence, *fire-breathing* is employed literally. The dragon is pictured as breathing real fire.

Sometimes words are used in a symbolic or nonliteral way in situations that do not "make sense" from a purely logical or realistic point of view. We call this nonliteral application of a word a **figurative** or **metaphorical** usage. For example:

> Suddenly my boss rushed into my office, *breathing fire.*

In this sentence *breathing fire* is not being used in a literal sense. That is, the boss was not actually breathing fire out of his nostrils. Rather, the expression is intended to convey graphically that the boss was very angry.

Exercises *In the space provided, write L for "literal" or F for "figurative" next to each of the following sentences to show how the italicized expression is being used.*

_____ **1.** She was so forgetful that she sometimes said her mind was a *sieve*.

_____ **2.** He strained his tea with a *sieve*.

_____ **3.** That suitcase weighed a *ton*!

Synonyms

A **synonym** is a word that has *the same* or *almost the same* meaning as another word. Here are some examples:

silent—quiet
ephemeral—transitory
happy—jovial

bellow—yell
pensive—thoughtful
proficient—skillful

Exercises *In each of the following groups, circle the word that is most nearly the* **synonym** *of the word in* **boldface** *type.*

1. amnesty
a. equanimity
b. culpability
c. gratitude
d. forgiveness

2. curtail
a. diminish
b. aggrandize
c. acknowledge
d. eschew

3. debase
a. raise
b. lower
c. deny
d. accept

4. aura
a. hemisphere
b. stratosphere
c. atmosphere
d. color

Antonyms

An **antonym** is a word that means *the opposite* of or *almost the opposite* of another word. Here are some examples:

dark—light
prudent—foolish
lax—strict

lethargic—energetic
gigantic—tiny
trivial—significant

Exercises *In each of the following groups, circle the word that is most nearly the* **antonym** *of the word in* **boldface** *type.*

1. berate
a. castigate
b. laud
c. equivocate
d. extenuate

2. erudite
a. encumbering
b. absorbing
c. scholarly
d. ignorant

3. galvanize
a. embroil
b. inhibit
c. elucidate
d. gesticulate

4. jejune
a. interesting
b. dry
c. southern
d. ecumenical

VOCABULARY STRATEGY: USING CONTEXT

How do you go about finding the meaning of an unknown or unfamiliar word that you come across in your reading? You might look the word up in a dictionary, of course, provided one is at hand. But there are two other useful strategies that you might employ to find the meaning of a word that you do not know at all or that is used in a way that you do not recognize. One strategy is to analyze the **structure** or parts of the word. (See pages 11 and 12 for more on this strategy.) The other strategy is to try to figure out the meaning of the word by reference to context.

When we speak of the **context** of a word, we mean the printed text of which that word is part. By studying the context, we may find **clues** that lead us to its meaning. We might find a clue in the immediate sentence or phrase in which the word appears (and sometimes in adjoining sentences or phrases, too); or we might find a clue in the topic or subject matter of the passage in which the word appears; or we might even find a clue in the physical features of a page itself. (Photographs, illustrations, charts, graphs, captions, and headings are some examples of such features.)

One way to use context as a strategy is to ask yourself what you know already about the topic or subject matter in question. By applying what you have learned before about deserts, for example, you would probably be able to figure out that the word *arid* in the phrase "the arid climate of the desert" means "dry."

The **Vocabulary in Context** exercises that appear in the Units and the **Vocabulary for Comprehension** and the **Choosing the Right Meaning** exercises that appear in the Reviews and Cumulative Reviews both provide practice in using context to determine the meaning of given words.

When you do the various word-omission exercises in this book, look for **context clues** built into the sentence or passage to guide you to the correct answer. Three types of context clues appear in the exercises in this book.

A **restatement clue** consists of a *synonym* for, or a *definition* of, the missing word. For example:

The summer humidity seemed to make everything wilt, and I could feel the _____ in the air.
a. wetness   b. pollen   c. excitement   d. boredom

In this sentence, *humidity* is a synonym of the missing word, *wetness*, and acts as a restatement clue for it.

A **contrast clue** consists of an *antonym* for, or a phrase that means the *opposite* of, the missing word. For example:

Though she was exhausted, she worked on the production with admirable (**energy,** lethargy).

In this sentence, *exhausted* is in contrast with the missing word, *energy*. This is confirmed by the presence of the word *though*. *Exhausted* thus functions as a contrast clue for *energy*.

An **inference clue** implies but does not directly state the meaning of the missing word or words. For example:

> It took a great deal of _____ to keep up with the rest of the pack as they sped across the broken and hilly _____ that separated them from the finish line in the cross country race.
>
> a. dispatch . . . apparel
> b. misgiving . . . repast
> c. stamina . . . terrain
> d. diversity . . . barrage

In this sentence, there are several inference clues: (a) *keep up with the rest of the pack* suggests the word *stamina* because people who keep up must by definition have stamina; the word *sped* suggests the same thing; (b) the words *broken* and *hilly* suggest *terrain* because they are both terms that describe terrain. Accordingly, all these words are inference clues because they suggest or imply, but do not directly state, the missing word or words.

Exercises

Use context clues to choose the word or words that complete each of the following sentences or sets of sentences.

1. It's better not to paraphrase lines from great works of literature if you can _____ them directly.

a. quote
b. copy
c. interpret
d. extrapolate

2. The town was the _____ it had been all year, and we trudged in thick boots through feet of white _____ every day on our way home from school.

a. wettest . . . rain
b. hottest . . . popcorn
c. quietest . . . air
d. coldest . . . snow

3. If you call my house before seven in the morning, it is (**unlikely, necessary**) that I will answer the phone.

VOCABULARY STRATEGY: WORD STRUCTURE

One important way to build your vocabulary is to learn the meaning of word parts that make up many English words. These word parts consist of **prefixes**, **suffixes**, and **roots**, or **bases**. A useful strategy for determining the meaning of an unknown word is to "take apart" the word and think about the parts. For example, when you look at the word parts in the word *invisible,* you find the prefix *in-* ("not") + the root *-vis-* ("see") + the suffix *-ible* ("capable of"). From knowing the meanings of the parts of this word, you can figure out that *invisible* means "not capable of being seen."

Following is a list of common prefixes. Knowing the meaning of a prefix can help you determine the meaning of a word in which the prefix appears.

Prefix	Meaning	Sample Words
bi-	two	bicycle
com-, con-	together, with	compatriot, contact
de-, dis-	lower, opposite	devalue, disloyal
fore-, pre-	before, ahead of time	forewarn, preplan
il-, im-, in-, ir, non-, un-	not	illegal, impossible, inactive, irregular, nonsense, unable
in-, im-	in, into	inhale, import
mid-	middle	midway
mis-	wrongly, badly	mistake, misbehave
re-	again, back	redo, repay
sub-	under, less than	submarine, subzero
super-	above, greater than	superimpose, superstar
tri-	three	triangle

Following is a list of common suffixes. Knowing the meaning and grammatical function of a suffix can help you determine the meaning of a word.

Noun Suffix	Meaning	Sample Nouns
-acy, -ance, -ence, -hood -ily -ment -ness, -ship	state, quality, or condition of, act or process of	adequacy, attendance, persistence, neighborhood, activity, judgment, brightness, friendship
-ant, -eer, -ent, -er, -ian, -ier, -ist, -or	one who does or makes something	contestant, auctioneer, resident, banker, comedian, financier, dentist, doctor
-ation, -ition, -ion	act or result of	organization, imposition, election

Verb Suffix	Meaning	Sample Verbs
-ate	to become, produce, or treat	validate, salivate, chlorinate
-en	to make, cause to be	weaken
-fy, -ify, -ize	to cause, make	liquefy, glorify, legalize

Adjective Suffix	Meaning	Sample Adjectives
-able, -ible	able, capable of	believable, incredible
-al, -ic,	relating to, characteristic of	natural, romantic
-ful, -ive, -ous	full of, given to, marked by	beautiful, protective, poisonous
-ish, -like	like, resembling	foolish, childlike
-less	lacking, without	careless

A **base** or **root** is the main part of a word to which prefixes and suffixes may be added. Many roots come to English from Latin, such as *-socio-,* meaning "society," or from Greek, such as *-logy-,* meaning "the study of." Knowing Greek and Latin roots can help you determine the meaning of a word such as *sociology,* which means "the study of society."

In the **Building with Classical Roots** sections of this book you will learn more about some of these Latin and Greek roots and about English words that derive from them. The lists that follow may help you figure out the meaning of new or unfamiliar words that you encounter in your reading.

Greek Root	Meaning	Sample Word
-astr-, -aster-, -astro-	star	astral, asteroid, astronaut
-auto-	self	autograph
-bio-	life	biography
-chron-, chrono-	time	chronic, chronological
-cosm-, -cosmo-	universe, order	microcosm, cosmopolitan
-cryph-, -crypt-	hidden, secret	apocryphal, cryptographer
-dem-, -demo-	people	epidemic, democracy
-dia-	through, across, between	diameter
-dog-, -dox-	opinion, teaching	dogmatic, orthodox
-gen-	race, kind, origin, birth	generation
-gnos-	know	diagnostic
-graph-, -graphy-, -gram-	write	graphite, autobiography, telegram
-log-, -logue-	speech, word, reasoning	logic, dialogue
-lys-	break down	analysis
-metr-, -meter-	measure	metric, kilometer
-micro-	small	microchip
-morph-	form, shape	amorphous
-naut-	sailor	cosmonaut
-phon-, -phone-, -phono-	sound, voice	phonics, telephone, phonograph
-pol-, -polis-	city, state	police, metropolis
-scop-, -scope-	watch, look at	microscope, telescope
-tele-	far off, distant	television
-the-	put or place	parentheses

Latin Root	Meaning	Sample Word
-cap-, -capt-, -cept-, -cip-	take	capitulate, captive, concept, recipient
-cede-, -ceed-, -ceas-, -cess-	happen, yield, go	precede, proceed, decease, cessation
-cred-	believe	incredible
-dic-, -dict-	speak, say, tell	indicate, diction
-duc-, -duct-, -duit-	lead, conduct, draw	educate, conduct, conduit
-fac-, -fact-, -fect-, -fic-, -fy-	make	faculty, artifact, defect, beneficial, clarify
-ject-	throw	eject
-mis-, -miss-, -mit-, -mitt-	send	promise, missile, transmit, intermittent
-note-, -not-	know, recognize	denote, notion
-pel-, -puls-	drive	expel, compulsive
-pend-, -pens-	hang, weight, set aside	pendulum, pension
-pon-, -pos-	put, place	component, position
-port-	carry	portable
-rupt-	break	bankrupt
-scrib-, -scribe-, -script-	write	scribble, describe, inscription
-spec-, -spic-	look, see	spectator, conspicuous
-tac-, -tag-, -tang-, -teg-	touch	contact, contagious, tangible, integral
-tain-, -ten-, -tin-	hold, keep	contain, tenure, retinue
-temp-	time	tempo
-ven-, -vent-	come	intervene, convention
-vers-, -vert-	turn	reverse, invert
-voc-, -vok-	call	vocal, invoke

VOCABULARY AND READING

Word knowledge is essential to reading comprehension. Quite simply, the more words you know, the easier it is to make sense of what you read. Your growing knowledge of word meanings combined with an ability to read carefully and think about what you read will help you succeed in school and do well on standardized tests, including the new SAT, the ACT, and the PSAT.

The **Vocabulary for Comprehension** exercises in this book will give you the opportunity to put your vocabulary knowledge and critical reading skills to use. Each exercise consists of a nonfiction reading passage followed by comprehension questions. The passages and questions are similar to those that you are likely to find on standardized tests.

Kinds of Questions

The questions on the reading sections of standardized tests are formulated in many different ways, but they are usually only of a small number of kinds, or types— the same ones that appear most frequently in the Vocabulary for Comprehension exercises in this book.

Main Idea Questions generally ask what the passage as a whole is about. Questions about the main idea may begin like this:

- The primary or main purpose of the passage is
- The primary focus of the passage is on
- The passage is best described as
- The passage is primarily concerned with
- The title that best describes the content of the passage is

Often the main idea is stated in the first paragraph of the passage. Sometimes, however, the first paragraph serves as an introduction and the main idea is included later on. When you answer questions about the main idea, you should make sure that the answers you choose reflect the focus of the entire passage and not just part of it. You may also be asked the main idea of a specific paragraph.

Detail Questions focus on important information that is explicitly stated in the passage. Often, however, the correct answer choices do not use the exact language of the passage. They are instead restatements, or paraphrases, of the text. So, for example, the answer to a question about "trash production and disposal" might use the term "waste management."

Vocabulary-in-Context Questions check your ability to use context to identify a word's meaning. All vocabulary-in-context questions include line references so that you can refer back to the passage to see how and in what context the word is used.

Here are some examples:

- **Condone** (line 6) most nearly means
- **Eminent** (line 8) is best defined as
- The meaning of **diffuse** (line 30) is

It is important to use context to check your answer choices, particularly when the vocabulary word has more than one meaning. Among the choices may be two (or more) correct meanings of the word in question. Your task is to choose the meaning that best fits the context.

Inference Questions ask you to make inferences or draw conclusions from the passage. These questions often begin like this:

- It can be inferred from the passage that
- The author implies that
- The passage suggests that
- Evidently the author feels that

The inferences you make and the conclusions you draw must be based on the information in the passage. Your own knowledge and reasoning come into play in understanding what is implied and in reaching conclusions that are logical.

Questions about Tone show your understanding of the author's attitude toward the subject of the passage. Words that describe tone, or attitude, are "feeling" words, for example, *indifferent, ambivalent, scornful, astonished, respectful.* These are typical questions:

- The author's attitude toward . . . is best described as
- The author's perspective is that of . . .
- Which word best describes the author's tone . . .

To determine the tone, it's important to pay attention to the author's choice of words and note your personal reaction. The author's attitude may be positive *(respectful, astonished)*, negative *(scornful)*, or neutral *(indifferent, ambivalent)*.

Questions about Author's Technique focus on the way a text is organized and the language the author uses. These questions ask you to think about structure and function. For example:

- The final paragraph serves to
- What is the function of the phrase . . . ?
- What does the author mean by . . . ?
- The author cites . . . in order to . . . .

To answer the questions, you must demonstrate an understanding of the way the author presents information and develops ideas.

Strategies

Here are some general strategies to help you in reading each passage and answering the questions.

- Read the introduction first. The introduction will provide a focus for the selection.

- Be an active reader. As you read, ask yourself questions about the passage, for example: What is this paragraph about? What does the writer mean here? Why does the writer include this information?

- Refer back to the passage when you answer the questions. In general, the order of the questions mirrors the organization of the passage, and many of the questions include paragraph or line references. It is often helpful to go back and reread before choosing an answer.

- Read carefully, and be sure to base your answer choices on the passage. There are answer choices that make sense, but are not based on the information in the passage. These are true statements, but incorrect answers. The correct answers are either restatements of ideas in the text or inferences that can be made from the text.

- Consider each exercise a learning experience. Keep in mind that your ability to answer the questions correctly shows as much about your understanding of the questions as about your understanding of the passage.

GRAMMAR AND WRITING

In order to write well, so that your meaning and your purpose are clearly understood, you must use words correctly; but, more than that, you must also make sure that what you write is grammatically correct. Knowing the rules of grammar, usage, and mechanics—the conventions of standard English—make your writing not just correct but more powerful and persuasive, too.

As a student you are regularly challenged to write effectively and correctly not only in your English classes but in your social studies, science, and history classes, too. Furthermore, high schools and colleges have raised their expectations for graduates. If you have taken a standardized test recently or are preparing to take one, you know this only too well. The writing and grammar sections of these tests have grown more demanding than ever.

On these grammar sections, questions usually appear in one or two multiple-choice formats. In one, you must decide if a mistake has been made in a sentence and, if one has been made, identify it. In another format, you must decide if an identified word or phrase is incorrect and, if it is incorrect, choose from several options the best way to correct it.

The **Grammar in Context** exercise that appears in each of the five Reviews in this book will provide you with opportunity to review and apply grammar and usage rules that are critical to good writing and that are frequently tested on the multiple-choice parts of standardized tests. In Level G, these topics are:

- Adjectives and adverbs
- Pronoun-antecedent agreement
- Pronoun reference and shift
- Dangling participles
- Faulty subordination

(For the sake of convenience, we sometimes use the term *grammar* to embrace all of the "rules" of English; but it's important to note that grammar, usage, and mechanics each represents a different aspect of writing. Grammar deals mostly with parts of speech and with parts of sentences and their relations. Usage, as the name suggests, concerns the way that words and phrases are used; usage topics would include, for example, irregular verbs, active and passive voice, subject-verb agreement, and double negatives. Mechanics deals with punctuation, capitalization, and spelling.)

There are many reasons to write and speak correctly other than to score well on standardized tests. You are judged by the way you write and speak. Your use of English is evaluated in the writing you do in school, on college applications, and in many different kinds of careers. You should be able to write and speak correctly when the situation calls for it—in a formal writing assignment, on a test, or in an interview. The more you practice standard English, the more comfortable and confident you will become when you write and speak.

WORKING WITH ANALOGIES

A verbal analogy expresses a relationship or comparison between sets of words. Normally, an analogy contains two pairs of words linked by a word or symbol that stands for an equals (=) sign. A complete analogy compares the two pairs of words and makes a statement about them. It asserts that the relationship between the first pair of words is the same as the relationship between the second pair.

In the **Analogies** exercises that appear in the Cumulative Reviews, you will be asked to complete analogies, that is, to choose the pair of words that best matches or parallels the relationship of the key, or given, pair of words. Here are two examples:

1. maple is to **tree** as
  a. acorn is to oak
  b. hen is to rooster
  c. rose is to flower
  d. shrub is to lilac

2. joyful is to **gloomy** as
  a. cheerful is to happy
  b. strong is to weak
  c. quick is to famous
  d. hungry is to starving

In order to find the correct answer to exercise 1, you must first determine the relationship between the two key words, **maple** and **tree**. In this case, that relationship might be expressed as "a maple is a kind (or type) of tree." The next step is to select from choices a, b, c, and d the pair of words that best reflects the same relationship. Clearly, the correct answer is (c); it is the only choice that parallels the relationship of the key words: a rose is a kind (or type) of flower, just as a maple is a kind (or type) of tree. The other choices do not express the same relationship.

In exercise 2, the relationship between the key words can be expressed as "joyful means the opposite of gloomy." Which of the choices best represents the same relationship? The answer, of course, is (b): "strong" means the opposite of "weak."

Here are examples of some other common analogy relationships:

Analogy	Key Relationship
big is to **large** as **little** is to **small**	**Big** means the same thing as **large**, just as **little** means the same thing as **small**.
brave is to **favorable** as **cowardly** is to **unfavorable**	The tone of **brave** is **favorable**, just as the tone of **cowardly** is **unfavorable**.
busybody is to **nosy** as **klutz** is to **clumsy**	A **busybody** is by definition someone who is **nosy**, just as a **klutz** is by definition someone who is **clumsy**.
cowardly is to **courage** as **awkward** is to **grace**	Someone who is **cowardly** lacks **courage**, just as someone who is **awkward** lacks **grace**.
visible is to **see** as **audible** is to **hear**	If something is **visible**, you can by definition **see** it, just as if something is **audible**, you can by definition **hear** it.
liar is to **truthful** as **bigot** is to **fair-minded**	A **liar** is by definition not likely to be **truthful**, just as a **bigot** is by definition not likely to be **fair-minded**.
eyes are to **see** as **ears** are to **hear**	You use your **eyes** to **see** with, just as you use your **ears** to **hear** with.

There are many different kinds of relationships represented in the analogy questions you will find in this book, but the key to solving any analogy is to find and express the relationship between the two key words.

This test contains a sampling of the words that are to be found in the exercises in this Level of VOCABULARY WORKSHOP. It will give you an idea of the types of words to be studied and their level of difficulty. When you have completed all the units, the Final Mastery Test at the end of this book will assess what you have learned. By comparing your results on the Final Mastery Test with your results on the Diagnostic Test below, you will be able to judge your progress.

Synonyms *In each of the following groups, circle the word or phrase that **most nearly** expresses the meaning of the word in **boldface** type in the given phrase.*

1. improvident behavior
a. conservative   b. funny   c. mysterious   d. rash

2. tended to **decry** our efforts
a. condemn   b. assist   c. hinder   d. finance

3. embellish a story
a. confirm   b. adorn   c. ridicule   d. translate

4. carping supervisors
a. cooperative   b. critical   c. efficient   d. clumsy

5. jettison the ballast
a. analyze   b. cast off   c. describe   d. conceal

6. an **overt** act
a. rebellious   b. obvious   c. nearly fatal   d. habitual

7. a **febrile** imagination
a. inhibited   b. feverish   c. disciplined   d. sentimental

8. an **insatiable** appetite
a. temporary   b. shallow   c. limitless   d. informed

9. germane to the problem
a. relevant   b. inappropriate   c. indispensable   d. foreign

10. spoke with the **distraught** parents
a. strict   b. permissive   c. agitated   d. indifferent

11. respond with **celerity**
a. intelligence   b. satisfaction   c. distrust   d. promptness

12. the **acclamation** of the crowd
a. applause   b. derision   c. indifference   d. criticism

13. a **utopian** community
a. restricted   b. backward   c. idealistic   d. successful

14. a **prepossessing** smile
a. engaging   b. sarcastic   c. tentative   d. timid

15. nothing but a **dilettante**
a. dabbler   b. skeptic   c. thief   d. lout

16. hallow the ground on which they fought
a. observe   b. consecrate   c. tread   d. profane

17. a minor **idiosyncrasy**
a. inclination   b. setback   c. error   d. peculiarity

18. received **intermittent** signals
a. interrupted   b. weak   c. clear   d. coded

19. accuse of **collusion**
a. theft   b. slander   c. conspiracy   d. negligence

20. tantamount to a victory
a. equivalent   b. opposed   c. favorable   d. unrelated

21. a **paucity** of resources
a. dearth   b. variety   c. oversupply   d. sample

22. used the Faust **motif**
a. theme   b. copyright   c. costume   d. scenery

23. dressed with **impeccable** taste
a. vulgar   b. modern   c. faultless   d. strange

24. a **sylvan** scene
a. marine   b. horrifying   c. wooded   d. urban

25. a **luminous** moon
a. sizeable   b. ostentatious   c. glowing   d. forbidding

26. allay our fears
a. analyze   b. intensify   c. lessen   d. ridicule

27. delineate the character
a. guess   b. portray   c. obscure   d. replace

28. a **delectable** dish
a. delightful   b. foreign   c. crude   d. expensive

29. belabor the point
a. ignore   b. sharpen   c. overwork   d. accept

30. attenuated the effect of the measure
a. questioned   b. diluted   c. enhanced   d. reassessed

Antonyms

*In each of the following groups, circle the word that is **most nearly opposite** in meaning to the word in **boldface** type in the given phrase.*

31. a **perfunctory** explanation
a. new   b. long   c. incisive   d. shallow

32. a **testy** reply
a. even-tempered   b. evasive   c. brilliant   d. impatient

33. exhumed the corpse
a. examined   b. unearthed   c. buried   d. revived

34. illusory gains
a. imaginary   b. actual   c. spectacular   d. supplemental

35. an **abstruse** theory
a. difficult   b. psychological   c. boring   d. straightforward

36. compose a **panegyric**
a. philippic   b. recipe   c. tribute   d. reply

37. sporadic precipitation
a. intermittent   b. steady   c. record   d. unseasonable

38. a **moot** point
a. indisputable   b. pertinent   c. new   d. debatable

39. an **obsequious** manner
a. fawning   b. courtly   c. overbearing   d. clumsy

40. the **acuity** of her mind
a. dullness   b. flexibility   c. tidiness   d. keenness

41. a **hapless** contestant
a. lucky   b. nervous   c. professional   d. brilliant

42. plenary powers
a. absolute   b. limited   c. acute   d. superhuman

43. manifest an interest in tennis
a. reveal   b. create   c. claim   d. conceal

44. a **pejorative** connotation
a. bad   b. colloquial   c. favorable   d. illegal

45. the **ephemeral** joys of summer
a. long-lasting   b. transitory   c. masculine   d. profound

46. a **defunct** organization
a. profitable   b. ongoing   c. charitable   d. dead

47. the man's **foibles**
a. wealth   b. background   c. children   d. strong suits

48. a **reputed** mobster
a. fearsome   b. celebrated   c. deceased   d. proven

49. lend **credence** to a statement
a. support   b. credibility   c. disbelief   d. eloquence

50. ubiquitous ants
a. scarce   b. omnipresent   c. aggressive   d. bestial

Definitions

Note carefully the spelling, pronunciation, part(s) of speech, and definition(s) of each of the following words. Then write the word in the blank space(s) in the illustrative sentence(s) following. Finally, study the lists of synonyms and antonyms given at the end of each entry.

1. acquisitive
(ə kwiz′ ə tiv)

(*adj.*) able to get and retain ideas or information; concerned with acquiring wealth or property

In an _____ society, there is a great deal of emphasis on buying and selling.

SYNONYMS: greedy, grasping, avaricious, retentive
ANTONYMS: altruistic, unretentive

2. arrogate
(a′ rə gāt)

(*v.*) to claim or take without right

The ambitious noblemen will put the young king under house arrest and _____ royal privileges to themselves.

SYNONYMS: expropriate, usurp, commandeer
ANTONYMS: relinquish, renounce, abdicate, abandon

3. banal
(bə nal′)

(*adj.*) hackneyed, trite, commonplace

The new play's _____ dialogue made it seem more like a soap opera than a serious drama.

SYNONYMS: stale, insipid
ANTONYMS: fresh, novel, original, new

4. belabor
(bi lā′ bər)

(*v.*) to work on excessively; to thrash soundly

His tendency to _____ the small points often made him miss the big picture.

SYNONYM: overwork

5. carping
(kär′ piŋ)

(*adj.*) tending to find fault, especially in a petty, nasty, or hairsplitting way; (*n.*) petty, nagging criticism

The trainee resigned after a week rather than put up with the _____ complaints of the sales manager.

Most artists choose to ignore the _____ of critics and simply go on with their work.

SYNONYMS: (*adj.*) nit-picking, caviling
ANTONYMS: (*adj.*) approving, uncritical

6. coherent
(kō hēr′ ənt)

(*adj.*) holding or sticking together; making a logical whole; comprehensible, meaningful

The physics teacher gave a surprisingly _____ description of quantum mechanics.

SYNONYMS: connected, unified, consistent, cohesive
ANTONYMS: muddled, chaotic, disjointed

7. congeal
(kən jēl′)

(v.) to change from liquid to solid, thicken; to make inflexible or rigid

If you do not wash your dishes right away, the food on them will _____ .

SYNONYMS: harden, jell, coagulate, solidify
ANTONYMS: melt, liquefy

8. emulate
(em′ yə lāt)

(v.) to imitate with the intent of equaling or surpassing the model

Most beginning writers try to _____ a great writer and later develop their own individual styles.

SYNONYMS: copy, mimic, rival, match, measure up to

9. encomium
(en kō′ mē əm)

(n.) a formal expression of praise, a lavish tribute

On Veterans Day, the President delivered a heartfelt _____ to those who died for their country.

SYNONYMS: panegyric, eulogy, commendation
ANTONYMS: condemnation, castigation, criticism

10. eschew
(es chü′)

(v.) to avoid, shun, keep away from

The young athletes promised the coach that they would train vigorously and _____ bad habits.

SYNONYMS: abstain from, steer clear of, forgo
ANTONYMS: embrace, adopt

11. germane
(jər mān′)

(adj.) relevant, appropriate, apropos, fitting

Bringing up examples from the past is not _____ to the present discussion.

SYNONYM: pertinent
ANTONYMS: irrelevant, extraneous, inappropriate

12. insatiable
(in sā′ shə bəl)

(adj.) so great or demanding as not to be satisfied

People with an _____ appetite for gossip often do not have compelling stories of their own.

SYNONYMS: unquenchable, ravenous, voracious

13. intransigent
(in tran′ sə jənt)

(adj.) refusing to compromise, irreconcilable

Little will get accomplished if the legislators of both parties maintain their _____ attitudes.

SYNONYMS: uncompromising, unyielding, obdurate
ANTONYMS: lukewarm, halfhearted, yielding

14. invidious
(in vid′ ē əs)

(*adj.*) offensive, hateful; tending to cause bitterness and resentment

Teachers should avoid making _____ comparisons between their students.

SYNONYMS: malicious, spiteful, prejudicial, pejorative
ANTONYMS: complimentary, flattering, ameliorative

15. largesse
(lär jes′)

(*n.*) generosity in giving; lavish or bountiful contributions

The university was the fortunate beneficiary of the _____ of many of its graduates.

SYNONYMS: liberality, munificence, bounty
ANTONYMS: stinginess, miserliness, niggardliness

16. reconnaissance
(ri kän′ ə səns)

(*n.*) a survey made for military purposes; any kind of preliminary inspection or examination

The field officer required a thorough _____ before ordering any troop movements.

SYNONYM: scouting expedition

17. substantiate
(səb stan′ shē āt)

(*v.*) to establish by evidence, prove; to give concrete or substantial form to

The prospector was unable to _____ his claim to the land where the gold was found.

SYNONYMS: verify, confirm, validate, authenticate
ANTONYMS: refute, disprove, invalidate

18. taciturn
(tas′ ə tərn)

(*adj.*) habitually silent or quiet, inclined to talk very little

Abraham Lincoln has the reputation of having a dour and _____ personality.

SYNONYMS: tight-lipped, uncommunicative, laconic
ANTONYMS: garrulous, loquacious, prolix, verbose

19. temporize
(tem′ pə rīz)

(*v.*) to stall or act evasively in order to gain time, avoid a confrontation, or postpone a decision; to compromise

For most of Shakespeare's greatest tragedy, the protagonist Hamlet chooses to _____ rather than act.

SYNONYMS: hedge, dillydally, procrastinate

20. tenable
(ten′ ə bəl)

(*adj.*) capable of being held or defended

The researchers put forth a _____ theory, but their conclusions would be reviewed carefully by others.

SYNONYMS: defensible, justifiable, maintainable
ANTONYMS: indefensible, unjustifiable

Completing the Sentence

From the words for this unit, choose the one that best completes each of the following sentences. Write the word in the space provided.

1. The novel contains an interesting study of a miser's _____ lust for gold and its evil effects on those around him.

2. Some of the episodes in the series were wonderfully fresh and original; others were just plain _____ .

3. I don't object to the inclusion of anecdotes in a serious lecture, but they should at the very least be _____ to the subject.

4. "There is no need for you to _____ the point," I replied, "when I already understand clearly what your criticism is."

5. There is nothing wrong with _____ the great singers of the past as long as you eventually develop a style that is all your own.

6. When the temperature outside dropped suddenly, the water in the ditch _____ into a mass of icy sludge.

7. Your essay would be a great deal tighter and more _____ if you removed all the extraneous information it now contains.

8. I would rather work at the most menial, ill-paying job than be the recipient of the government's _____ .

9. The purpose of military _____ remains the same whether cavalry or helicopters are used: to learn as much as possible about the enemy.

10. I doubt very much that he can _____ his assertion that he won two gold medals in the 1956 Olympics.

11. Despite the _____ and nit-picking of a few petty minds, I feel we have substantially improved our local school system of late.

12. In any crisis, the longer a person _____ , the greater the danger is likely to become.

13. In my humble opinion, there is absolutely no justification for making such _____ distinctions between the two types of product.

14. Never having any money in one's pockets can be a real trial for someone born with the _____ instincts of a pack rat.

15. Students who seek high grades must learn to _____ the joys of the one-eyed monster, the TV set.

16. As a result of recent research, earlier theories about the origin of the universe are no longer _____ .

17. In spite of his size, he was so _____ that we tended to forget that he was even in the room.

18. By whose authority did you _____ to yourself the right to decide how the club's money would be spent?

19. Even the most severe critics showered _____ on the young writer for the remarkable narrative power of her first novel.

20. How can we "meet them halfway" when they are so _____ in their opposition to what we propose to do?

Synonyms

*Choose the word from this unit that is **the same** or **most nearly the same** in meaning as the **boldface** word or expression in the given phrase. Write the word on the line provided.*

1. harp on the same point again and again _____

2. the **grasping** real estate developer _____

3. tries to **copy** her social graces _____

4. tends to **hedge** when confronted by direct questions _____

5. the **nit-picking** comments of a perfectionist _____

6. the **voracious** hunger _____

7. led the **scouting expedition** into the jungle _____

8. was thanked for her **munificence** _____

9. could not **verify** the alibi _____

10. received a well-deserved **commendation** _____

11. blood that does not **coagulate** _____

12. was **pertinent** to the investigation _____

13. obdurate on certain points _____

14. a **justifiable** reason for disagreeing _____

15. tried to **usurp** control of the finances _____

Antonyms

*Choose the word from this unit that is **most nearly opposite** in meaning to the **boldface** word or expression in the given phrase. Write the word on the line provided.*

16. made a very **complimentary** remark _____

17. questioned the **garrulous** witness _____

18. the **novel** lyrics to that song _____

19. a **disjointed** essay on foreign policy _____

20. adopted the use of technology _____

Choosing the Right Word

Circle the **boldface** word that more satisfactorily completes each of the following sentences.

1. Aristotle had such a(n) (**tenable, acquisitive**) mind that his writings are a veritable gold mine of odd and interesting information.

2. The mood of easy cordiality with which we began the meeting soon (**congealed, temporized**) into icy politeness.

3. "That word has such (**invidious, germane**) connotations in modern American parlance," I said, "that I would hesitate to use it, even in jest."

4. In that moment of grief, the conventional expressions of sympathy I had always considered (**tenable, banal**) were surprisingly comforting.

5. The speech was so filled with (**encomiums, reconnaissance**) that I found it hard to believe that the subject of all this acclaim was plain old me.

6. When the evidence of his misconduct became irrefutable, he saw that his position was not (**banal, tenable**) and resigned.

7. I am proud to have it said of me that I am stubborn and (**invidious, intransigent**) when genuine moral issues are involved.

8. His figure bears witness to his (**acquisitive, insatiable**) appetite for the pleasures of the table.

9. Ethelred the Unready was so reluctant to face the Vikings who invaded his kingdom that in effect he (**arrogated, temporized**) himself off the throne.

10. After I mowed the lawn for an hour, he gave me a whole dollar with the air of a feudal lord bestowing (**largesse, intransigence**) on a grateful serf.

11. The poor woman was in such a state of shock after the accident that she couldn't give a (**coherent, taciturn**) account of what had happened.

12. Your critical comments about my "lack of social background" may be true, but they are not (**coherent, germane**) to my qualifications for office.

13. Aerial (**reconnaissance, encomium**) of the enemy's positions provided the general with the information he needed to plan his attack.

14. What evidence can you offer to (**substantiate, eschew**) the assertion that capital punishment does not deter potential murderers?

15. In our attempt to improve the quality of life in America, we should not be too quick to (**eschew, cohere**) old ideas simply because they are old.

16. The new batting champion in our softball league is a(n) (**insatiable, taciturn**) young man who prefers to let his bat to do his talking for him.

17. Suddenly a band of ruffians set upon us and began to (**congeal, belabor**) us with blows and curses.

18. After the editor read the story, he returned it to the author with only a few (**carping, coherent**) criticisms of minor faults penciled in the margin.

19. Even a very imperfect human being may sometimes have virtues of mind or character that are worthy of (**carping, emulation**).

20. The Constitution is uniquely designed to provide protection against those who might seek to (**substantiate, arrogate**) undue power to themselves.

Vocabulary in Context

*Read the following passage, in which some of the words you have studied in this unit appear in **boldface** type. Then complete each statement given below the passage by circling the letter of the item that is **the same** or **almost the same** in meaning as the highlighted word.*

All That Glitters

(Line)

While the decades following the American Civil War were troubled by two serious economic depressions and rampant political corruption epitomized by the machinations of Boss Tweed at Tammany Hall in New York City, they were also a period of unprecedented economic growth and opportunity. "Robber Barons" with an
(5) apparently **insatiable** hunger for success amassed huge empires unregulated by anti-monopoly laws or income taxes. Mark Twain dubbed this era of growth, industry, and contrasting poverty "The
(10) Gilded Age" in a novel of the same name. The title sums up the **acquisitive** energy and desire to display wealth that seemed to possess every level of American society in that freewheeling era. The
(15) former distaste for the energetic pursuit of money was **eschewed** and replaced by an uncritical admiration for those who acquired great wealth. Getting rich quick was now the dream of millions, and it was
(20) upstart entrepreneurs like Cornelius Vanderbilt and Andrew Carnegie whom the masses wished to **emulate**.

THE "BRAINS"

THAT ACHIEVED THE TAMMANY VICTORY AT THE ROCHESTER DEMOCRATIC CONVENTION.

Lampoon of Tammany Hall corruption published in *Harper's Magazine*

When French Premier Georges Clemenceau visited the U.S. during the
(25) Gilded Age, he intimated that the effects of capitalism on American society were **invidious**, and that the nation had gone from a stage of barbarism to one of decadence—without achieving anything in between. But Clemenceau's observation does not tell the whole story. While there was an increasing disparity between the working and leisure classes during this time, a new economy increased the overall
(30) standard of living so that laborers were less dependent on the **largesse** of their employers, and more able to care for themselves.

---

1. The meaning of **insatiable** (line 5) is
  a. admirable   c. unquenchable
  b. lifelong   d. humble

2. The meaning of **acquisitive** (line 11) is
  a. enthusiastic   c. unflagging
  b. remarkable   d. grasping

3. Eschewed (line 16) most nearly means
  a. embraced   c. digested
  b. shunned   d. blamed

4. Emulate (line 22) is best defined as
  a. copy   c. condemn
  b. discuss   d. escape

5. Invidious (line 26) most nearly means
  a. malicious   c. original
  b. clever   d. controversial

6. Largesse (line 30) most nearly means
  a. display   c. munificence
  b. decency   d. modesty

Definitions

Note carefully the spelling, pronunciation, part(s) of speech, and definition(s) of each of the following words. Then write the word in the blank space(s) in the illustrative sentence(s) following. Finally, study the lists of synonyms and antonyms given at the end of each entry.

1. accost
(ə käst′)

(v.) to approach and speak to first; to confront in a challenging or aggressive way

The nobleman was _____ by beggars on his way to the castle.

SYNONYMS: buttonhole, approach, confront
ANTONYMS: evade, avoid, shun

2. animadversion
(an ə mad vər′ zhən)

(n.) a comment indicating strong criticism or disapproval

The inexperienced filmmaker was disheartened by the _____ of the film critic.

SYNONYMS: rebuke, reproof
ANTONYMS: praise, compliment

3. avid
(av′ id)

(adj.) desirous of something to the point of greed; intensely eager

Most writers are also _____ readers who have loved books since childhood.

SYNONYMS: keen, enthusiastic, grasping
ANTONYMS: reluctant, indifferent, unenthusiastic

4. brackish
(brak′ ish)

(adj.) having a salty taste and unpleasant to drink

The shipwrecked passengers adrift on the lifeboat became ill after drinking _____ water.

SYNONYMS: briny, saline
ANTONYMS: fresh, clear, sweet

5. celerity
(sə ler′ ə tē)

(n.) swiftness, rapidity of motion or action

Although the heavy snowfall was not expected, the highway department responded with surprising _____.

SYNONYMS: promptness, alacrity, speed
ANTONYMS: slowness, sluggishness, dilatoriness

6. devious
(dē′ vē əs)

(adj.) straying or wandering from a straight or direct course; done or acting in a shifty or underhanded way

The interrogator used _____ methods to try to get the suspect to incriminate himself.

SYNONYMS: roundabout, indirect, tricky, sly, artful
ANTONYMS: direct, straightforward, open, aboveboard

7. gambit
(gam′ bit)

(*n.*) in chess, an opening move that involves risk or sacrifice of a minor piece in order to gain a later advantage; any opening move of this type

Asking an interesting stranger about his or her job is a popular party _____.

SYNONYMS: ploy, stratagem, ruse, maneuver

8. halcyon
(hal′ sē ən)

(*n.*) a legendary bird identified with the kingfisher; (*adj.*) of or relating to the halcyon; calm, peaceful; happy, golden; prosperous, affluent

The teacher read the legend of the _____, a mythic bird that nested in a calm sea.

The woman often spoke of the _____ days of her childhood.

SYNONYMS: (*adj.*) tranquil, serene, placid, palmy
ANTONYMS: (*adj.*) turbulent, chaotic, tumultuous

9. histrionic
(his trē än′ ik)

(*adj.*) pertaining to actors and their techniques; theatrical, artificial; melodramatic

Upon receiving his award, the young actor gave a

_____ speech.

SYNONYMS: affected, stagy
ANTONYMS: low-keyed, muted, untheatrical, subdued

10. incendiary
(in sen′ dē er ē)

(*adj.*) deliberately setting or causing fires; designed to start fires; tending to stir up strife or rebellion; (*n.*) one who deliberately sets fires, arsonist; one who causes strife

The arsonist planted an _____ device in the basement of the store.

The radical _____ was sentenced to life imprisonment.

SYNONYMS: (*adj.*) inflammatory, provocative, (*n.*) firebrand
ANTONYMS: (*adj.*) soothing, quieting, (*n.*) peacemaker

11. maelstrom
(māl′ strəm)

(*n.*) a whirlpool of great size and violence; a situation resembling a whirlpool in violence and destruction

Many innocent people caught in the _____ of the revolution lost their lives and property.

SYNONYMS: vortex, chaos, turbulence, tumult

12. myopic
(mī äp′ ik)

(*adj.*) nearsighted; lacking a broad, realistic view of a situation; lacking foresight or discernment

The _____ foreign policy of the last administration has led to serious problems with our allies.

SYNONYM: shortsighted
ANTONYM: farsighted

13. overt
(ō vert')

(*adj.*) open, not hidden, expressed or revealed in a way that is easily recognized

In order for Congress to declare war, the President must demonstrate an _____ threat.

SYNONYMS: clear, obvious, manifest, patent
ANTONYMS: secret, clandestine, covert, concealed

14. pejorative
(pə jôr' ə tiv)

(*adj.*) tending to make worse; expressing disapproval or disparagement, derogatory, deprecatory, belittling

The lawyer was accused of making a _____ remark when referring to the defendant's background.

ANTONYMS: complimentary, ameliorative

15. propriety
(prə prī' ə tē)

(*n.*) the state of being proper, appropriateness; (*pl.*) standards of what is proper or socially acceptable

The social worker questioned the _____ of the police's request to see confidential records.

SYNONYMS: fitness, correctness, decorum
ANTONYMS: unseemliness, inappropriateness

16. sacrilege
(sak' rə lij)

(*n.*) improper or disrespectful treatment of something held sacred

The anthropologist was accused of committing a _____ when she disturbed an ancient burial ground.

SYNONYMS: desecration, profanation, defilement

17. summarily
(sə mer' ə lē)

(*adv.*) without delay or formality; briefly, concisely

As soon as there was evidence of criminal wrongdoing, the official was _____ ousted from his post.

SYNONYMS: promptly, peremptorily, abruptly

18. suppliant
(səp' lē ənt)

(*adj.*) asking humbly and earnestly; (*n.*) one who makes a request humbly and earnestly, a petitioner, suitor

He made a _____ address to the parole board.

Stranded in the deserted city of Moscow, Napoleon had to turn to the Czar not as a conqueror but as a _____.

19. talisman
(tal' iz mən)

(*n.*) an object that serves as a charm or is believed to confer magical powers, an amulet, fetish

Most people do not believe that rabbit's feet and other _____ actually bring good luck.

20. undulate
(ən' dyə lāt)

(*v.*) to move in waves or with a wavelike motion; to have a wavelike appearance or form

The baseball fans began to _____ as they cheered, so that they appeared to move in a wave.

SYNONYMS: ripple, fluctuate, rise and fall

**Completing
the Sentence**

*From the words for this unit, choose the one that best
completes each of the following sentences. Write the
word in the space provided.*

1. To our dismay, we discovered that the water we had worked so hard to bring to the
surface was too _____ for human consumption.

2. As an employee of the local polling service last summer, it was my job to
_____ people on the street and ask their opinions.

3. Many a rich southern planter saw all his or her financial resources swallowed up in
the _____ of the Civil War.

4. After the prisoner had been found guilty of treason, he was led before a firing squad
and _____ executed.

5. Saying that "people who live in glass houses shouldn't throw stones" is not an
effective response to their _____ on your conduct.

6. During the rainy season, the highway sank at so many points that its surface began
to _____ like the track for a roller coaster.

7. I stand before you an abject _____, hoping against hope for a
sign of your forgiveness.

8. My brother is such a(n) _____ collector of toy soldiers that I
sometimes think our house has been invaded by a pint-sized army.

9. The suffix *-ling* often has a(n) _____ connotation, as in the word
princeling, derived from *prince*.

10. On the return trip, we cut straight across the meadows rather than take the more
_____ path along the river.

11. In Grandmother's day, standards of _____ required that a young
lady wear a hat and gloves when she went out in public.

12. The _____ with which he accepted our invitation to dinner
suggested that he was badly in need of a good meal.

13. The tons of _____ material ignited and turned the waste disposal
plant into a roaring inferno.

14. In the eyes of most Americans, people who burn or spit on our flag are guilty of an
intolerable _____.

15. We looked back on those _____ years before the war broke out as
a kind of "golden age" in our history.

16. Any book on chess strategy usually discusses the standard opening moves, such
as the "knight's _____."

17. The Japanese attack on Pearl Harbor was a(n) _____ act of war.

18. Down in the main square, a wrinkled old peasant was selling charms and _____ to ward off the evil eye.

19. To be really convincing on stage, an opera singer must possess both vocal and _____ abilities.

20. His pale face, hunched shoulders, and _____ stare showed that he had spent his life poring over old books and documents.

Synonyms

*Choose the word from this unit that is **the same** or **most nearly the same** in meaning as the **boldface** word or expression in the given phrase. Write the word on the line provided.*

1. a tireless **petitioner**   _____

2. a lucky **amulet**   _____

3. the **vortex** of public opinion   _____

4. **ripple** in the current   _____

5. was taken in by her **stratagem**   _____

6. outraged by the **desecration**   _____

7. apologized for his unnecessary **rebuke**   _____

8. swam in the **briny** water   _____

9. **abruptly** resigned from the Cabinet   _____

10. behaved with her usual **decorum**   _____

11. memories of our **serene** beginnings   _____

12. **confronted** the thief at the door   _____

13. completed the job with **alacrity**   _____

14. their **derogatory** references to his past   _____

15. took an **indirect** route   _____

Antonyms

*Choose the word from this unit that is **most nearly opposite** in meaning to the **boldface** word or expression in the given phrase. Write the word on the line provided.*

16. identified the **peacemaker**   _____

17. made a very **low-keyed** plea for mercy   _____

18. one of the most **reluctant** participants   _____

19. known for **farsighted** thinking   _____

20. took **secret** action to avoid a crisis   _____

Choosing the Right Word

Circle the **boldface** word that more satisfactorily completes each of the following sentences.

1. His reckless words had an (**incendiary, overt**) effect on the already excited crowd, and large-scale rioting resulted.

2. He is the kind of person who is concerned not with real moral values but simply with appearances and (**propriety, celerity**).

3. He regarded his Phi Beta Kappa key as a(n) (**talisman, animadversion**) that would open all doors and win him universal acceptance.

4. After years of failure to sell a single story, the young writer described himself bitterly as "a(n) (**pejorative, avid**) collector of rejection slips."

5. She was buffeted about in a veritable (**gambit, maelstrom**) of emotions, caused mainly by her own dissatisfaction with herself.

6. His methods were so complicated and his purposes so (**avid, devious**) that we were not sure if he was spying on the enemy or on us.

7. Without even considering the new evidence that I was prepared to present, they (**deviously, summarily**) denied my appeal to reopen the case.

8. In an age when the United States has truly global responsibilities, we can ill afford leaders with (**myopic, pejorative**) points of view.

9. The adoring fan regarded my negative comments about his favorite singer as tantamount to (**maelstrom, sacrilege**).

10. I certainly do not claim that my performance in office was beyond criticism, but I deeply resent (**animadversions, maelstroms**) on my honesty.

11. Although all politicians must have some ability to dramatize themselves, it is very easy to overdo the (**proprieties, histrionics**).

12. As the defendant left the courtroom, he was (**gambited, accosted**) by a group of reporters seeking his reaction to the verdict.

13. Walt tends to react slowly, but when he feels that his own interests are at stake he can move with striking (**celerity, myopia**).

14. Since the word appeasement is associated with disastrous concessions to Adolf Hitler, it has acquired a(n) (**pejorative, overt**) connotation.

15. John Masefield's poem "Sea Fever" has an (**avid, undulating**) rhythm that actually gives one the feeling of being on a rolling ship.

16. "His acts of defiance have been so (**myopic, overt**) and premeditated that I have no choice but to fire him," she said sadly.

17. Instead of imbibing the (**brackish, suppliant**) waters of superstition, let us refresh ourselves with long drafts of pure, clean common sense.

18. "I realize that this kind of financial (**gambit, sacrilege**) has its risks," she said, "but I expect it to pay off handsomely in the end."

19. Nary a ripple disturbed the (**halcyon, brackish**) calm of the sea on that glorious summer's afternoon.

20. The infatuated schoolboy, in one of his more restrained expressions, described himself as "a (**sacrilege, suppliant**) at the altar of love."

Vocabulary in Context

*Read the following passage, in which some of the words you have studied in this unit appear in **boldface** type. Then complete each statement given below the passage by circling the letter of the item that is **the same** or **almost the same** in meaning as the highlighted word.*

The Wonder Around Us

(Line)

Most people today have a far greater appreciation of the preciousness of the land and sea than the general public living just a half century ago. In the 1940s and 1950s, many held the **myopic** view that natural resources were limitless and impervious to pollution. The marine biologist Rachel Carson (1907–1964) was one of the first scientists to challenge these widely held assumptions. She did so by (5) writing a series of evocative books about the sea, culminating in the 1951 bestseller, *The Sea Around Us*. To the surprise of many, Carson found an **avid** audience for her

unique blend of science and lyricism and became one of the pioneers of the growing ecological movement. (10)

Through her imaginative prose, Carson made the **brackish** waters of the world's oceans come alive for her readers. She helped them see that the ocean was not a deep, dark, empty (15) abyss, but a living home to a fascinating array of plants and animals.

Carson also dramatized the intricate relationship between wind and water. The rotation of the earth, water (20) temperature, and wind combine to produce the great ocean currents— giant global **maelstroms** that carry the sea's waters in roughly circular

The endangered blue whale is indigenous to oceans all over the world.

patterns. The wind also whips up the ocean waters into waves that **undulate** across (25) the sea's surface. Carson explained that these waves vary from the smallest ripples to giant mountains of water, called *tsunamis*, that travel up to 600 miles per hour—with a sometimes startling **celerity**—and cause great damage when they come ashore. No matter what force of nature Carson evoked, she never failed to make her reader feel a part of the process she was describing, and to respect the earth and seas. (30)

---

1. The meaning of **myopic** (line 3) is
a. imaginative
b. enlightened
c. democratic
d. shortsighted

2. Avid (line 7) most nearly means
a. enthusiastic
b. grateful
c. critical
d. varied

3. Brackish (line 12) is best defined as
a. frigid
b. briny
c. deep
d. mysterious

4. The meaning of **maelstroms** (line 23) is
a. whirlpools
b. explosions
c. motors
d. earthquakes

5. Undulate (line 25) most nearly means
a. creep
b. sing
c. ripple
d. reflect

6. Celerity (line 28) most nearly means
a. quantity
b. cost
c. speed
d. time

34 ■ Unit 2

Definitions

Note carefully the spelling, pronunciation, part(s) of speech, and definition(s) of each of the following words. Then write the word in the blank space(s) in the illustrative sentence(s) following. Finally, study the lists of synonyms and antonyms given at the end of each entry.

1. articulate
(*v.*, är tik′ yə lāt;
adj., är tik′ yə lit)

(*v.*) to pronounce distinctly; to express well in words; to connect by a joint or joints; (*adj.*) expressed clearly and forcefully; able to employ language clearly and forcefully; jointed

Few people can _____ their emotions during times of stress.

The most _____ student in the class was chosen to mediate the debate.

SYNONYMS: (*v.*) pronounce, elucidate; (*adj.*) eloquent
ANTONYMS: (*v.*) mumble, slur; (*adj.*) tongue-tied, halting

2. cavort
(kə vôrt′)

(*v.*) to romp or prance around exuberantly; to make merry

The actors in the musical _____ on stage.

SYNONYM: gambol

3. credence
(krēd′ əns)

(*n.*) belief, mental acceptance

The government and the public failed to give _____ to the reports of an impending water shortage.

SYNONYMS: credit, trust, confidence
ANTONYMS: disbelief, skepticism, incredulity

4. decry
(di krī′)

(*v.*) to condemn, express strong disapproval; to officially depreciate

Every arm of government and every educational institution should _____ bigotry in all its forms.

SYNONYMS: denounce, censure, devalue
ANTONYMS: tout, commend, extol, laud, praise

5. dissemble
(di sem′ bəl)

(*v.*) to disguise or conceal, deliberately give a false impression

The young man was unable to _____ his feelings and admitted to having committed the crime.

SYNONYMS: dissimulate, mask, feign

6. distraught
(dis trôt′)

(*adj.*) very much agitated or upset as a result of emotion or mental conflict

The workforce became _____ in the wake of the 1929 stock market crash.

SYNONYMS: frantic, distracted
ANTONYMS: calm, composed, collected

7. eulogy
(yü′ lə jē)

(*n.*) a formal statement of commendation; high praise

The best friend and longtime law partner of the deceased delivered the _____ at the funeral.

SYNONYMS: panegyric, encomium, tribute, testimonial
ANTONYMS: philippic, diatribe, invective

8. evince
(i vins′)

(*v.*) to display clearly, to make evident, to provoke

The crowd did not _____ any signs of panic but moved in an orderly fashion to the nearest exits.

SYNONYMS: exhibit, manifest, occasion

9. exhume
(eks hyüm′)

(*v.*) to remove from a grave; to bring to light

Suspecting foul play, the coroner issued an order to _____ the body immediately.

SYNONYMS: disinter, unearth, uncover
ANTONYMS: bury, inter

10. feckless
(fek′ ləs)

(*adj.*) lacking in spirit and strength; ineffective, weak; irresponsible, unreliable

Although a _____ youth, he eventually matured into a hard-working and responsible citizen.

SYNONYMS: feeble, helpless, incompetent, ineffectual
ANTONYMS: competent, capable, effective

11. murky
(mər′ kē)

(*adj.*) dark and gloomy, obscure; lacking in clarity and precision

Many visitors have claimed to see a mysterious creature in the _____ waters of Loch Ness in Scotland.

SYNONYMS: dim, cloudy, unclear
ANTONYMS: clear, transparent, lucid, limpid

12. nefarious
(nə fâr′ ē əs)

(*adj.*) wicked, depraved, devoid of moral standards

Brutus and Cassius hatched a _____ plot to assassinate Julius Caesar on the steps of the Roman Senate.

SYNONYMS: iniquitous, reprehensible
ANTONYMS: virtuous, honorable, praiseworthy, meritorious

13. piquant
(pē′ kənt)

(*adj.*) stimulating to the taste or mind; spicy, pungent; appealingly provocative

The chef was an expert in making those _____ dishes that are characteristic of South Indian cooking.

SYNONYMS: tangy, zestful
ANTONYMS: bland, insipid, tasteless, mild

14. primordial
(prī môr′ dē əl)

(*adj.*) developed or created at the very beginning; going back to the most ancient times or earliest stage; fundamental, basic

The _____ stages of most civilizations are founded on common needs met by common goals.

SYNONYMS: original, primeval, primal

15. propinquity
(prō piŋ′ kwə tē)

(*n.*) nearness in place or time; kinship

The _____ of the two cities has created a greater metropolitan area that in effect is one city.

SYNONYMS: proximity, similarity
ANTONYMS: remoteness, distance

16. unwonted
(un wōn′ tid)

(*adj.*) not usual or expected; not in character

The listless student answered with _____ spirit when the subject of military tactics was raised.

SYNONYMS: unusual, uncommon, unexpected, atypical
ANTONYMS: usual, customary, typical

17. utopian
(yü tō′ pē ən)

(*adj.*) founded upon or involving a visionary view of an ideal world; impractical

A number of American religious groups like the Shakers have built separate communities based on _____ schemes.

SYNONYM: idealistic
ANTONYMS: realistic, pragmatic

18. verbiage
(vər′ bē ij)

(*n.*) language that is too wordy or inflated in proportion to the sense or content, wordiness; a manner of expression

The contract was full of meaningless _____ that seemed designed to confuse the lay person.

SYNONYMS: verbosity, prolixity, diction, jargon

19. verdant
(vər′ dənt)

(*adj.*) green in tint or color; immature in experience or judgment

The tourists on safari traveled over the _____ grasslands of Kenya in search of native wildlife.

SYNONYMS: artless, naíve
ANTONYMS: scorched, sere, barren, arid

20. viscous
(vis′ kəs)

(*adj.*) having a gelatinous or gluey quality, lacking in easy movement or fluidity

The varnish left a _____ residue on the wood that was hard to remove.

SYNONYMS: gummy, sticky, thick
ANTONYMS: runny, watery, aqueous

Completing the Sentence

From the words for this unit, choose the one that best completes each of the following sentences. Write the word in the space provided.

1. The assembly speaker couldn't be understood because he mumbled his words instead of _____ them clearly.

2. For as far as the eye could see, _____ fields of unripe corn swayed gently in the morning breeze.

3. An educated citizenry will not give _____ to wild charges of extremists seeking to undermine our political and economic system.

4. How could we draw any clear ideas from a talk that was so disorganized, confused in language, and generally _____?

5. Sadly, the _____ schemes of high-minded idealists usually founder on the rocks of practical realities.

6. Such spices as red pepper make many of the sauces used in Cajun cooking delightfully _____.

7. I believe there is an overall design to the universe that has been visible ever since the first thing crawled out of the _____ ooze.

8. In the hands of our hopelessly _____ producer, what should have been a surefire hit turned into a resounding fiasco.

9. When new evidence turned up in the case, the court ordered the coroner to _____ the victim's body and reexamine it.

10. Though diesel fuels are not as thick as motor oil, they are a good deal more _____ than regular gasoline.

11. Though I prefer to be as open and aboveboard as possible, I have learned that it is sometimes wiser or more tactful to _____.

12. When Bill was told that he had made the varsity wrestling team, he began to _____ around the gym like a young colt.

13. The NCAA has in recent years cracked down hard on such _____ practices as "shaving points."

14. He clothes his puny ideas in such highfalutin _____ that they resemble gnats in top hats and tails.

15. The new chairman _____ what she called the "deplorable tendency of so many Americans to try to get something for nothing."

16. Even at an early age, my sister _____ a strong interest in studying medicine.

17. When news of the school fire ran through town, _____ parents rushed to the scene of the blaze.

18. Every Memorial Day, the Mayor delivers a(n) _____ extolling the selfless devotion of those who have died in defense of this country.

19. Since my apartment is in such close _____ to my office, I usually walk to work.

20. I have always regarded the man as something of a daredevil, but on this occasion he approached the problem with _____ caution.

Synonyms
*Choose the word from this unit that is **the same** or **most nearly the same** in meaning as the **boldface** word or expression in the given phrase. Write the word on the line provided.*

1. did **exhibit** true remorse _____

2. **primeval** history _____

3. burdened by unnecessary **verbosity** _____

4. a very **tangy** salad dressing _____

5. distinguished by **uncommon** courtesy _____

6. full of **idealistic** plans _____

7. the **iniquitous** traitor and spy _____

8. a slightly **gummy** coating of wax _____

9. **gamboled** in the wading pool _____

10. tried to **dissimulate** when confronted _____

11. **uncovered** the buried treasure _____

12. feared for the **helpless** child _____

13. an unwelcome **proximity** _____

14. tried to calm the **frantic** parents _____

15. could not make out the **unclear** image _____

Antonyms
*Choose the word from this unit that is **most nearly opposite** in meaning to the **boldface** word or expression in the given phrase. Write the word on the line provided.*

16. watered the **arid** lawn _____

17. managed to **mumble** a quick response _____

18. rose to **commend** the new regime _____

19. published her lengthy **diatribe** _____

20. treated the idea with **skepticism** _____

Circle the **boldface** word that more satisfactorily completes each of the following sentences.

1. Far from being unpleasant, her slight foreign accent added an extra dash of spice to her already (**primordial, piquant**) personality.

2. Trying to read your (**viscous, utopian**) prose is just like trying to swim upstream through custard.

3. An accomplished hypocrite usually finds it very easy to (**dissemble, decry**) his or her true feelings as circumstances dictate.

4. The new mayor is a curious mixture of the hardheaded pragmatist and the (**utopian, murky**) reformer.

5. The book has an interesting plot, but the author has practically smothered it in endless (**verbiage, eulogy**).

6. Though the work hadn't seen the light of day for over a century, a daring impresario (**cavorted, exhumed**) and staged it to great public acclaim.

7. Not surprisingly, the address was a notably evenhanded affair in which the speaker cleverly mixed (**eulogy, verbiage**) with admonition.

8. The investigating committee (**decried, dissembled**) the use of substandard materials and slovenly workmanship in the housing project.

9. One of the duties of a President is to (**cavort, articulate**) the policies and programs of his administration in a forceful and convincing way.

10. The United States is cooperating with the other nations of the world in an effort to check the (**feckless, nefarious**) trade in narcotics.

11. (**Exhumed, Distraught**) with grief, they sat motionless for hours, staring blankly into space.

12. The extraordinary musical talents of Wolfgang Amadeus Mozart (**evinced, dissembled**) themselves at an amazingly early age.

13. Despite all the reports of "miraculous" cures, you would be well advised to withhold (**verbiage, credence**) until the drug has been fully tested.

14. The behavior of armies in wartime often evinces the (**murky, primordial**) blood lust that civilized people have not yet fully overcome.

15. When life was easy he was all dash and confidence, but in times of trouble his essentially (**piquant, feckless**) character came to the fore.

16. The (**credence, propinquity**) of our ideas on handling the problem made it very easy for my colleague and me to produce the report in record time.

17. From the bridge, the rescue team could just make out the blurred image of a car beneath the (**murky, unwonted**) waters of the river.

18. Unfortunately, the (**nefarious, verdant**) hopes and aspirations of my youth have been somewhat blighted by the icy blasts of reality.

19. From the deck of our luxury liner, we occasionally caught sight of schools of porpoises (**cavorting, evincing**) playfully in the waves.

20. His (**viscous, unwonted**) interest in the state of my finances strengthened my suspicions that he was about to ask for a loan.

Read the following passage, in which some of the words you have studied in this unit appear in **boldface** type. Then complete each statement given below the passage by circling the letter of the item that is **the same** or **almost the same** in meaning as the highlighted word.

The Great Green World

(Line)

Forests developed in marshlands about 365 million years ago. These **primordial** tracts covered the earth for eons, providing food and shelter first for animals and later for human beings. In fact, sixty percent of the earth's landmass was covered with forest until humans began clearing great

(5) swaths of timber for farmland and town-building. Although many **decry** the loss of so much forest habitat, few realize that today forests still occupy thirty percent of the planet.

The forest ecosystem is a very complex,

(10) interdependent environment that **evinces** a great variety of plants and animals that range from huge, towering trees to low shrubs and mosses to invisible, microscopic bacteria that break down larger organisms. This natural recycling process returns

(15) minerals to the soil where they can again be used by plants to make food. There are also different types of forests, depending on climate, soil, water, and geography. These include the **verdant** rain forests of the tropics, the mixed deciduous forests of the

(20) temperate zones, the cold boreal or northern forests with their short growing season, the grassy tree-pocked savannas of Africa, and the **murky** evergreen forests of the wet Pacific Northwest.

Actual life for forest creatures may contradict our

(25) **utopian** visions of a wild paradise. In reality, every animal, bird, and plant in the forest must compete with others of its kind and with similar species for food, breeding space, and water. Many plants and animals live by feeding on others, creating and sustaining a complex food chain. The

(30) truth of forest life is that, although individuals die, species survive and so does the forest, unless human beings disturb its delicate balance.

Hikers dwarfed by a California redwood tree

1. The meaning of **primordial** (line 1) is
a. agricultural   c. expansive
b. mysterious   d. original

2. Decry (line 6) most nearly means
a. extol   c. bemoan
b. denounce   d. publicize

3. Evinces (line 10) is best defined as
a. destroys   c. hides
b. boasts   d. exhibits

4. The meaning of **verdant** (line 18) is
a. barren   c. green
b. noisy   d. frightening

5. Murky (line 22) most nearly means
a. wet   c. dim
b. merry   d. wild

6. Utopian (line 25) most nearly means
a. idealistic   c. charitable
b. futuristic   d. primitive

Vocabulary for Comprehension

Read the following passage, in which some of the words you have studied in Units 1–3 appear in **boldface** *type. Then answer questions 1–12 on page 43 on the basis of what is* <u>stated</u> *or* <u>implied</u> *in the passage and in the introductory statement.*

Although the Chicago fire caused enormous destruction, the city recovered quickly, as this passage shows.

(Line)

On the evening of October 8, 1871, at around 9 o'clock, the city of Chicago went up in flames. The exact **incendiary** agent remains unknown,
(5) but historians have **substantiated** the Chicago Fire Department's discovery that the blaze began in or near the barn of Mr. and Mrs. Patrick O'Leary, on the southwest side of the city.
(10) Official **credence**, however, has not been extended to the popular belief that it all started when the O'Leary's cow knocked over a lighted lantern.

Whatever the initial spark, the city
(15) was a tinderbox. That summer had been unusually dry, and almost all the buildings, bridges, and even the sidewalks were made of wood. Construction over the previous years
(20) had proceeded rapidly and with little attention to fire safety. The **feckless** city council ignored all pleas to improve the level of fire protection, either by bolstering the fire
(25) department or by passing zoning laws. As a result, the city of Chicago averaged about two fires a day.

Driven by a strong wind out of the southwest, the October 8 fire was
(30) already out of control by the time the exhausted Chicago firefighters (who had been working the day before on another large fire) arrived. The wind

carried the flames to the center of
(35) the city, where they consumed nearly every structure in their path. In a panic, the **distraught** population fled northward toward Lincoln Park and Lake Michigan.
(40) The fire raged for more than twenty-four hours until it rained on the morning of October 10.

In the days that followed, **reconnaissance** missions were
(45) conducted over the rubble that remained of homes, businesses, and tunnels. Three hundred were dead, nearly 100,000 were homeless, and property damage
(50) amounted to $200 million. Yet, four years later, Chicago was almost completely rebuilt. And today, the Chicago Fire Academy stands on the site of the O'Leary cowshed.

1. The primary purpose of the passage is to
   a. expose the incompetence of the city council
   b. focus on the heroism of the firefighters
   c. tell the story of the Chicago fire of 1871
   d. highlight the geography of Chicago
   e. compare the Chicago fire with the San Francisco earthquake of 1906

2. The meaning of **incendiary** (line 3) is
   a. causative
   b. criminal
   c. foreign
   d. subversive
   e. inflammatory

3. **Substantiated** (line 5) most nearly means
   a. ignored
   b. verified
   c. dismissed
   d. disputed
   e. analyzed

4. From the passage, it is clear that
   a. Mr. and Mrs. O'Leary were responsible for setting the fire
   b. the fire started when the O'Learys' cow knocked over a lighted lantern
   c. no one really knows how or where the fire started
   d. the fire started in or near the O'Learys' barn
   e. the fire spread slowly but steadily

5. **Credence** (line 10) is best defined as
   a. acceptance
   b. pardon
   c. enthusiasm
   d. mourning
   e. condemnation

6. Which of the following best describes the organizational structure of paragraph 2 (lines 14–27)?
   a. order of importance
   b. chronological order
   c. spatial order
   d. comparison and contrast
   e. cause and effect

7. The meaning of **feckless** (line 21) is
   a. popular
   b. corrupt
   c. incompetent
   d. conservative
   e. effective

8. From the passage, you can reasonably infer that all of the following played a role in the spread of the fire EXCEPT
   a. the unusually dry summer
   b. a strong wind
   c. the minimal attention to safety in construction
   d. the fleeing population
   e. the exhaustion of the firefighters

9. **Distraught** (line 37) is best defined as
   a. frightened
   b. frantic
   c. disheveled
   d. angry
   e. bemused

10. **Reconnaissance** (line 44) is best defined as
    a. calm evacuation
    b. court decision
    c. slow deliberation
    d. scouting expedition
    e. detailed analysis

11. The effect of the last sentence in the passage (lines 52–54) might best be described as
    a. ironic
    b. tragic
    c. farcical
    d. melancholy
    e. fanciful

12. Which of the following best describes the author's attitude toward the subject of the passage?
    a. disillusioned
    b. satiric
    c. enthusiastic
    d. factual
    e. skeptical

Grammar in Context

In the sentence "Construction over the previous years had pro-ceeded rapidly and with little attention to fire safety" (lines 19–21 on page 42), the word *little* is an **adjective**. Adjectives tell *what kind*, *which one*, *how many*, or *how much*. Adjectives always modify a noun or pronoun. The word *rapidly* in the sen-tence is an **adverb**. Adverbs tell *where*, *when*, *in what way*, or *to what extent*. An adverb modifies a verb, an adjective, or another adverb. Sometimes the same word can be either an adjective or an adverb, depending on how it is used in the sentence. For example in the sentence "Determining the cause of the fire posed a hard challenge for investigators," *hard* is an adjective. But in the sentence "Firefighters worked hard to extinguish the blaze," *hard* is an adverb.

Many adverbs are formed by adding the suffix *–ly* to an adjective: for example, *rapid* and *rapidly*. Keep in mind, though, that not all words ending in *–ly* are adverbs. A few of these words are adjectives: for example, *gingerly*, *leisurely*, and *ungainly*. A few others may be either adjectives or adverbs: for example, *early* and *daily*.

On the lines provided, identify each underlined word as an adjective or an adverb.

1. The <u>specific</u> cause of the Chicago fire was never determined <u>exactly</u>.

_____

2. The <u>most</u> <u>likely</u> location for the origin of the blaze was the O'Learys' barn.

_____

3. It was <u>widely</u> rumored that the O'Learys' cow knocked over a lighted lantern.

_____

4. In Chicago, the summer of 1871 had been <u>unusually</u> dry.

_____

5. Ignoring <u>urgent</u> pleas to improve fire protection, the city council proved to be <u>incompetent</u>.

_____

6. As a result, <u>several</u> fires broke out in the city on a <u>daily</u> basis.

_____

7. <u>Distraught</u> citizens fled <u>northward</u> toward Lincoln Park and Lake Michigan.

_____

8. The buildings destroyed by the fire included dozens of <u>stately</u> homes.

_____

Two-Word Completions

Circle the pair of words that best complete the meaning of each of the following passages.

1. Little did we realize, as we _____ blithely on the beach during those _____ and cloudless days of spring 1914, that the world was moving inexorably into the maelstrom of total war.

   a. evinced . . . piquant
   b. belabored . . . utopian

   c. emulated . . . insatiable
   d. cavorted . . . halcyon

2. For what must have been the first and only time in his life, the overly cautious general did not _____ or vacillate but committed his troops to battle with _____ celerity.

   a. arrogate . . . overt
   b. temporize . . . unwonted

   c. carp . . . myopic
   d. dissemble . . . feckless

3. Someone who is by nature as skeptical as I am usually refuses to give any _____ to the kinds of wild allegations thrown about in an election until they have been _____ by solid evidence.

   a. credence . . . substantiated
   b. celerity . . . decried

   c. largesse . . . exhumed
   d. propriety . . . eschewed

4. Despite the somewhat strident _____ of some professional critics and the inane _____ of a few literary pedants, the work enjoyed a notable popular success.

   a. encomiums . . . largesse
   b. verbiage . . . eulogies

   c. animadversions . . . carping
   d. gambits . . . sacrilege

5. From the top of the mountain that summer afternoon, I looked out on a(n) _____ panorama of fields and pasturelands through which countless streams and rivulets _____ like so many serpents slithering lazily across a carpet.

   a. murky . . . articulated
   b. avid . . . congealed

   c. verdant . . . undulated
   d. primordial . . . cavorted

6. Someone with a _____ nature is generally very good at _____, while more honest people give off unconscious cues that they are not telling the truth.

   a. distraught . . . emulating
   b. devious . . . dissembling

   c. ubiquitous . . . strategizing
   d. acquisitive . . . decrying

Read each sentence carefully. Then circle the item that best completes the statement below the sentence.

By decrying the nation's currency, the government hoped to both spur exports and curb inflation. (2)

1. The word **decrying** in line 1 is used to mean

a. denouncing   b. devaluating   c. condemning   d. supporting

Unfortunately, the procurement specifications were framed in technical verbiage that only those thoroughly versed in such matters could understand. (2)

2. In line 1 the word **verbiage** most nearly means

a. prolixity   b. jargon   c. verbosity   d. code

The space vehicle was equipped with an articulated boom designed to deploy and retrieve small satellites and scientific devices. (2)

3. The best definition for the word **articulated** in line 1 is

a. elucidated   b. state-of-the-art   c. well-spoken   d. jointed

The ultimatum delivered to the besieged American forces at Bastogne in December 1944 is reputed to have evinced the succinct response "Nuts!" (2)

4. The best definition for the **evinced** in line 2 is

a. displayed   b. demanded   c. provoked   d. exhibited

The narrator of Edgar Allan Poe's tale "Descent Into the Maelstrom" tells the harrowing story of his deliverance from a gigantic vortex. (2)

5. In line 1 the word **maelstrom** most nearly means

a. chaos   b. turbulence   c. mine   d. whirlpool

Fire marshals soon apprehended the incendiary responsible for the conflagration that reduced to smoking embers the historic waterfront hotel. (2)

6. The word **incendiary** in line 1 is used to mean

a. arsonist   b. rabble-rouser   c. agitator   d. criminal

Antonyms

In each of the following groups, circle the word or expression that is most nearly the **opposite** of the word in **boldface** type.

1. propriety
a. tactfulness
b. correctness
c. morality
d. unseemliness

2. avid
a. enthusiastic
b. indifferent
c. quick
d. intelligent

3. myopic
a. sincere
b. scholarly
c. farsighted
d. foolish

4. coherent
a. recent
b. disjointed
c. strange
d. workable

5. nefarious
a. intelligent
b. feasible
c. new
d. meritorious

6. propinquity
a. remoteness
b. importance
c. size
d. splendor

7. largesse
a. haste
b. rudeness
c. stinginess
d. skill

8. overt
a. concealed
b. obvious
c. humorous
d. unnecessary

9. animadversions
a. compliments
b. salaries
c. backgrounds
d. quirks

10. germane
a. irrelevant
b. worthy
c. unprotected
d. disloyal

11. acquisitive
a. fault-finding
b. deliberate
c. altruistic
d. retentive

12. substantiate
a. refute
b. introduce
c. report
d. confirm

13. tenable
a. scientific
b. indefensible
c. interesting
d. complicated

15. murky
a. salty
b. turbulent
c. clear
d. polluted

14. piquant
a. bland
b. foreign
c. expensive
d. spicy

16. taciturn
a. arrogant
b. mean
c. stupid
d. garrulous

Word Families

A. *On the line provided, write the word you have learned in Units 1–3 that is related to each of the following nouns.*
EXAMPLE: acquisitiveness—**acquisitive**

1. utopia, utopianism _____
2. viscosity _____
3. murkiness, murk _____
4. myopia _____
5. coherence _____
6. banality _____
7. undulation _____
8. piquancy _____
9. intransigence _____
10. emulation _____
11. deviousness _____
12. substantiation _____
13. exhumation, exhumer _____
14. articulation, articulator, articulateness _____
15. arrogation _____

B. *On the line provided, write the word you have learned in Units 1–3 that is related to each of the following verbs.*
EXAMPLE: acquire—**acquisitive**

16. eulogize _____
17. cohere _____
18. supplicate _____
19. satiate _____
20. reconnoiter _____

Word Associations

In each of the following groups, circle the word that is best defined or suggested by the given phrase.

1. what a person who vacillates would probably do in a crisis
   a. cavort   b. temporize   c. propound   d. articulate

2. going back to the time of the first appearance of life on this planet
   a. primordial   b. feckless   c. viscous   d. taciturn

3. what a nitpicker seems always to be doing
   a. cavorting   b. decrying   c. articulating   d. carping

4. one who is unwilling to compromise
   a. tenable   b. invidious   c. intransigent   d. pejorative

5. hiding one's disappointment behind a brave smile
   a. arrogate   b. congeal   c. dissemble   d. evince

6. the rate at which gossip travels
   a. celerity   b. encomium   c. maelstrom   d. credence

7. lavish tips given to waiters, parking lot attendants, etc.
   a. eulogy   b. gambit   c. credence   d. largesse

8. too agitated to continue
   a. articulate   b. distraught   c. utopian   d. primordial

9. so nearsighted that one can't see the woods for the trees
   a. avid   b. unwonted   c. myopic   d. devious

10. rolling hills and lush meadows in springtime
    a. verdant   b. brackish   c. intractable   d. germane

11. how you might properly characterize a cliché
    a. piquant   b. insatiable   c. banal   d. halcyon

12. "So he came up to me and asked me for a quarter."
    a. accost   b. eschew   c. emulate   d. exhume

13. improper use of a house of worship
    a. suppliant   b. sacrilege   c. animadversion   d. verbiage

14. will consider only matters directly related to the question under discussion
    a. incendiary   b. germane   c. pejorative   d. suppliant

15. a grasping society
    a. feckless   b. acquisitive   c. overt   d. primordial

16. avoid bad habits
    a. eschew   b. evince   c. belabor   d. articulate

17. disparaging remark
    a. verdant   b. coherent   c. halcyon   d. pejorative

18. a rabbit's foot
    a. talisman   b. gambit   c. suppliant   d. animadversion

19. condemn publicly
    a. temporize   b. decry   c. exhume   d. substantiate

20. appropriateness
    a. eulogy   b. credence   c. propriety   d. verbiage

Building with Classical Roots

cred—to believe

This root appears in **credence** (page 35). Some other words based on the same root are listed below.

accreditation	**credibility**	**creditor**	**credulity**
credentials	**creditable**	**credo**	**credulous**

From the list of words above, choose the one that corresponds to each of the brief definitions below. Write the word in the blank space in the illustrative sentence below the definition.

1. references, testimonials, or other (usually written) evidence of identity or status (*"that which provides a basis for belief"*)

The security guard demanded to see their _____ before they could enter the building.

2. inclined to believe very readily, gullible

The naïve young man seemed as _____ as a child.

3. worthiness of belief

At the hearing, a panel of experts questioned the _____ of the advertisement.

4. a statement or summary of faith or fundamental belief; an authoritative statement of religious belief (*"I believe"*)

The _____ of our hiking club is "Take only pictures; leave only footprints."

5. bringing or deserving credit or honor

Despite limited rehearsal time, the cast did a(n) _____ job on that play.

6. an undue readiness to believe; a lack of critical judgment

The wily con artists exploited their victim's _____.

7. official authorization or approval (often used in regard to academic affairs)

The college received _____ as an institution of higher learning.

8. a person or an organization to which money is owed

The bank denied her request for a loan when they saw that she had made late payments to past _____.

From the list of words above, choose the one that best completes each of the following sentences. Write the word in the space provided.

1. In view of the number of weeks he'd been absent from class with the chicken pox, he gave a very _____ performance on the math final.

2. The salesperson making those absurd claims about the used car was clearly trying to take advantage of our _____.

3. The new medical school will convene classes as soon as it receives its official _____ from the state.

4. A physician's _____ is aptly summarized in the noble ideas and attitudes set forth in the Hippocratic Oath.

5. The applicant submitted her résumé, along with several _____ such as a diploma and written references from former employers, in order to get the job.

6. After a series of financial setbacks, the entrepreneur was forced to dodge a relentless wave of _____ .

7. The plot involved a series of coincidences so farfetched as to tax the patience of even the most _____ of readers.

8. The attorney attacked the _____ of the star witness by demonstrating that he had a poor reputation for honesty and reliability.

Circle the **boldface** word that more satisfactorily completes each of the following sentences.

1. In researching day-care centers for her son, Ms. Lopez always asked to see the most recent documents of (**accreditation, credo**).

2. We could tell by the (**creditable, credulous**) looks on their faces that the children completely believed our story about flying carpets.

3. The first thing she did with her prize money was to pay off all her (**credentials, creditors**).

4. My doctor's office is decorated with framed diplomas, certificates, awards, and other (**credentials, credulities**) that attest to her excellent training.

5. Each week that they met, the boy scouts recited their (**accreditation, credo**).

6. During the 1960s, widespread distrust of government led to the "(**credibility, creditor**) gap"—a general lack of confidence in statements made by public officials.

7. The children tried to take advantage of their babysitter's (**credulity, credibility**) when they told him they were allowed eight cookies apiece.

8. In the American film classic *Gone with the Wind*, the ever-resourceful Scarlett O'Hara creates a (**credulous, creditable**) ball gown out of green velvet drapes.

Definitions

Note carefully the spelling, pronunciation, part(s) of speech, and definition(s) of each of the following words. Then write the word in the blank space(s) in the illustrative sentence(s) following. Finally, study the lists of synonyms and antonyms given at the end of each entry.

1. atrophy
(aʹ trə fē)

(*n.*) the wasting away of a body organ or tissue; any progressive decline or failure; (*v.*) to waste away

The _____ of the downtown business district began when two huge malls opened.

The patient's muscles have _____.

SYNONYMS: (*n.*) degeneration, deterioration; (*v.*) wither
ANTONYMS: (*n.*) growth, development; (*v.*) mature, develop

2. bastion
(basʹ chən)

(*n.*) a fortified place, stronghold

Contrary to popular belief, the military is not always a _____ of political conservatism.

SYNONYMS: citadel, rampart, bulwark, parapet

3. concord
(känʹ kôrd)

(*n.*) a state of agreement, harmony, unanimity; a treaty, pact, covenant

A spirit of _____ was restored when the company compensated its employees.

ANTONYMS: disagreement, strife, discord

4. consummate
(*v.*, känʹ sə māt;
adj., kənʹ sə mət)

(*adj.*) complete or perfect in the highest degree; (*v.*) to bring to a state of completion or perfection

Michelangelo's paintings on the ceiling of the Sistine Chapel in the Vatican are works of _____ artistry.

The lawyers could not _____ the settlement until the two parties met face to face.

SYNONYMS: (*adj.*) masterful; (*v.*) clinch, conclude
ANTONYMS: (*v.*) launch, initiate, begin, kick off

5. disarray
(dis ə rāʹ)

(*n.*) disorder, confusion; (*v.*) to throw into disorder

The burgled apartment was in a state of _____.

If you leave the window open, a breeze may _____ the papers on the desktop.

SYNONYMS: (*n.*) disorganization; (*v.*) dishevel, mess up
ANTONYMS: (*n.*) organization, order, tidiness

6. exigency
(ekʹ sə jən sē)

(*n.*, *often pl.*) urgency, pressure; urgent demand, pressing need; an emergency

The governor emphasized the _____ of the situation by requesting the immediate dispatch of rescue teams.

SYNONYM: requirement, crisis

7. flotsam
(flät′ səm)

(*n.*) floating debris; homeless, impoverished people

After the two ships collided, the survivors clung to various pieces of _____ and hoped for rescue.

SYNONYM: floating wreckage

8. frenetic
(frə net′ ik)

(*adj.*) frenzied, highly agitated

When a court order was issued, the social services department made a _____ search for the missing report.

SYNONYMS: frantic, overwrought
ANTONYMS: calm, controlled, relaxed, leisurely

9. glean
(glēn)

(*v.*) to gather bit by bit; to gather small quantities of grain left in a field by the reapers

By means of painstaking investigation, the detectives will eventually _____ the truth.

SYNONYMS: collect, cull, pick up

10. grouse
(graủs)

(*n.*) a type of game bird; a complaint; (*v.*) to complain, grumble

The patient's latest _____ was that he did not get any dessert with his dinner the night before.

Those who just stand around and _____ about their low salaries are not likely to get raises.

SYNONYMS: (*v.*) gripe, kvetch, bellyache

11. incarcerate
(in kär′ sə rāt)

(v.) to imprison, confine, jail

They will _____ the convicted felon at the state penitentiary.

SYNONYMS: intern, immure
ANTONYMS: liberate, release, free

12. incumbent
(in kəm′ bənt)

(*adj.*) obligatory, required; (*n.*) one who holds a specific office at the time spoken of

Voting on election day is a duty _____ on all Americans who value a democratic government.

The _____ has the advantage when standing for reelection but does not have a guarantee of victory.

SYNONYMS: (*adj.*) mandatory, necessary
ANTONYMS: (*adj.*) optional, unnecessary

13. jocular
(jäk′ yə lər)

(*adj.*) humorous, jesting, jolly, joking

After receiving the news that she was ahead in the polls, the candidate was in a delightfully _____ mood.

SYNONYMS: waggish, facetious, droll, witty
ANTONYMS: humorless, solemn, grave, earnest, grim

14. ludicrous
(lüd' ə krəs)

(*adj.*) ridiculous, laughable, absurd

Her comment was so _____ that we finally understood that she was joking.

SYNONYMS: risible, preposterous
ANTONYMS: heartrending, poignant, pathetic

15. mordant
(môr' dənt)

(*adj.*) biting or caustic in thought, manner, or style; sharply or bitterly harsh

The actor was upset by the _____ criticism of the gossip columnist who seemed out to ruin his reputation.

SYNONYMS: acrimonious, acidulous, sardonic, scathing
ANTONYMS: bland, mild, gentle, soothing

16. nettle
(net' əl)

(*n.*) a prickly or stinging plant; (*v.*) to arouse displeasure, impatience, or anger; to vex or irritate severely

If you are pricked by a _____, aloe cream will soothe and reduce the sting.

The principal was _____ by the student's disrespectful behavior.

SYNONYMS: (*v.*) peeve, annoy, incense, gall, irk
ANTONYMS: (*v.*) please, delight, soothe, pacify

17. pecuniary
(pi kyü' nē er ē)

(*adj.*) consisting of or measured in money; of or related to money

The couple was forced by _____ considerations to sell their large home and buy a smaller one.

SYNONYMS: monetary, financial

18. pusillanimous
(pyü sə lan' ə məs)

(*adj.*) contemptibly cowardly or mean-spirited

It is often said that bullies, when tested, are the most _____ people of all.

SYNONYMS: craven, lily-livered
ANTONYMS: stouthearted, courageous, daring

19. recumbent
(ri kəm' bənt)

(*adj.*) in a reclining position, lying down, in the posture of one sleeping or resting

The tired toddlers were _____ on the couch after playing all afternoon in the yard.

SYNONYMS: prone, prostrate, supine, inactive
ANTONYMS: erect, upright, energetic, dynamic

20. stratagem
(strat' ə jəm)

(*n.*) a scheme to outwit or deceive an opponent or to gain an end

The defense attorney used a clever _____ to curry sympathy for her client.

SYNONYMS: ruse, trick, ploy, subterfuge

From the words for this unit, choose the one that best completes each of the following sentences. Write the word in the space provided.

1. I get my best ideas while lying down; the _____ position seems to stimulate my brain.

2. It was pleasant to see the usually quiet and restrained Mr. Baxter in such a(n) _____ and expansive mood.

3. The _____ that we observed here and there in the harbor bore mute testimony to the destructive power of the storm.

4. Since I had had only one year of high-school French, my attempts to speak that language on my trip to Paris were pretty _____.

5. The high ground east of the river formed a natural _____, which we decided to defend with all the forces at our disposal.

6. I regret that Nancy was _____ by my unfavorable review of her short story, but I had to express my opinion honestly.

7. Almost every case of muscle or tissue _____ is the result of disease, prolonged disuse, or changes in cell nutrition.

8. The _____ of my present financial situation demand that I curtail all unnecessary expenses for at least a month.

9. It is _____ on all of us to do whatever we can to help our community overcome this crisis.

10. Even critics of our penal system admit that so long as hardened criminals are _____, they can't commit further crimes.

11. Despite all their highfalutin malarky about helping the poor, I suspect that their interest in the project is purely _____.

12. The purpose of our _____ was to draw in the safety so that Tom could get behind him to receive a long pass.

13. The defeated army fled in such _____ that before long it had become little more than a uniformed mob.

14. As soon as he struck the opening chords of the selection, we realized that we were listening to a(n) _____ master of the piano.

15. Though next to nothing is known about Homer, historians have been able to _____ a few odd facts about him from studying his works.

16. Shakespeare's Timon of Athens is a disillusioned misanthrope who spends his time hurling _____ barbs at the rest of mankind.

17. Peace is not just the absence of war but a positive state of _____ among the nations of the world.

18. I have yet to meet an adult who did not _____ about the taxes he or she had to pay.

19. Most people regarded the government's attempt to avert a war by buying off the aggressor as not only shameful but _____.

20. People who are used to the unhurried atmosphere of a country town often find it hard to cope with the _____ pace of big-city life.

Synonyms

*Choose the word from this unit that is **the same** or **most nearly the same** in meaning as the **boldface** word or expression in the given phrase. Write the word on the line provided.*

1. **floating wreckage** in the harbor

2. **gripes** about every change in the routine

3. received **financial** compensation

4. the ill-conceived **ruse**

5. **collected** tidbits of information

6. a longtime **bulwark** of resistance

7. **prostrate** on a hospital bed

8. **craven** behavior

9. enthusiasm that **withered**

10. left the room in a state of **disorganization**

11. a handshake that **clinched** the deal

12. **immured** for years in a dank dungeon

13. **irks** her coworkers with senseless chatter

14. the **obligatory** responsibilities of the new administrator

15. the **requirements** of a wartime economy

Antonyms

*Choose the word from this unit that is **most nearly opposite** in meaning to the **boldface** word or expression in the given phrase. Write the word on the line provided.*

16. maintained a **leisurely** pace

17. **disagreement** among the family members

18. the **poignant** story

19. a **gentle** reproof

20. a **humorless** manner

Choosing the Right Word

*Circle the **boldface** word that more satisfactorily completes each of the following sentences.*

1. We were fascinated by the (**mordant, frenetic**) scene on the floor of the stock exchange as brokers struggled to keep up with sudden price changes.

2. Before the ceremony began, we all bowed our heads and prayed for unity, peace, and (**concord, atrophy**) among all nations.

3. It has been said that the only way to handle a (**nettle, stratagem**), or any difficult problem, without being stung is to grasp it firmly and decisively.

4. There are few things in life as (**frenetic, ludicrous**) as an unqualified person trying to assume the trappings of authority.

5. In the shelter, I saw for the first time people who'd been beaten and discouraged by life—the so-called derelicts and (**flotsam, incumbents**) of the great city.

6. Do you really think that those (**jocular, recumbent**) remarks are appropriate on such a solemn occasion?

7. The affairs of our city are in such (**disarray, flotsam**) that the state may have to intervene to restore some semblance of order.

8. I have always regarded our schools and colleges as citadels of learning and (**bastions, stratagems**) against ignorance and superstition.

9. The huge influx of wealth that resulted from foreign conquests led in part to the physical and moral (**atrophy, flotsam**) of the Roman ruling class.

10. A born leader is someone who can rise to the (**incumbents, exigencies**) of any crisis that he or she may be confronted with.

11. Comfortably (**recumbent, frenetic**) in the shade of the elm tree, I watched the members of the football team go through a long, hard workout.

12. In Victorian times, fashionable ladies (**disarrayed, incarcerated**) their waists in tight corsets to achieve a chic "hourglass" figure.

13. I noticed with approval that his (**pecuniary, mordant**) remarks were intended to deflate the pompous and unmask the hypocritical.

14. All that I needed to (**consummate, nettle**) the most important deal of my career was her signature on the dotted line.

15. During the 19th century, it was fashionable to spend a few weeks in the fall hunting (**grouse, nettles**), pheasants, and other game birds.

16. Of the ten Congressional seats in our state, only one was won by a new member; all the other winners were (**incumbents, bastions**).

17. To feel fear in difficult situations is natural, but to allow one's conduct to be governed by fear is (**jocular, pusillanimous**).

18. We were able to (**consummate, glean**) only a few shreds of useful information from his long, pretentious speech.

19. What we need to cope with this crisis is not cute (**grouping, stratagems**) but a bold, realistic plan and the courage to carry it out.

20. The only way we'll really be able to increase productivity is to offer our employees a few solid (**frenetic, pecuniary**) incentives to work harder.

Read the following passage, in which some of the words you have studied in this unit appear in **boldface** type. Then complete each statement given below the passage by circling the letter of the item that is **the same** or **almost the same** in meaning as the highlighted word.

Tea Time

(Line)

Although people today tend to think of colonial Boston as a **bastion** of revolutionary fervor, anti-British sentiment there grew slowly in the 1760s and 1770s. Not surprisingly, the provocation that eventually turned many loyal colonists against their mother country was **pecuniary**. In 1767 a financially strapped British

(5) Parliament placed duties, or taxes, on several items imported into the American colonies. This **nettled** the colonists because they had no representatives in the British Parliament to speak against the taxes on their behalf.

The British government, on the other hand, saw the taxes as fair since it had

(10) incurred huge debts in the French and Indian War—a war the British believed benefited their American subjects. In the end, the British government repealed all of the taxes except the

(15) one on tea. In 1773 the British provoked the colonists once again when they decreed that the British East India Company would be the exclusive seller of tea to the American

(20) colonies. Such a monopoly was a clear threat to the businesses of local tea merchants.

Boston Tea Party reenactment

When three shiploads of tea arrived in Boston Harbor in December 1773,

(25) the colonists developed a **stratagem** to foil the British. Before the tea could be sold, colonists disguised as Indians boarded the ships and emptied 342 chests of tea into the harbor. The next morning the empty chests were mere **flotsam**, and the British had not earned a penny on tea. This incident has since been given the **jocular** title the Boston Tea Party, but unlike most tea parties, it did nothing to bring

(30) the colonists and the British together.

---

1. The meaning of **bastion** (line 1) is
a. broadcaster   c. citadel
b. cesspool   d. fountainhead

2. Pecuniary (line 4) most nearly means
a. superficial   c. premeditated
b. financial   d. unnecessary

3. Nettled (line 6) is best defined as
a. incensed   c. confused
b. amused   d. delighted

4. The meaning of **stratagem** (line 25) is
a. ruse   c. code
b. costume   d. company

5. Flotsam (line 27) most nearly means
a. paper   c. trinkets
b. symbols   d. wreckage

6. Jocular (line 29) most nearly means
a. appropriate   c. facetious
b. primitive   d. famous

Definitions

Note carefully the spelling, pronunciation, part(s) of speech, and definition(s) of each of the following words. Then write the word in the blank space(s) in the illustrative sentence(s) following. Finally, study the lists of synonyms and antonyms given at the end of each entry.

1. acuity
(ə kyü′ ə tē)

(*n.*) sharpness (particularly of the mind or senses)

The _____ of most people's hearing diminishes as they grow older.

SYNONYMS: keenness, acuteness
ANTONYMS: dullness, obtuseness

2. delineate
(di lin′ ē āt)

(*v.*) to portray, sketch, or describe in accurate and vivid detail; to represent pictorially

The architects will _____ the main features of their plan at the next client meeting.

SYNONYMS: depict, picture, render

3. depraved
(di prāvd′)

(*adj.*) marked by evil and corruption, devoid of moral principles

Oscar Wilde's novel *The Picture of Dorian Gray* is about a _____ man whose portrait reveals his wickedness.

SYNONYMS: perverted, degenerate, vicious, corrupt
ANTONYMS: moral, virtuous, upright, uncorrupted

4. enervate
(en′ ər vāt)

(*v.*) to weaken or lessen the mental, moral, or physical vigor of; enfeeble, hamstring

Unfortunately, the great musician's mind was _____ by disease in the last decade of her life.

SYNONYMS: impair, cripple, paralyze
ANTONYMS: invigorate, strengthen, buttress

5. esoteric
(es ə ter′ ik)

(*adj.*) intended for or understood by only a select few, private, secret

The fraternity developed a set of _____ rites that had to be performed by anyone seeking membership.

SYNONYMS: occult, cryptic, arcane, recondite
ANTONYMS: accessible, comprehensible, intelligible

6. fecund
(fek′ und)

(*adj.*) fruitful in offspring or vegetation; intellectually productive

The remarkably _____ mind of Albert Einstein produced theories that revolutionized the science of physics.

SYNONYMS: fertile, teeming, prolific
ANTONYMS: infertile, barren, unproductive

7. fiat
(fē ət)

(*n.*) an arbitrary order or decree; a command or act of will or consciousness

The ruler instituted several new _____.

SYNONYMS: edict, dictum, ukase

8. figment
(fig′ mənt)

(*n.*) a fabrication of the mind; an arbitrary notion

The silhouette of a man on the porch was a mere _____ of your overheated imagination.

SYNONYMS: creation, invention, fancy

9. garner
(gär′ nər)

(*v.*) to acquire as the result of effort; to gather and store away, as for future use

Over the years, the writer was able to _____ some wisdom that she passed on to others in her books.

SYNONYMS: collect, accumulate, accrue
ANTONYMS: scatter, squander, waste, dissipate

10. hallow
(hal′ ō)

(*v.*) to set apart as holy or sacred, sanctify, consecrate; to honor greatly, revere

In the Gettysburg Address, Lincoln _____ the battlefield on which the Union soldiers fought and died.

SYNONYMS: venerate, bless
ANTONYMS: desecrate, defile, profane

11. idiosyncrasy
(id ē ə siŋ′ krə sē)

(*n.*) a peculiarity that serves to distinguish or identify

The fact that the plurals of some nouns are formed irregularly is an _____ of English grammar.

SYNONYMS: eccentricity, quirk, mannerism

12. ignominy
(ig′ nə min ē)

(*n.*) shame and disgrace

He went from glory to _____.

SYNONYMS: dishonor, humiliation, disrepute, odium
ANTONYMS: honor, glory, acclaim

13. mundane
(mən dān′)

(*adj.*) earthly, worldly, relating to practical and material affairs; concerned with what is ordinary

The painter left all _____ concerns to her sister while she single-mindedly pursued her artistic goals.

SYNONYMS: prosaic, humdrum, routine, sublunary
ANTONYMS: heavenly, unworldly, spiritual, transcendental

14. nuance
(nü′ äns)

(*n.*) a subtle or slight variation (as in color, meaning, quality), delicate gradation or shade of difference

In his writing, the poet paid close attention to every

_____ of meaning in the words he chose.

SYNONYMS: shade, nicety, refinement

15. overweening
(ō vər wē ′niŋ)

(*adj.*) conceited, presumptuous; excessive, immoderate

It was the _____ confidence of the candidate that prevented her from acknowledging her weaknesses.

SYNONYMS: arrogant, unbridled, inflated
ANTONYMS: restrained, understated, modest, meek

16. penchant
(pen′ chənt)

(*n.*) a strong attraction or inclination

A teacher with a _____ for belaboring the obvious is bound to be boring.

SYNONYMS: proclivity, propensity, predilection
ANTONYMS: disinclination, aversion

17. reputed
(ri pyüt′ id)

(*adj.*) according to reputation or general belief; having widespread acceptance and good reputation; (*part.*) alleged

Although he is the _____ head of a crime syndicate, he has never spent time in jail.

SYNONYMS: putative, reputable, supposed
ANTONYMS: proven, corroborated, authenticated

18. sophistry
(säf′ ə strē)

(*n.*) reasoning that seems plausible but is actually unsound; a fallacy

The couple was beguiled into buying a bigger house than they needed by the clever _____ of the broker.

SYNONYMS: specious reasoning

19. sumptuous
(səmp′ chü əs)

(*adj.*) costly, rich, magnificent

The _____ feast honoring the king's birthday was followed by musical entertainment.

SYNONYMS: lavish, munificent, opulent, splendid
ANTONYMS: skimpy, meager, stingy, niggardly, spartan

20. ubiquitous
(yü bik′ wə təs)

(*adj.*) present or existing everywhere

The _____ eye of the TV camera threatens to rob citizens of any sense of privacy.

SYNONYMS: omnipresent, pervasive, universal
ANTONYMS: restricted, limited, rare, scarce

Completing the Sentence

From the words for this unit, choose the one that best completes each of the following sentences. Write the word in the space provided.

1. The man is _____ to have mob connections, but so far no one has actually substantiated the allegation.

2. During the eleven years of his "personal rule," King Charles I bypassed Parliament and ruled England by royal _____.

3. The phonograph is but one of the wonderful new devices that sprang from the _____ mind of Thomas Edison, our most prolific inventor.

4. American-style fast-food shops have gained such popularity all over the world that they are now truly _____.

5. His constant use of the word *fabulous,* even for quite ordinary subjects, is a(n) _____ that I could do without.

6. The passing years lessened her physical vigor but in no way diminished the _____ of her judgment.

7. I was so _____ by the oppressive heat and humidity of that awful afternoon that I could barely move.

8. Music can often express a(n) _____ of mood or feeling that would be difficult to put into words.

9. The ground in which those soldiers are buried was _____ by the blood they shed on it.

10. Analysis will show that his "brilliant exposition" of how we can handle the pollution problem without cost to anyone is the merest _____.

11. His _____ sense of superiority dominates his personality in much the same way as his beetling brow dominates his face.

12. The marathon not only brought in huge sums of money for Africa's starving masses but also _____ much sympathy for their plight.

13. May I interrupt this abstruse discussion and turn your attention to more _____ matters—like what's for dinner?

14. You may have many good traits, but I do not admire your _____ for borrowing things and failing to return them.

15. The artist's sketch not only _____ the model's appearance accurately, but also captured something of her personality.

16. "Your suspicion that I am constantly making fun of you behind your back is a mere _____ of your overheated brain," I replied.

17. There is quite a difference between the austere furnishings of my little apartment and the _____ accommodations of a luxury hotel.

18. He was a changed young man after he suffered the _____ of expulsion from West Point for conduct unbecoming a gentleman.

19. Most people I know are so busy dealing with the ordinary problems of life that they have no time for _____ philosophical speculation.

20. Beneath the man's cultivated manner and impeccable grooming there lurked the _____ mind of a brutal sadist.

Synonyms

*Choose the word from this unit that is **the same** or **most nearly the same** in meaning as the **boldface** word or expression in the given phrase. Write the word on the line provided.*

1. known for his **propensity** for exaggeration _____

2. a distinct **shade** of meaning _____

3. as a result of a general **edict** _____

4. a **supposed** heir to a huge fortune _____

5. an **eccentricity** of speech _____

6. **depicted** the view from the balcony _____

7. sought **occult** knowledge in ancient books _____

8. the latest **fabrication** of his imagination _____

9. their **omnipresent** sense of dread _____

10. known for the **keenness** of her wit _____

11. a truly **vicious** attack on an innocent person _____

12. the **fertile** products of a lively intelligence _____

13. **weakened** by the relentless repetition _____

14. **collects** data from many sources _____

15. deceived by the **specious reasoning** of a lawyer _____

Antonyms

*Choose the word from this unit that is **most nearly opposite** in meaning to the **boldface** word or expression in the given phrase. Write the word on the line provided.*

16. **desecrated** the tombs of their ancestors _____

17. a man of **modest** aspirations _____

18. the **unworldly** side of life _____

19. made a **meager** meal _____

20. the **glory** of her situation _____

Choosing the Right Word

Circle the **boldface** word that more satisfactorily completes each of the following sentences.

1. It is only in superior mental powers, not in physical strength or (**ignominy, acuity**) of the senses, that human beings surpass other living things.

2. Cleopatra took her own life rather than suffer the (**figment, ignominy**) of being led through the streets of Rome in chains.

3. Like a true fanatic, he considers anyone who disagrees with him on any issue to be either feebleminded or (**depraved, mundane**).

4. Your language is indeed clever and amusing, but your argument is nothing but a piece of outright (**sophistry, idiosyncrasy**).

5. In a democracy, the government must rule by persuasion and consent—not by mere (**fiat, sophistry**).

6. The conversation between the computer programmers was so (**esoteric, ubiquitous**) that I wasn't sure whether they were speaking English.

7. Her imagination is like a (**fecund, depraved**) field in which new ideas spring up like so many ripe ears of corn.

8. In that rarefied atmosphere, I was afraid to ask about anything quite so (**sumptuous, mundane**) as the location of the john.

9. We will never abandon a cause that has been (**garnered, hallowed**) by the achievements and sacrifices of so many noble people.

10. Someone with a pronounced (**penchant, figment**) for saying the wrong thing might justly be described as a victim of "foot-in-mouth" disease.

11. I appreciate all those kind expressions of gratitude for my services, but I had hoped also to (**garner, nuance**) some greenbacks.

12. Probably no complaint of young people is more (**ubiquitous, depraved**) than "My parents don't understand me!"

13. Scandal and corruption may so (**enervate, delineate**) an administration that it can no longer function effectively.

14. He means well, but we cannot tolerate his highly (**idiosyncratic, fecund**) behavior in an organization that depends on discipline and teamwork.

15. How I'd love to knock the wind out of the sails of that lout's (**fecund, overweening**) conceit!

16. Two synonyms are rarely exactly the same because (**fiats, nuances**) of tone or applicability make each of the words unique.

17. The alert defense put up by our team completely neutralized our opponents' (**reputedly, sumptuously**) unstoppable passing attack.

18. A true sign of intellectual maturity is the ability to distinguish the (**figments, penchants**) of wishful thinking from reality.

19. The (**sumptuous, ubiquitous**) banquet was a pleasant change of pace from the spartan fare to which I had become accustomed.

20. Few writers have J. D. Salinger's remarkable ability to (**delineate, garner**) the emotions and aspirations of the average teenager.

Read the following passage, in which some of the words you have studied in this unit appear in **boldface** type. Then complete each statement given below the passage by circling the letter of the item that is **the same** or **almost the same** in meaning as the highlighted word.

Lights! Action! Paint!

(Line)

The age-old aspiration of painters to **delineate** reality in recognizable forms was consciously abandoned in the United States in the 1940s and 1950s by a group of artists working mostly in New York. The most prominent member of the group was Wyoming-born Jackson Pollock. Other major figures included Willem de Kooning, Mark Rothko, and Barnett Newman. Although critics were quick to lump these (5) painters together under the rather **esoteric** label Abstract Expressionist, each one had an individual style, ranging from the explosive energy of Pollock's action paintings to the serene comtemplativeness of Rothko's color (10) field canvasses.

Pollock at work on one of his famous action paintings

Despite each artist's **idiosyncratic** technique, the critics continued to point to a set of common practices that marked these painters as members of a distinct movement in (15) modern art. These commonalties included a **penchant** for working on a huge scale, an interest in the surface qualities and flat plane of the canvas, and a preference for an all-over aesthetic in which no one area of the painting (20) is emphasized over any other. One product of Pollock's **fecund** mind, his series of "action paintings" of the 1940s, is a well-known example of these Abstract Expressionist traits. Instead of using the traditional easel and brush, Pollock laid a canvas on the floor (25) and moved around it rhythmically, pouring and dripping paint on it from a can.

The utter abstraction and seeming randomness of these revolutionary paintings initially baffled the public, but Pollock did succeed in **garnering** widespread critical acclaim, public recognition, and considerable financial rewards before his untimely death in a car accident in 1956 at the age of forty-four. (30)

---

1. The meaning of **delineate** (line 1) is
a. heighten
b. deny
c. escape
d. depict

2. Esoteric (line 6) most nearly means
a. cryptic
b. kind
c. critical
d. catchy

3. Idiosyncratic (line 12) is best defined as
a. excellent
b. similar
c. eccentric
d. delightful

4. Penchant (line 17) most nearly means
a. propensity
b. reputation
c. weakness
d. dislike

5. The meaning of **fecund** (line 22) is
a. fertile
b. insightful
c. brilliant
d. expository

6. Garnering (line 28) most nearly means
a. belittling
b. acquiring
c. ignoring
d. demanding

Definitions

Note carefully the spelling, pronunciation, part(s) of speech, and definition(s) of each of the following words. Then write the word in the blank space(s) in the illustrative sentence(s) following. Finally, study the lists of synonyms and antonyms given at the end of each entry.

1. abject
(ab′ jekt)

(*adj.*) degraded; base, contemptible; cringing, servile; complete and unrelieved

In the American dream, those who work hard can escape lives of _____ poverty.

SYNONYMS: wretched, miserable, ignoble, sheer, utter
ANTONYMS: lofty, noble, exalted

2. agnostic
(ag näs′ tik)

(*n.*) one who believes that nothing can be known about God; a skeptic; (*adj.*) without faith, skeptical

Although he was a confirmed _____, he supported the rights of others to practice their religion.

Her _____ tendencies made it difficult for her to subscribe to any set of religious beliefs.

SYNONYM: (*n.*) doubter
ANTONYM: (*n.*) believer

3. complicity
(kəm plis′ ə tē)

(*n.*) involvement in wrongdoing; the state of being an accomplice

If you know a crime is going to be committed but do nothing to prevent it, you may be accused of

_____.

SYNONYMS: connivance, collusion
ANTONYMS: noninvolvement, innocence

4. derelict
(der′ ə likt)

(*n.*) someone or something that is abandoned or neglected; (*adj.*) left abandoned; neglectful of duty

The family complained about the unsightly collection of _____ cars in their neighbor's driveway.

SYNONYMS: (*n.*) vagrant; (*adj.*) remiss, delinquent
ANTONYMS: (*adj.*) punctilious, conscientious, scrupulous

5. diatribe
(dī′ ə trīb)

(*n.*) a bitter and prolonged verbal attack

The senator's speech was more of a _____ than a reasoned address.

SYNONYMS: harangue, tirade
ANTONYMS: panegyric, encomium, eulogy

6. effigy
(ef′ ə jē)

(*n.*) a crude image of a despised person

The night before the battle, the troops burned the despised enemy leader in _____.

SYNONYMS: figure, figurine, likeness

7. equity
(ek′ wət ē)

(*n.*) the state or quality of being just, fair, or impartial; fair and equal treatment; something that is fair; the money value of a property above and beyond any mortgage or other claim

Prompted by considerations of _____, the father decided to divide his estate equally among his children.

SYNONYMS: justice, fairness, impartiality
ANTONYMS: injustice, unfairness, bias, prejudice

8. inane
(in ān′)

(*adj.*) silly, empty of meaning or value

The politician made an _____ reply to the interviewer's probing question.

SYNONYMS: vapid, idiotic, moronic, fatuous
ANTONYMS: sensible, meaningful, profound

9. indictment
(in dīt′ mənt)

(*n.*) the act of accusing; a formal accusation

The Grand Jury delivered the _____ for murder after deliberating in secret for two weeks.

SYNONYMS: charge, accusation

10. indubitable
(in dü′ bə tə bəl)

(*adj.*) certain, not to be doubted or denied

You cannot argue with _____ truths.

SYNONYMS: unquestionable, indisputable
ANTONYMS: questionable, debatable, dubious

11. intermittent
(in tər mit′ ənt)

(*adj.*) stopping and beginning again, sporadic

The pulled muscle in her back gave her _____ pains for about a week.

SYNONYMS: fitful, spasmodic, random
ANTONYMS: continuous, uninterrupted

12. moot
(müt)

(*adj.*) open to discussion and debate, unresolved; (*v.*) to bring up for discussion; (*n.*) a hypothetical law case argued by students

The class agreed that the question of whether Jefferson should have retaliated sooner against the Barbary Pirates was a _____ point.

The committee members decided to _____ the issue to the full Congress at the earliest opportunity.

The law student prepared for the _____ court.

SYNONYMS: (*adj.*) debatable, questionable; (*v.*) broach
ANTONYMS: (*adj.*) undebatable, indisputable, self-evident

13. motif
(mō tēf′)

(*n.*) a principal idea, feature, theme, or element; a repeated or dominant figure in a design

The collector admired the unusual Asian _____ that was woven into the fabric of the tapestry.

14. neophyte
(nē′ ə fīt)

(*n.*) a new convert, beginner, novice

In comparison to an experienced wilderness hiker, he is a mere _____ in the woods.

SYNONYMS: tenderfoot, tyro, rookie
ANTONYMS: veteran, past master, expert, pro

15. perspicacity
(pər spə kas′ ət ē)

(*n.*) keenness in observing and understanding

The birdwatcher scans the surrounding trees and fields with the same _____ as a hawk looking for prey.

SYNONYMS: acuity, acumen, discernment
ANTONYMS: dullness, obtuseness

16. plenary
(plēn′ ə rē)

(*adj.*) complete in all aspects or essentials; absolute; attended by all qualified members

Because of its importance, the case was presented at a _____ session of the Superior Court.

SYNONYMS: unlimited, unrestricted
ANTONYMS: limited, restricted, incomplete

17. surveillance
(sər vā′ ləns)

(*n.*) a watch kept over a person; careful, close, and disciplined observation

The police kept the suspect under strict _____ after she was released due to lack of evidence.

SYNONYMS: observation, scrutiny, monitoring

18. sylvan
(sil′ vən)

(*adj.*) pertaining to or characteristic of forests; living or located in a forest; wooded, woody

Once upon a time, Hansel and Gretel walked down a _____ path, leaving only breadcrumbs in their wake.

SYNONYMS: forested, arcadian

19. testy
(tes′ te)

(*adj.*) easily irritated; characterized by impatience and exasperation

The lawyer's _____ remarks during cross-examination probably affected her credibility with the jury.

SYNONYMS: irritable, peevish, waspish, petulant
ANTONYMS: even-tempered, imperturbable, unexcitable

20. travesty
(trav′ ə stē)

(*n.*) a grotesque or grossly inferior imitation; a disguise, especially the clothing of the opposite sex; (*v.*) to ridicule by imitating in a broad or burlesque fashion

Instead of modernizing Shakespeare's "Twelfth Night," they made a _____ of it.

The Restoration dramatists _____ the snobbery of the upper classes in their satirical comedies.

SYNONYMS: (*n.*) burlesque, parody, caricature, farce

Completing the Sentence

From the words for this unit, choose the one that best completes each of the following sentences. Write the word in the space provided.

1. Though some writers have emphasized Jefferson's human weaknesses, his greatness is also a(n) _____ part of the historic record.

2. Since he neither affirms nor denies the existence of God, I'd classify him as a(n) _____ rather than an atheist.

3. During the emergency, the mayor assumed _____ authority and did whatever was needed to provide essential services.

4. It was such a(n) _____ remark that I couldn't keep myself from laughing derisively when I heard it.

5. "Simple _____ demands that we distribute the tax burden as fairly as possible among the populace," the Senator remarked.

6. How can you call that a(n) _____ question when it is quite clearly a simple matter of right and wrong?

7. I would be _____ in my duty to you if I did not warn you against the bad effects of smoking cigarettes.

8. Since the accused was never really given a chance to defend himself, his so-called "trial" was nothing but a(n) _____ of justice.

9. The overthrown dictator was hanged in _____ before a vast throng in the town square.

10. Those who saw the young woman being assaulted and did nothing to help her were guilty of _____ in the crime.

11. At the slightest sound of thunder, my dog Rover dives under the bed in a state of _____ terror.

12. In her garland of leaves and acorns, the child looked very much like some _____ spirit from an Arthurian myth.

13. Throughout the period that the spy thought he had gone undetected, he was actually under close _____ by the CIA.

14. For years, we carried on a(n) _____ correspondence, sometimes allowing months to pass before a letter was answered.

15. Every time we did something to anger him, he delivered an intemperate _____ lambasting our "hopeless irresponsibility."

16. In Wagner's operas, brief musical _____ associated with the characters or their actions recur again and again.

17. The fact that so many released prisoners return to a life of crime is in itself a terrifying _____ of our penal system.

18. How could a mere _____ in the teaching profession question the judgment of so experienced an educator?

19. I'd say that the phrase "having a short fuse" aptly describes my boss's decidedly _____ disposition.

20. The _____ of her analysis not only clarified the nature of the problem but also suggested its most promising solution.

Synonyms

*Choose the word from this unit that is **the same** or **most nearly the same** in meaning as the **boldface** word or expression in the given phrase. Write the word on the line provided.*

1. a crude **likeness** _____

2. a familiar **theme** in her poetry _____

3. put under **scrutiny** _____

4. a mere **parody** of fair play _____

5. the **forested** slopes of the Rockies _____

6. announced the formal **charge** to the press _____

7. admired for his uncommon **acuity** _____

8. was given **unlimited** power to govern _____

9. indoctrinated the **rookie** _____

10. a **doubter** in every aspect _____

11. **remiss** in discharging her responsibilities _____

12. guilty of **collusion** _____

13. could not contain her own **tirade** _____

14. the **vapid** chatter of thoughtless critics _____

15. a **debatable** issue _____

Antonyms

*Choose the word from this unit that is **most nearly opposite** in meaning to the **boldface** word or expression in the given phrase. Write the word on the line provided.*

16. the **continuous** flow of water _____

17. a history of **injustice** _____

18. the **dubious** strength of the foundation _____

19. calmed the **even-tempered** child _____

20. her **lofty** plea for understanding _____

Choosing the Right Word

*Circle the **boldface** word that more satisfactorily completes each of the following sentences.*

1. Today's forecast calls for variable cloudiness with (**abject, intermittent**) periods of rain.

2. Only an (**intermittent, abject**) coward would stand idly by while a defenseless old woman was mugged in the street.

3. All of a sudden, a strange young man rushed onto the speaker's platform and launched into a (**travesty, diatribe**) against "big government."

4. After over 30 years in Congress, he retains the idealism of the (**agnostic, neophyte**) but has gained the practical wisdom of the veteran.

5. As he sat before the fire absentmindedly puffing on his pipe, Grandfather seemed the very epitome of (**plenary, sylvan**) contentment.

6. According to voodoo belief, one can get rid of an enemy by making a tiny (**effigy, motif**) of him and sticking it full of pins.

7. My studies have convinced me that the one dominant (**motif, diatribe**) in American history has been the expansion of democracy.

8. The picture shows the three Graces dancing in a forest clearing, while nymphs, satyrs, and other (**sylvan, indubitable**) creatures cavort among the trees.

9. "I vetoed that idea when it was first (**mooted, indicted**) years ago," the Governor said, "and I have never regretted my decision."

10. The awkward pause in the conversation became even more painful when he interjected his (**plenary, inane**) attempts at humor.

11. His extraordinary ability to (**moot, travesty**) the works of popular writers is largely due to his keen eye for the ridiculous.

12. What qualities will he have to fall back on when his (**indubitable, testy**) charm and good looks begin to wear thin?

13. Though the book was written by an avowed (**agnostic, derelict**), it enjoyed a certain popularity with the faithful.

14. How can I be accused of (**indictment, complicity**) in that plot when I did not even know the conspirators?

15. Bag ladies and other homeless (**neophytes, derelicts**) roam our streets in increasing numbers.

16. Observers on the ground keep close (**surveillance, equity**) on air traffic at a busy airport by means of various electronic devices, such as radar.

17. Though I can sometimes be as (**testy, derelict**) as an irate wasp, I normally do not lose my temper very easily.

18. The historian had long been noted for the soundness of his scholarship and the (**complicity, perspicacity**) of his judgment.

19. His disgraceful behavior since he left college is in itself a(n) (**indictment, surveillance**) of the lax, overindulgent upbringing he received.

20. Since she is a fair-minded woman, I'm sure she will present both sides of the controversy with admirable (**equity, effigy**).

Read the following passage, in which some of the words you have studied in this unit appear in **boldface** type. Then complete each statement given below the passage by circling the letter of the item that is **the same** or **almost the same** in meaning as the highlighted word.

Judicial Heights

(Line)

The Supreme Court is the most powerful judicial body in the United States and, possibly, the world. But this esteemed branch of the American government has not always commanded quite so much respect. In its early days the court had to fight off **intermittent** infringements on its authority by the executive and legislative
(5) branches of the American government. Most challenging, it also had to assert its authority over fractious state and local courts in order to bolster the power of the federal government.
(10) The first justices were appointed to the Supreme Court by George Washington. They were all members of Washington's Federalist party and thus intensely sympathetic to his policies. These
(15) **neophytes** could not see any role for themselves beyond personal and party loyalty, and, as a result, the young court quickly became a hotbed of partisan controversy. Two of the first three justices,
(20) John Jay and Oliver Ellsworth, resigned after a few years, and the third, John Rutledge, was refused confirmation by a

Located in the nation's capital, the U.S. Supreme Court is open to the public year-round.

testy Senate after he had already served four months on the bench. The Court's most **abject** hour occurred, however, when Justice Samuel Chase, an outspoken
(25) Federalist, was impeached (but not convicted) by anti-Federalist forces in Congress following the election of Republican Thomas Jefferson.
The judicial tide turned in 1800 with the appointment of John Marshall by President John Adams. For 35 years the distinguished Judge Marshall steadily moved the Court toward what he saw as its rightful role: supreme arbiter of the
(30) Constitution. His **indubitable** integrity, personal courage, and judicial **perspicacity** permanently advanced the power and prestige of the Court.

---

1. The meaning of **intermittent** (line 4) is
a. rightful
c. sporadic
b. malicious
d. clever

2. Neophytes (line 15) most nearly means
a. novices
c. criminals
b. patriots
d. fools

3. Testy (line 23) is best defined as
a. indecisive
c. powerful
b. irritable
d. divided

4. The meaning of **abject** (line 24) is
a. triumphant
c. moving
b. memorable
d. ignoble

5. Indubitable (line 30) most nearly means
a. remarkable
c. political
b. indisputable
d. questionable

6. Perspicacity (line 30) most nearly means
a. manipulation
c. discernment
b. training
d. reputation

Vocabulary for Comprehension

*Read the following passage, in which some of the words you have studied in Units 4–6 appear in **boldface** type. Then answer questions 1–12 on page 73 on the basis of what is* <u>stated</u> *or* <u>implied</u> *in the passage and in the introductory statement.*

As this passage shows, zoos have served a wide range of purposes during their long history.

(Line)

Zoos, or at least collections of **incarcerated** animals, have existed for millennia. The purpose of capturing and caging animals, however, has
(5) changed over time. In ancient Egypt, certain animals were deified or else considered very closely connected to gods. These animals were held in cages in temple complexes and
(10) treated as objects of worship. In a sense, these ancient zoos were **hallowed** grounds, but it is difficult not to see them as existing more for the benefit of humans than for animals.
(15) In the classical world, private menageries, or collections of exotic animals, were **ubiquitous** among **overweening** rulers who wished to advertise their power and wealth.
(20) The modern conception of a zoo emerged in Victorian England. In fact, the word *zoo* derives from the London zoological garden, which was established in the late nineteenth
(25) century. The purpose of this zoo, according to its founder Sir Stamford Raffles, was scientific study, not the "vulgar admiration" of animals. Despite Raffles's **fiat**, however, zoos
(30) on both sides of the Atlantic soon focused on entertaining the large crowds that paid money to view the animals. While exposure to both rare and commonplace creatures
(35) benefited many zoo patrons, the animals often suffered. The creatures, which had been either taken captive in the wild or bred in captivity, were usually housed singly
(40) in tiny metal cages or other bare enclosures, where they paced nervously or lay **recumbent** in a bored stupor.

Finally, with the rise of ecological
(45) consciousness in the 1970s, the bars began to come down in zoos all over the world. Increasingly, captive animals were placed in roomier, more natural environments not only for their
(50) own well-being but also as a way of educating the public about the need to preserve wild habitats.

1. The meaning of **incarcerated** (line 2) is
a. immense
b. exotic
c. imaginary
d. confined
e. dangerous

2. The primary purpose of the passage is
a. to compare modern zoos with ancient ones
b. to argue that zoos unjustifiably deprive wild animals of their freedom
c. to expose the shocking conditions in modern zoos
d. to present some aspects of the historical development of zoos
e. to offer insights into the religion of ancient Egypt

3. Hallowed (line 12) most nearly means
a. fertile
b. sacred
c. neutral
d. breeding
e. forbidden

4. Ubiquitous (line 17) is best defined as
a. pervasive
b. prohibited
c. unusual
d. traditional
e. coveted

5. The meaning of **overweening** (line 18) is
a. feuding
b. brutal
c. arrogant
d. benevolent
e. weak

6. According to the author, in the classical world private menageries of exotic animals served to
a. insure the progress of science
b. entertain large crowds of visitors
c. strengthen traditional religious attitudes
d. advertise the power and wealth of rulers
e. celebrate foreign conquests

7. The author states that the modern conception of a zoo emerged
a. in Victorian England
b. during the late Middle Ages in France
c. in China around 1900
d. during the Italian Renaissance
e. in the United States during the late nineteenth century

8. From paragraph 2 (lines 20–43), one can reasonably infer that the author
a. believes that zoo admission should be free
b. sympathizes with the animals' suffering
c. thinks that zoos are vital for scientific progress
d. rejects the techniques of captive breeding
e. thinks that zoos should be abolished

9. Fiat (line 29) most nearly means
a. title
b. request
c. decree
d. wealth
e. opinion

10. The organization of the passage as a whole is best defined as
a. chronological order
b. cause and effect
c. comparison and contrast
d. order of importance
e. spatial order

11. Recumbent (line 42) most nearly means
a. prostrate
b. contented
c. injured
d. relaxed
e. ignored

12. The tone of the final paragraph (lines 44–52) is best described as
a. satirical
b. positive
c. skeptical
d. humorous
e. philosophical

Grammar in Context

In the sentence "In a sense, these ancient zoos were hallowed grounds, but it is difficult not to see them as existing more for the benefit of humans than for animals" (lines 10–14 on page 72), the pronoun *them* refers to the noun *zoos*. A pronoun usually refers to a noun or another pronoun. This word is called the pronoun's **antecedent**. Proper **pronoun-antecedent agreement** requires that a pronoun agree with its antecedent in number and gender.

Singular pronouns are used to refer to antecedents such as *anyone, each, either, everyone, neither, no one, nothing,* and *someone.* A plural pronoun is used to refer to two or more singular antecedents connected by *and.* A singular pronoun is used to refer to two or more singular antecedents joined by *or* or *nor.* When a singular and a plural antecedent are joined by *or* or *nor,* the pronoun usually agrees with the nearer antecedent. If a pronoun's antecedent may be either masculine or feminine, use both the masculine and feminine pronouns to refer to it.

On the lines provided, rewrite each of the sentences or pairs of sentences to eliminate any errors in pronoun-antecedent agreement. Write "correct" if the sentence is correct.

1. In ancient Egypt, certain animals were highly respected for its close connections to the gods.

_____

_____

2. Each of these animals had their own mythology, or collection of tales.

_____

_____

3. Through collecting exotic animals, rulers wished to advertise his or her power and wealth.

_____

_____

4. The modern concept of zoos had their start in Victorian England.

_____

_____

5. Neither full-grown African lions nor an adult giraffe likes its close confinement.

_____

_____

6. Beginning in the 1970s, ecological consciousness has had their effect on zoos.

_____

_____

7. Nowadays each zoo visitor will have to make up their minds about the animals' well-being.

_____

_____

Two-Word Completions

Circle the pair of words that best complete the meaning of each of the following passages.

1. After the battle, the officer who had failed to carry out his orders was arrested by the military police, charged with _____ of duty, and _____ in the stockade, pending a court-martial.
   a. atrophy . . . garnered
   b. dereliction . . . incarcerated
   c. travesty . . . mooted
   d. ignominy . . . hallowed

2. Despite the harried officer's _____ attempts to steady his troops after the left flank had been turned, they fled from the field in such _____ that their departure was more of a rout than a retreat.
   a. consummate . . . ignominy
   b. ludicrous . . . equity
   c. intermittent . . . concord
   d. frenetic . . . disarray

3. I'm extremely circumspect about what I say or do in the office because my boss is so _____ that it is easy to _____ or exasperate him.
   a. mordant . . . disarray
   b. abject . . . moot
   c. testy . . . nettle
   d. jocular . . . enervate

4. Vincent van Gogh was indeed a(n) _____ technician, able to _____ every nuance of nature's variegated panorama with a mere stroke of the brush.
   a. ubiquitous . . . hallow
   b. indubitable . . . enervate
   c. consummate . . . delineate
   d. sylvan . . . travesty

5. Although the man is certainly thought to have been involved in the crime, no _____ has yet been brought against him because the authorities have not been able to assemble enough evidence to establish his _____ beyond a reasonable doubt.
   a. indictment . . . complicity
   b. surveillance . . . equity
   c. exigency . . . acuity
   d. figment . . . perspicacity

6. Edward R. Murrow will hold a place in history as a journalist who saw in 1950s television the potential to educate, and not simply to entertain. He felt it was the _____ responsibility of all journalists to act as a(n) _____ against both zealotry and indifference.
   a. consummate . . . fiat
   b. plenary . . . grouse
   c. overweening . . . indictment
   d. incumbent . . . bastion

Choosing the Right Meaning

Read each sentence carefully. Then circle the item that best completes the statement below the sentence.

Many of this nation's Founding Fathers have been widely honored, but perhaps none has been so universally hallowed as its first president, George Washington. (2)

1. In line 2 the word **hallowed** most nearly means
a. sanctified   b. emulated   c. consecrated   d. venerated

The real business of the convention was conducted not so much in the plenary sessions as in preliminary, backroom caucuses. (2)

2. The word **plenary** in line 1 most nearly means
a. absolute   b. unlimited   c. fully attended   d. unrestricted

Although the source for the controversial story was undeniably a reputed one, the managing editor declined to print the article without independent verification of its accuracy. (2)

3. The best definition for the word **reputed** in line 1 is
a. alleged   b. supposed   c. reputable   d. anonymous

The lender would agree to the loan only on the condition that the borrowers offer as security the equity they held in their home. (2)

4. In line 2 the word **equity** is used to mean
a. impartiality   b. justice   c. furnishings   d. financial interest

"I, King Pericles, have lost
This Queen, worth all our mundane cost," (2)
　　　(Shakespeare, *Pericles*, III, 2, 70–71)

5. The word **mundane** in line 2 most nearly means
a. worldly   b. ordinary   c. routine   d. humdrum

Antonyms

*In each of the following groups, circle the word or expression that is most nearly the **opposite** of the word in **boldface** type.*

1. acuity
a. orderliness
b. breadth
c. flexibility
d. obtuseness

2. fecund
a. fertile
b. large
c. barren
d. serious

3. indubitable
a. dubious
b. trenchant
c. surprising
d. new

4. equity
a. result
b. meaning
c. injustice
d. cause

5. ludicrous
a. chaotic
b. heartrending
c. unusual
d. lengthy

6. intermittent
a. sudden
b. continuous
c. seasonal
d. imminent

7. mordant
a. gentle
b. repellent
c. caustic
d. savage

8. neophyte
a. advocate
b. enemy
c. beginner
d. expert

9. inane
a. explicit
b. unexpected
c. profound
d. fatuous

11. pusillanimous
a. craven
b. ravenous
c. daring
d. corpulent

13. ignominy
a. criticism
b. publicity
c. odium
d. acclaim

15. consummate
a. report
b. initiate
c. study
d. clinch

10. sumptuous
a. open
b. meager
c. secret
d. lavish

12. frenetic
a. frantic
b. haphazard
c. relaxed
d. indolent

14. depraved
a. corrupt
b. intelligent
c. curious
d. virtuous

16. concord
a. strife
b. harmony
c. determination
d. curiosity

A. *On the line provided, write the word you have learned in Units 4–6 that is related to each of the following nouns.*
EXAMPLE: consummation—**consummate**

1. inanity, inanition _____

2. incarceration, incarcerator _____

3. fecundity, fecundation _____

4. mordancy _____

5. sumptuousness _____

6. depravity, depravedness, depraver, depravation _____

7. enervation _____

8. jocularity _____

9. testiness _____

10. delineation, delineator _____

11. frenzy _____

12. ubiquity, ubiquitousness _____

13. ludicrousness _____

14. pusillanimity _____

15. reputation, repute _____

B. *On the line provided, write the word you have learned in Units 4–6 that is related to each of the following verbs.*
EXAMPLE: sophisticate—**sophisticated**

16. doubt _____

17. indict _____

18. deprave _____

19. repute _____

20. intermit _____

Word Associations

In each of the following groups, circle the word that is best defined or suggested by the given phrase.

1. the woman who now represents this district in Congress
a. fiat   b. penchant   c. incumbent   d. derelict

2. senseless chatter
a. esoteric   b. plenary   c. sumptuous   d. inane

3. a strong inclination toward the outdoor life
a. travesty   b. penchant   c. effigy   d. fiat

4. sanctify
a. hallow   b. grouse   c. atrophy   d. nettle

5. the need of the moment
a. exigency   b. diatribe   c. travesty   d. figment

6. irritable and peevish behavior
a. testy   b. inane   c. depraved   d. ubiquitous

7. a plan to keep our surprise party a secret
a. equity   b. stratagem   c. indictment   d. acuity

8. gather knowledge bit by bit
a. enervate   b. nettle   c. glean   d. consummate

9. a habit of stirring coffee with a fork, rather than a spoon
a. surveillance   b. complicity   c. atrophy   d. idiosyncrasy

10. a matter of dollars and cents
a. abject   b. intermittent   c. moot   d. pecuniary

11. a cabin in a heavily wooded area
a. mordant   b. overweening   c. abject   d. sylvan

12. keep a round-the-clock watch on the suspect
a. surveillance   b. diatribe   c. fiat   d. equity

13. wreckage that was washed up on the beach
a. adversity   b. bastion   c. disarray   d. flotsam

14. never slows down and relaxes
a. frenetic   b. consummate   c. plenary   d. jocular

15. the sole defender of democracy in that part of the world
a. nuance   b. bastion   c. derelict   d. agnostic

16. the literary theme of a man destroyed by his own ambitions
a. sophistry   b. motif   c. indictment   d. complicity

17. intend to cause embarrassment or annoyance
a. incarcerate   b. enervate   c. garner   d. nettle

18. spent most of the summer lying on the beach
a. depraved   b. sumptuous   c. esoteric   d. recumbent

19. possesses a remarkable keenness of insight into human nature
a. concord   b. neophyte   c. diatribe   d. perspicacity

20. the product of a fevered brain or overactive imagination
a. travesty   b. flotsam   c. figment   d. ignominy

gno(s)—to know

Building with Classical Roots

This Greek root appears in **agnostic** (page 65). Note that in some words based on the root **gno-**, the **o** in the base may not appear in the final form of the word; this is the case in **cognate**. Some other words based on this root are listed below.

cognate	**cognizant**	**gnostic**	**prognosis**
cognition	**diagnose**	**ignore**	**recognize**

From the list of words above, choose the one that corresponds to each of the brief definitions below. Write the word in the blank space in the illustrative sentence below the definition.

1. related by family or origin; related in nature, character, quality, or function; a person or thing related to another

The Sanskrit word for king—*rajah*—is a _____ of the Latin *rex*.

2. to disregard deliberately; to pay no attention to; to refuse to consider

If we just _____ Rover, he will eventually stop begging for food at the table.

3. a prediction of the probable course of a disease; a probable forecast or estimate

With modern treatment options, patients who contract this once-fatal disease now have an excellent _____ for full recovery.

4. the broad mental process by which knowledge is acquired, including aspects of awareness, perception, reasoning, judgment, memory, and intuition; knowledge

After a serious blow to the head, her _____ was impaired for several weeks.

5. to identify a disease or condition based on observation, examination, and analysis

A podiatrist is trained to _____ and treat a range of problems of the foot.

6. to know, identify, or show awareness of something from past experience or knowledge; to accept as a fact; to acknowledge a thing's existence, validity, or authority; to approve of or appreciate

The school board has come to _____ the positive impact of art and music classes.

7. of, relating to, or possessing intellectual or spiritual knowledge

Many religions observe a _____ doctrine, where emphasis is placed on the pursuit of spiritual and intellectual knowledge.

8. fully informed; conscious; aware

As a result of a 1966 court decision, all arrested suspects must be made _____ of their Miranda rights.

From the list of words on page 79, choose the one that best completes each of the following sentences. Write the word in the blank space provided.

1. High-speed Internet connections and extensive medical databases make it possible for doctors to _____ certain conditions without actually seeing the patient.

2. Had she been _____ of the rugged terrain, she'd have avoided that route.

3. Ignoring her doctor's pessimistic _____, grandmother insisted on inviting the entire family to her home for a festive holiday party.

4. "I'd like this august body to _____ my esteemed colleague from Iowa," boomed the senior senator from Arkansas.

5. Poet Richard Wilbur once described the Garden of Eden as the "_____ splendor [from which] all things came. . . ."

6. Although they may respond to certain sensations, comatose individuals do not experience _____ in the way that fully conscious people do.

7. A flourishing society must not _____ its failings, but instead address and try to fix them.

8. In a short book of poetry published in 1891, Herman Melville included an eight-line fragment from a lost _____ poem believed to have been written in the twelfth century.

---

*Circle the **boldface** word that more satisfactorily completes each of the following sentences.*

1. To devise a meaningful survey, an astute pollster must be (**cognizant, gnostic**) of the current issues most likely to influence respondents.

2. Dedicated (**ignorant, gnostic**) believers sought to understand the nature of the soul and its relationship to the world.

3. One fascinating branch of neuroscience examines and analyzes the physical characteristics of (**prognosis, cognition**) and related brain function.

4. Clever teachers have written funny (**cognate, cognizant**) poems to help students learn foreign words by using the vocabulary they already know in their own language.

5. Salmon who swim upstream to spawn in the fresh waters where they were born are believed to (**recognize, diagnose**) their original home by some primal sense of smell.

6. I've finally learned to (**recognize, ignore**) those annoying messages that tell me that my computer has committed a fatal error; I just reboot and start over.

7. A good business plan should include a reasoned (**prognosis, cognition**) for future growth.

8. It's never easy to (**cognate, diagnose**) a baby's illness because an infant cannot describe his or her symptoms or provide a medical history.

Analogies

In each of the following, circle the item that best completes the comparison.

1. intransigent is to **compromise** as
a. dour is to carp
b. honest is to dissemble
c. friendly is to oblige
d. irresolute is to temporize

2. acquisitive is to **garner** as
a. perspicacious is to glean
b. agnostic is to dissemble
c. depraved is to belabor
d. distraught is to cavort

3. consummate is to **perfection** as
a. myopic is to perspicacity
b. esoteric is to accessibility
c. plenary is to completeness
d. taciturn is to propriety

4. pejorative is to **disparaging** as
a. jocular is to ludicrous
b. moot is to indubitable
c. abject is to lofty
d. pusillanimous is to craven

5. inane is to **acuity** as
a. overt is to brevity
b. unwonted is to status
c. banal is to originality
d. feckless is to allure

6. articulate is to **mouth** as
a. taste is to lip
b. scan is to eye
c. grouse is to heel
d. accost is to foot

7. germane is to **relevance** as
a. coherent is to consistency
b. derelict is to genuineness
c. piquant is to humanity
d. utopian is to practicality

8. diatribe is to **animadversions** as
a. eulogy is to rebukes
b. harangue is to accolades
c. encomium is to compliments
d. panegyric is to reprimands

9. detective is to **surveillance** as
a. saint is to sacrilege
b. scout is to reconnaissance
c. witch is to appropriation
d. artist is to travesty

10. testy is to **nettle** as
a. serene is to disturb
b. callous is to move
c. articulate is to numb
d. sensitive is to hurt

Choosing the Right Meaning

Read each sentence carefully. Then circle the item that best completes the statement below the sentence.

"What judgment shall I dread, doing no wrong?
You have among you many a purchased slave, (2)
Which, like your asses and your dogs and mules,
You use in abject and in slavish parts (4)
Because you bought them. . . ." (Shakespeare, *The Merchant of Venice,* IV, 1, 89–93)

1. In line 4 the word **abject** most nearly means

a. servile   b. unrelieved   c. wretched   d. cringing

The Transcontinental Treaty of 1819, a territorial concord between Spain and
America that for the first time drew the boundary of the United States from (2)
ocean to ocean, was chiefly the work of future President John Quincy Adams.

2. The word **concord** in line 1 is used to mean

a. harmony   b. unanimity   c. pact   d. misunderstanding

George Eliot introduces the hero of her 1861 novel *Silas Marner* as a miserly, avid
weaver who cares for nothing on earth so much as his hoard of gold coins.   (2)

3. The word **avid** in line 1 is best defined as

a. enthusiastic   b. keen   c. eager   d. grasping

The chief incumbency of the President is, in the succinct words of the inaugural oath,
"to preserve, protect, and defend the Constitution of the United States."   (2)

4. The best definition for the word **incumbency** in line 1 is

a. term   b. officeholder   c. aide   d. duty

In the comedies—especially those that involve mistaken identity—Shakespeare
often hinges a turn of plot on the appearance of a character in travesty.   (2)

5. In line 2 the word **travesty** is used to mean

a. burlesque   b. disguise   c. farce   d. caricature

Two-Word Completions

*Circle the pair of words that best complete the meaning
of each of the following sentences.*

1. Even after the last _____ of enemy resistance had fallen to our
troops, the sound of _____ sniper fire occasionally broke the
stillness of the summer evening.
a. bastion . . . intermittent   c. maelstrom . . . incendiary
b. gambit . . . pejorative   d. nuance . . . recumbent

2. So much industrial waste has been dumped into that once clear lake that it has now
become a _____ cesspool covered with all kinds of unsightly and
potentially dangerous _____.
a. primordial . . . concord   c. fecund . . . verbiage
b. verdant . . . largesse   d. murky . . . flotsam

3. Though most Northerners were not _____ proponents of war with
the South, many of them responded to President Lincoln's call to arms with
exemplary _____.
a. mordant . . . ignominy   c. primordial . . . exigency
b. avid . . . celerity   d. reputed . . . disarray

4. It is a truly sad commentary on modern city life that bag ladies and other homeless
_____ are becoming as _____ as traffic lights
on the streets of our larger urban centers.
a. suppliants . . . histrionic   c. derelicts . . . ubiquitous
b. agnostics . . . hallowed   d. incumbents . . . overweening

5. Since the Roman emperors were autocrats who ruled their vast empire by
_____, the democratic institutions of the Republic slowly
_____ and died.
a. complicity . . . dissembled   c. fiat . . . atrophied
b. penchant . . . evinced   d. sophistry . . . groused

Enriching Your Vocabulary

Read the passage below. Then complete the exercise at the bottom of the page.

Stepping Up to the Plate

When baseball batters step up to home plate, they ready themselves—physically and mentally—to face the opposing pitcher whose job it is to strike them out. The expression *step up to the plate,* taken from the terminology of baseball, has become a part of everyday language. People who step up to the plate take their turn putting their skill, talent, experience, or reputation on the line as they accept their unique moment of competitive confrontation.

Many words, phrases, and colorful expressions that enrich the English language have their origins in sports and games. This should come as no surprise, since athletics and recreation play such important roles in our daily lives. One such word, *gambit* (Unit 2), is derived from an opening move in chess. In standard usage, gambit has come to mean any early move made at the cost of something minor that will hopefully lead to future advantage. What does it mean to describe a political candidate as the *front-runner?* This term, from racing, refers to the competitor who clearly holds the lead.

Chess was invented in Asia centuries ago, and many words and expressions associated with it have been incorporated into the English language.

In Column A below are 8 more words and phrases that come from the world of sports and games. With or without a dictionary, match each sports word or phrase to its meaning in Column B.

Column A

_____ **1.** have an ace up one's sleeve

_____ **2.** kick off

_____ **3.** long shot

_____ **4.** Monday-morning quarterback

_____ **5.** par for the course

_____ **6.** pinch-hit

_____ **7.** showboating

_____ **8.** throw in the towel

Column B

a. what is expected according to an accepted standard, common sense, or previous experience (golf)

b. a bet or venture that has only a slight chance of success (horse racing)

c. to start, initiate, or commence (football)

d. person who is prepared to explain, *after* a defeat or disappointment, what should have been done to achieve success (football)

e. seeking to impress by acting in an ostentatious manner; grandstanding (baseball)

f. to have an effective resource held in reserve for use at a strategic point (card playing)

g. to serve as a substitute (baseball)

h. to give up, surrender, or admit defeat (boxing)

Definitions

Note carefully the spelling, pronunciation, part(s) of speech, and definition(s) of each of the following words. Then write the word in the blank space(s) in the illustrative sentence(s) following. Finally, study the lists of synonyms and antonyms given at the end of each entry.

1. allay
(ə lā′)

(*v.*) to calm or pacify, set to rest; to lessen or relieve

The politician made a speech in order to _____ his constituents' fears.

SYNONYMS: reduce, alleviate, moderate
ANTONYMS: aggravate, exacerbate, intensify

2. bestial
(bes′ chəl)

(*adj.*) beastlike; beastly, brutal; subhuman in intelligence and sensibility

In beating their prisoner, the guards were guilty of a truly

_____ act.

SYNONYMS: animal, depraved, loathsome
ANTONYMS: human, humane, clement, virtuous, upright

3. convivial
(kən viv′ ē əl)

(*adj.*) festive, sociable, having fun together, genial

Thanksgiving dinner at Grandmother's house is always

a _____ family gathering.

SYNONYMS: fun-loving, jovial, merry
ANTONYMS: dour, grim, sullen, unsociable

4. coterie
(kō′ tə rē)

(*n.*) a circle of acquaintances; a close-knit, often exclusive, group of people with a common interest

Robert Browning and his _____ had ideas about poetry that seemed revolutionary in their day.

SYNONYMS: clique, set

5. counterpart
(kaůnt′ ər pärt)

(*n.*) a person or thing closely resembling or corresponding to another; a complement

I have to admit I was frightened of my _____ on the other team because she held the high-jump record.

SYNONYM: match

6. demur
(di mər′)

(*v.*) to object or take exception to; (*n.*) an objection

The rank and file will _____ if they are not consulted regularly by the union leadership.

The speech in favor of the proposal was drowned out by a

chorus of _____ from the senate floor.

SYNONYMS: (*v.*) protest, object to
ANTONYMS: (*v.*) assent to, consent to, accept, agree to

7. effrontery
(ə frən' tə rē)

(*n.*) shameless boldness, impudence

After having been suspended for disrespectful behavior, the student had the _____ to talk back to his teacher again.

SYNONYMS: gall, chutzpah, nerve, impertinence, cheek
ANTONYMS: shyness, diffidence, timidity

8. embellish
(em bel' ish)

(*v.*) to decorate, adorn, touch up; to improve by adding details

The best storytellers _____ their tales in ways that help readers visualize the setting.

SYNONYMS: ornament, garnish
ANTONYMS: strip, mar, disfigure

9. ephemeral
(i fem' ər əl)

(*adj.*) lasting only a short time, short-lived

Only the greatest of writers and artists achieve anything other than _____ popularity.

SYNONYMS: fleeting, transient, evanescent, transitory
ANTONYMS: durable, long-lasting, permanent, perpetual

10. felicitous
(fə lis' ə təs)

(*adj.*) appropriate, apt, well chosen; marked by well-being or good fortune, happy

In view of the high prices for home heating oil, the mild winter was a _____ turn of events.

SYNONYMS: fortunate, well-put
ANTONYMS: inappropriate, inept, graceless, unhappy

11. furtive
(fər' tiv)

(*adj.*) done slyly or stealthily, sneaky, secret, shifty; stolen

The girl was caught taking a _____ glance at the test paper of the student sitting next to her.

SYNONYMS: clandestine, covert, surreptitious
ANTONYMS: forthright, aboveboard, open

12. garish
(gar' ish)

(*adj.*) glaring; tastelessly showy or overdecorated in a vulgar or offensive way

The storefront was painted in _____ colors so that it would attract the attention of passersby.

SYNONYMS: gaudy, flashy, tawdry
ANTONYMS: subdued, muted, understated, quiet

13. illusory
(i lü' sə rē)

(*adj.*) misleading, deceptive; lacking in or not based on reality

Police state tactics provide an _____ sense of security in an unjust society.

SYNONYMS: specious, spurious, fanciful, imaginary
ANTONYMS: actual, real, factual, objective

14. indigent
(in' də jənt)

(*adj.*) needy, impoverished

The number of homeless and _____
persons has increased since the economy took a downturn.

SYNONYMS: penniless, poverty-stricken, destitute
ANTONYMS: wealthy, affluent, prosperous

15. inordinate
(in ôr' də nət)

(*adj.*) far too great, exceeding reasonable limits, excessive

The press showered the popular actor with
_____ praise for what seemed
a rather ordinary performance.

SYNONYMS: exorbitant, extravagant
ANTONYMS: moderate, reasonable, equitable

16. jettison
(jet' ə sən)

(*v.*) to cast overboard, get rid of as unnecessary or burdensome

The captain ordered the crew to _____
the ballast so the ship could move more quickly through
the water.

SYNONYMS: cast off, discard, dump, junk, abandon
ANTONYMS: conserve, retain, hold on to, keep

17. misanthrope
(mis' ən thrōp)

(*n.*) a person who hates or despises people

The millionaire _____ left all her
money to an animal shelter and not a penny to a single
human being.

SYNONYMS: people-hater

18. pertinacious
(pər tə nā' shəs)

(*adj.*) very persistent; holding firmly to a course of action or a
set of beliefs; hard to get rid of, refusing to be put off or denied

The defense attorney was as _____
as a bulldog in his cross-examination of the witness.

SYNONYMS: stubborn, dogged, determined

19. picayune
(pik ē yün')

(*adj.*) of little value or importance, paltry, measly; concerned
with trifling matters, small-minded

A supervisor who fusses about every _____
fault of the workers will lower morale and productivity.

SYNONYMS: inconsequential, piddling, trifling
ANTONYMS: important, significant, huge, gigantic

20. raiment
(rā' mənt)

(*n.*) clothing, garments

When the chorus in the Greek tragedy hears that the king
has died, they tear their _____ in
anguish.

SYNONYMS: apparel, attire

Completing the Sentence

From the words for this unit, choose the one that best completes each of the following sentences. Write the word in the space provided.

1. A busy administrator in today's high-pressure business world just doesn't have time to deal with such _____ concerns as making coffee.

2. Recent developments in that part of the world have intensified rather than _____ our fears of a renewed conflict.

3. He is entitled to reasonable compensation for the damage to his car, but the demands he has made are totally _____.

4. The "Old 400" was a very small and exclusive _____ of prominent families that dominated East Coast society for decades.

5. When Charles V retired to a Spanish monastery, he exchanged the costly _____ of a king for the simple habit of a monk.

6. The crew of the freighter _____ most of its cargo in a desperate effort to keep the sinking ship afloat.

7. A good deal of sad experience has taught me that my youthful hopes of getting something for nothing are entirely _____.

8. Who wouldn't have had fun among such a(n) _____ group of people?

9. In the Victorian era, designers _____ women's dresses with all sorts of elaborate frills and flounces.

10. Since we all agreed that the proposal seemed to offer the best solution to our problem, It was accepted without _____.

11. The disastrous stock market crash of 1929 left many a wealthy speculator as _____ as the proverbial church mouse.

12. Though I don't consider myself much of a diplomat, I think I handled that delicate situation in a particularly _____ manner.

13. The _____ manner in which he sidled into the room and tried to avoid being noticed actually drew attention to his presence.

14. "If at first you don't succeed, try, try again" seems to be the motto of that _____ young woman.

15. Jonathan Swift so came to loathe human folly, vice, and hypocrisy that he died a virtual _____.

16. At the Casablanca Conference in 1943, President Roosevelt and his military aides met with their British _____ to map military strategy for the Western Allies.

17. The man's features suddenly contorted into a(n) _____ mask, more reminiscent of a hobgoblin than a human being.

18. The _____ movie palaces of an earlier era have given way to smaller theaters, decorated in a simpler, more austere style.

19. Many a now-forgotten "movie great" has discovered to his or her chagrin that fame may indeed be as _____ as a passing shower.

20. He had the _____ to come into my own home to tell me what I should do to help him.

Synonyms

*Choose the word from this unit that is **the same** or **most nearly the same** in meaning as the **boldface** word or expression in the given phrase. Write the word on the line provided.*

1. the **dogged** researcher   _____

2. donned fashionable **attire**   _____

3. an influential **set** of friends   _____

4. willingly **abandoned** their prejudices   _____

5. their **apt** meeting   _____

6. had the **gall** to demand an apology   _____

7. prone to **fanciful** get-rich-quick schemes   _____

8. will surely **relieve** his anxiety   _____

9. her **complement** at the rival company   _____

10. condemned the militia's **depraved** behavior   _____

11. **protested** when asked to leave   _____

12. a well-known **people-hater**   _____

13. **ornamented** with high-sounding phrases   _____

14. ignore those **inconsequential** objections   _____

15. the **fleeting** nature of power   _____

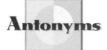

Antonyms

*Choose the word from this unit that is **most nearly opposite** in meaning to the **boldface** word or expression in the given phrase. Write the word on the line provided.*

16. their **forthright** attempt to withdraw   _____

17. **moderate** increases in profits   _____

18. the **wealthy** inhabitants of the big cities   _____

19. a very **grim** lunch meeting   _____

20. **understated** taste in home furnishings   _____

Choosing the Right Word

*Circle the **boldface** word that more satisfactorily completes each of the following sentences.*

1. The Presidency is the "toughest job in the world" because it makes such (**bestial, inordinate**) demands on a person's time, energy, and ingenuity.

2. The famous sleuth pursued his investigation with all the (**pertinacity, conviviality**) of a lion stalking its dinner.

3. "You mean you had the (**effrontery, demur**) to ask for a raise when everyone knows you've been goofing off lately?" I asked in amazement.

4. An emotion so fickle and (**ephemeral, pertinacious**) does not deserve to be categorized as "love."

5. The kind of (**garish, picayune**) theatrical makeup used by circus clowns is not suitable for an elegant fashion model.

6. Nothing we could say seemed to (**demur, allay**) her grief over the loss of her dog.

7. The proofreader didn't notice any significant flaws in the writing, but he did find a few (**ephemeral, picayune**) defects in the typesetting.

8. To anyone as fond of horses as I am, the stable and the tack room provide as (**indigent, convivial**) an atmosphere as one could wish for.

9. If installment buying is not carefully controlled, the benefits that can accrue from it may prove wholly (**illusory, inordinate**).

10. I am flattered that you want me to chair the meeting, but I must (**demur, embellish**) on the grounds of my youth and inexperience.

11. I can always come up with the crushing rejoinder, the dazzling witticism, or the (**furtive, felicitous**) phrase—about an hour after I need it!

12. When the facts of a matter speak so plainly for themselves, we shouldn't seek to (**jettison, embellish**) them.

13. Somehow, it depresses me to think that with the approach of winter this magnificent old tree will surrender all its leafy (**effrontery, raiment**).

14. She has neither the starry-eyed optimism of the idealist nor the mordant cynicism of the (**coterie, misanthrope**).

15. Though the Federal government does much to help the (**indigent, illusory**), private charities play no small part in their welfare.

16. Often the antonym of a given English word is not so much its opposite as its (**embellishment, counterpart**)—for example, *actor* and *actress*.

17. Every dynamic and successful society must be able to (**jettison, allay**) ideas and institutions that have outlived their usefulness.

18. As the rock star's popularity began to skyrocket, what had been a small (**coterie, raiment**) of admirers became an unruly mob.

19. The atrocities committed by the (**garish, bestial**) commanders of such concentration camps as Auschwitz appalled the civilized world.

20. When I returned to the office earlier than expected, I caught the little snoop (**felicitously, furtively**) going through the papers on my desk.

Read the following passage, in which some of the words you have studied in this unit appear in **boldface** *type. Then complete each statement given below the passage by circling the letter of the item that is* **the same** *or* **almost the same** *in meaning as the highlighted word.*

Hello Dolley!

(Line)

Dolley Madison (1768–1849), wife of the fourth President of the United States, James Madison, was the first great Washington hostess and an outstanding First Lady. In 1794 she married then Congressman James Madison of Virginia. Despite their differences (he was seventeen years older), their marriage was a

The state dining room of the White House where Dolley Madison entertained statesmen and socialites alike

long and **felicitous** one. In fact, her warmth (5) and personal grace seemed the perfect **counterpart** to Madison's formality and social awkwardness. After Madison became President, Mrs. Madison proved a political and social asset as well. Her letters to him (10) reveal her shrewd evaluation of the issues of the day, and an ease of communication between husband and wife on matters beyond the domestic and social.

As First Lady, Dolley Madison was best (15) known for her **convivial** Wednesday evening receptions at the White House, where influential politicians and dignitaries met and mingled. At a time of intense rivalry between political parties, these gatherings helped to **allay** some of the (20) festering bitterness between the Federalists and the Republicans, making it easier for Madison to handle a divided Congress.

Dolley Madison also brought a new sense of informality and individualism to prim and (25) proper Washington society. She set tongues wagging, for example, when she wore a buff-

colored velvet dress with a very **garish** purple bonnet, trimmed in white satin and feathers, to the Inaugural Ball. Misgivings about her unusual **raiment**, however, always gave way to pleasure at her ability to put others at ease. (30)

---

1. Felicitous (line 5) most nearly means
   a. prosperous   c. happy
   b. peaceful   d. miserable

2. The meaning of **counterpart** (line 7) is
   a. complement   c. contrast
   b. response   d. tribute

3. Convivial (line 16) is best defined as
   a. controversial   c. fashionable
   b. genial   d. famous

4. The meaning of **allay** (line 20) is
   a. sharpen   c. publicize
   b. hide   d. moderate

5. Garish (line 28) most nearly means
   a. stylish   c. large
   b. expensive   d. gaudy

6. Raiment (line 29) most nearly means
   a. attire   c. speech
   b. ancestry   d. personality

Definitions

Note carefully the spelling, pronunciation, part(s) of speech, and definition(s) of each of the following words. Then write the word in the blank space(s) in the illustrative sentence(s) following. Finally, study the lists of synonyms and antonyms given at the end of each entry.

1. allege
(ə lej')

(*v.*) to assert without proof or confirmation

The newspaper tabloid _____ that the movie star and the director were having creative differences.

SYNONYMS: claim, contend
ANTONYMS: prove, deny

2. arrant
(ar' ənt)

(*adj.*) thoroughgoing, out-and-out; shameless, blatant

In Shakespeare's tragedy the audience sees clearly that Iago is an _____ scoundrel, but Othello is blind to his treachery.

SYNONYMS: egregious, unmitigated

3. badinage
(bad ə näzh')

(*n.*) light and playful conversation

I enjoy the delightful _____ between stars like Spencer Tracy and Katherine Hepburn in 1940s movies.

SYNONYMS: banter, persiflage, repartee
ANTONYM: sermon

4. conciliate
(kən sil' ē āt)

(*v.*) to overcome the distrust of, win over; to appease, pacify; to reconcile, make consistent

Because of the weakness of our army, we had to try to _____ the enemy.

SYNONYM: placate, mollify, propitiate
ANTONYMS: antagonize, alienate, estrange

5. countermand
(kaùn' tər mand)

(*v.*) to cancel or reverse one order or command with another that is contrary to the first

Today's directive clearly _____ all previous instructions on how to exit the building in case of fire.

SYNONYMS: recall, revoke
ANTONYMS: reaffirm, reassert

6. echelon
(esh' ə län)

(*n.*) one of a series of grades in an organization or field of activity; an organized military unit; a steplike formation or arrangement

Although the civil servant began in the lower _____ of government service, he rose quickly through the ranks.

SYNONYMS: level, rank

7. exacerbate
(eg zas′ ər bāt)

(*v.*) to make more violent, severe, bitter, or painful

Shouting and name-calling are sure to _____ any quarrel.

SYNONYMS: aggravate, intensify, worsen
ANTONYMS: alleviate, mitigate, ameliorate

8. fatuous
(fach′ ü əs)

(*adj.*) stupid or foolish in a self-satisfied way

In order to discredit the candidate, the columnist quoted some of his more _____, self-serving remarks.

SYNONYMS: silly, vapid, inane, doltish, vacuous
ANTONYMS: sensible, intelligent, perceptive, bright

9. irrefutable
(ir i fyü′ tə bəl)

(*adj.*) impossible to disprove; beyond argument

The jury felt the prosecution presented them with _____ evidence of the defendant's guilt.

SYNONYMS: indisputable, incontrovertible, undeniable
ANTONYMS: disputable, indefensible, untenable

10. juggernaut
(jəg′ ər nôt)

(*n.*) a massive and inescapable force or object that crushes whatever is in its path

Any population that has experienced the _____ of war firsthand will not easily forget its destructive power.

11. lackadaisical
(lak ə dā′ zə kəl)

(*adj.*) lacking spirit or interest, halfhearted

The team's performance in the late innings was _____ because they were so far ahead.

SYNONYMS: listless, indolent, indifferent, lax
ANTONYMS: energetic, vigorous, wholehearted

12. litany
(lit′ ə nē)

(*n.*) a prayer consisting of short appeals to God recited by the leader alternating with responses from the congregation; any repetitive chant; a long list

Whenever she talks about her childhood, she recites an interminable _____ of grievances.

SYNONYMS: rigmarole, catalog, megillah

13. macabre
(mə käb′ rə)

(*adj.*) grisly, gruesome; horrible, distressing; having death as a subject

The continuing popularity of horror movies suggests that one way to score at the box office is to exploit the _____ .

SYNONYMS: grotesque, grim, ghoulish

14. paucity
(pô′ sə tē)

(*n.*) an inadequate quantity, scarcity, dearth

The senate campaign was marred by a _____ of original ideas.

SYNONYM: lack
ANTONYMS: abundance, glut, plenitude, deluge

15. portend
(por tənd′)

(*v.*) to indicate beforehand that something is about to happen; to give advance warning of

In Shakespeare's plays, disturbances in the heavens usually _____ disaster or trouble in human affairs.

SYNONYMS: bode, foretell, foreshadow, suggest

16. raze
(rāz)

(*v.*) to tear down, destroy completely; to cut or scrape off or out

The town _____ the old schoolhouse to make room for a larger, more modern school complex.

SYNONYMS: pull down, demolish, shave off
ANTONYMS: build, construct, raise, erect

17. recant
(ri kant′)

(*v.*) to withdraw a statement or belief to which one has previously been committed, renounce, retract

On the stand, the defendant _____ the guilty admissions she had made in her confession to the police.

SYNONYMS: repudiate, disavow
ANTONYMS: reaffirm, reassert

18. saturate
(sach′ ə rāt)

(*v.*) to soak thoroughly, fill to capacity; to satisfy fully

A sponge that is _____ with water swells up but does not drip.

SYNONYMS: permeate, drench, flood, imbue
ANTONYM: drain

19. saturnine
(sat′ ər nīn)

(*adj.*) of a gloomy or surly disposition; cold or sluggish in mood

Ebenezer Scrooge, the main character of Dickens's *A Christmas Carol*, has a decidedly _____ temperament.

SYNONYMS: sullen, morose
ANTONYMS: lighthearted, cheerful, vivacious

20. slough
(sləf)

(*v.*) to cast off, discard; to get rid of something objectionable or unnecessary; to plod through as if through mud; (*n.*) a mire; a state of depression

At New Year's time, many people resolve to _____ off bad habits and start living better, healthier lives.

The advancing line of tanks became bogged down in a

_____.

SYNONYMS: (*v.*) shed, slog
ANTONYMS: (*v.*) take on, acquire, assume

Completing the Sentence

From the words for this unit, choose the one that best completes each of the following sentences. Write the word in the space provided.

1. However much it may cost me, I will never _____ the principles to which I have devoted my life.

2. No sooner had the feckless tsar decreed a general mobilization than he _____ his order, only to reissue it a short time later.

3. Though some "home remedies" appear to alleviate the symptoms of a disease, they may in fact _____ the condition.

4. Ms. Ryan's warnings to the class to "review thoroughly" seemed to me to _____ an usually difficult examination.

5. The men now being held in police custody are _____ to have robbed eight supermarkets over the last year.

6. Her friendly manner and disarming smile helped to _____ those who opposed her views on the proposal.

7. The service in honor of the miners trapped in the underground collapse included prayers and _____.

8. We object to the policy of _____ historic old buildings to make way for unsightly parking lots.

9. You are not going to do well in your job if you continue to work in such a(n) _____ and desultory manner.

10. The enemy's lines crumpled before the mighty _____ of our attack like so much wheat before a harvester.

11. As a snake _____ off its old skin, so he hoped to rid himself of his weaknesses and develop a new and better personality.

12. My shirt became so _____ with perspiration on that beastly day that I had to change it more than once during the match.

13. After he made that absurd remark, a(n) _____ grin of self-congratulation spread like syrup across the lumpy pancake of his face.

14. "I find it terribly depressing to be around people whose dispositions are so _____ and misanthropic," I remarked.

15. The breaking news story concerned corruption among the highest _____ of politics.

16. Only someone with a truly _____ sense of humor would decide to use a hearse as the family car or a coffin as a bed.

17. "It seems to me that such _____ hypocrisy is indicative of a thoroughly opportunistic approach to running for office," I said sadly.

18. The seriousness of the matter under discussion left no room for the type of lighthearted _____ encountered in the locker room.

19. At first I thought it would be easy to shoot holes in their case, but I soon realized that their arguments were practically _____.

20. His four disastrous years in office were marked by a plenitude of promises and a(n) _____ of performance.

Synonyms

*Choose the word from this unit that is **the same** or **most nearly the same** in meaning as the **boldface** word or expression in the given phrase. Write the word on the line provided.*

1. the **indisputable** evidence

2. the **banter** of the morning talk show hosts

3. the **egregious** corruption of the officials

4. **claimed** that a crime had been committed

5. **foreshadows** dangers to come

6. an idea that **permeates** all aspects of society

7. will **aggravate** tensions between the rivals

8. a long **rigmarole** of questions and answers

9. a **listless** response from voters

10. the upper **levels** of power

11. tried to **placate** both sides in the dispute

12. **revoked** the outgoing President's orders

13. wore a very **grotesque** mask

14. crushed by the **force** of progress

15. **slog** through the seemingly endless files

Antonyms

*Choose the word from this unit that is **most nearly opposite** in meaning to the **boldface** word or expression in the given phrase. Write the word on the line provided.*

16. a growing **abundance** of cheap labor

17. given to **lighthearted** predictions

18. known for his **sensible** opinions

19. has **reaffirmed** her support of free trade

20. **constructed** a downtown shopping district

Choosing the Right Word

*Circle the **boldface** word that more satisfactorily completes each of the following sentences.*

1. By (**portending, sloughing**) off the artificiality of her first book, the novelist arrived at a style that was simple, genuine, and highly effective.

2. By denying your guilt without offering any explanation of your actions, you will only (**recant, exacerbate**) an already bad situation.

3. Not surprisingly, the committee's final report was an incongruous mixture of the astute and the (**irrefutable, fatuous**).

4. Stephen King's book *Danse* (***Macabre, Lackadaisical***) surveys popular and obscure horror fiction of the twentieth century.

5. With incredible unconcern, the nobles of Europe immersed themselves in social frivolities as the fearful (**juggernaut, litany**) of World War I steamrolled ineluctably toward them.

6. She excused herself from lending me the money I so desperately needed by (**conciliating, alleging**) that she had financial troubles of her own.

7. Over the years, hard work and unstinting devotion to duty have raised me from one (**echelon, paucity**) of company management to the next.

8. Economists believe that the drop in automobile sales and steel production (**countermands, portends**) serious problems for business in the future.

9. We have many capable and well-meaning people in our organization, but it seems to me that there is a (**paucity, juggernaut**) of real leadership.

10. It is a good deal easier to (**raze, allege**) an old building than it is to destroy a time-honored social institution.

11. I never ask anyone "How are you?" anymore because I am afraid I will be treated to an endless (**litany, badinage**) of symptoms and ailments.

12. His attempts at casual (**badinage, echelon**) did not conceal the fact that he was acutely embarrassed by his blunder.

13. What possible purpose will be served by setting up yet another hamburger stand in an area already (**saturated, sloughed**) with fast-food shops?

14. His debating technique is rooted in the firm belief that anything bellowed in a loud voice is absolutely (**saturnine, irrefutable**).

15. Our excitement at visiting the world-famous ruins was dampened by the (**lackadaisical, arrant**) attitude of the bored and listless guide.

16. In earlier times, people whose views conflicted with "received opinion" often had to (**recant, portend**) their ideas or face the consequences.

17. Only a(n) (**arrant, macabre**) knave would be capable of devising such an incredibly underhanded and treacherous scheme.

18. The authority of the Student Council is not absolute because the principal can (**countermand, exacerbate**) any of its decisions.

19. Someone with such a (**fatuous, saturnine**) outlook on life doesn't make an agreeable traveling companion, especially on a long journey.

20. The views of the two parties involved in this dispute are so diametrically opposed that it will be almost impossible to (**conciliate, saturate**) them.

Read the following passage, in which some of the words you have studied in this unit appear in **boldface** type. Then complete each statement given below the passage by circling the letter of the item that is **the same** or **almost the same** in meaning as the highlighted word.

The Grass Might Be Greener

(Line)

In December 2000 President Bill Clinton signed the historic Comprehensive Everglades Restoration Plan, a 7.8 billion-dollar project to rescue a unique natural habitat that was **irrefutably** on the brink of destruction. Before the twin **juggernauts** of development and agriculture transformed Florida's landscape,
(5) the seasonally **saturated** lands known as the Everglades stretched from just south of Orlando to the Florida Keys. This 60-mile wide ecosystem was comprised of sawgrass marshes, wet prairies, muddy **sloughs**, and hardwood swamps. What made the region unique was the unpredictable changes in weather patterns that
(10) created very wet and very dry periods. Indigenous wildlife adapted to these changes over the centuries, but the growing human population of South Florida wanted to control the flooding and secure a reliable water supply.
(15) In 1947 ten feet of rain fell on South Florida, flooding most of the region, including parts of Miami. The residents agitated for government assistance, and to **conciliate** them, the Army Corps of Engineers initiated a massive flood
(20) control project. Beginning in 1948, and for the next thirty years, an intricate network of canals and levees was built across the region, managing water flow for the benefit of farmers and the general population. These canals effectively cut
(25) off the northern Everglades from the southern

This Everglades alligator may live as long as 35 years and weigh as much as 500 pounds.

wetlands. This **exacerbated** conditions in the southern region not only because water flow was reduced, but also because fertilizers contaminated what water remained.

The bill President Clinton signed is meant to reverse these trends and restore as
(30) much as 1.7 billion gallons of fresh water to the Everglades ecosystem.

---

1. Irrefutably (line 3) most nearly means
  a. remarkably   c. arguably
  b. indisputably   d. irreversibly

2. The meaning of **juggernauts** (line 4) is
  a. engines   c. benefits
  b. forces   d. industries

3. Saturated (line 5) is best defined as
  a. flooded   c. neglected
  b. cultivated   d. varied

4. The meaning of **sloughs** (line 7) is
  a. fields   c. ponds
  b. trails   d. mires

5. Conciliate (line 18) most nearly means
  a. silence   c. placate
  b. reward   d. divert

6. Exacerbated (line 26) most nearly means
  a. changed   b. improved
  b. favored   d. worsened

Definitions

Note carefully the spelling, pronunciation, part(s) of speech, and definition(s) of each of the following words. Then write the word in the blank space(s) in the illustrative sentence(s) following. Finally, study the lists of synonyms and antonyms given at the end of each entry.

1. acclamation
(ak lə mā′ shən)

(*n.*) a shout of welcome; an overwhelming verbal vote of approval

It is very rare for a presidential candidate to be nominated by _____ from the convention floor.

SYNONYMS: ovation, cheering, plaudits
ANTONYMS: booing, hissing, jeers, catcalls

2. bucolic
(byü käl′ ik)

(*adj.*) characteristic of the countryside, rural; relating to shepherds and cowherds, pastoral

The Elizabethans who wrote of shepherds in ideal country settings were imitating the Greek _____ poets.

SYNONYM: rustic
ANTONYMS: urban, metropolitan

3. calumniate
(kə ləm′ nē āt)

(*v.*) to slander; to accuse falsely and maliciously

Not only did the artist's enemy seek to discredit her while she was alive but tried to _____ her memory as well.

SYNONYMS: defame, libel
ANTONYMS: flatter, whitewash, praise

4. chary
(châr′ ē)

(*adj.*) extremely cautious, hesitant, or slow (to); reserved, diffident

Since so many funds had been spent with so few results, they were _____ about appropriating more money.

SYNONYMS: wary, skittish
ANTONYMS: heedless, reckless, incautious

5. collusion
(kə lü′ zhən)

(*n.*) secret agreement or cooperation

Years later, it was discovered that senior members of the company had been in _____ with the enemy.

SYNONYMS: conspiracy, plot, connivance, cahoots

6. dilettante
(dil′ ə tänt)

(*n.*) a dabbler in the arts; one who engages in an activity in an amateurish, trifling way; (*adj.*) superficial

Many people dismissed the poster artists of the 1960s as mere _____ with nothing serious to say about life or art.

SYNONYMS: amateur, trifler
ANTONYM: professional

7. imperturbable
(im pər tər' bə bəl)

(*adj.*) not easily excited; emotionally steady

The witness remained _____
throughout the grueling cross-examination.

SYNONYMS: unflappable, unexcitable, serene, unruffled
ANTONYM: excitable

8. increment
(in' krə mənt)

(*n.*) an enlargement, increase, addition

Employees were added to the work force in _____
of five to save money on training costs.

SYNONYMS: accretion, gain
ANTONYMS: loss, reduction, decrease

9. mandate
(man' dāt)

(*n.*) an authoritative command, formal order, authorization;
(*v.*) to issue such an order

The peacekeepers were sent into the war-torn country
under a UN _____ to protect
minority populations.

The environmental protection agency has _____
that all automobiles pass an annual emissions test.

SYNONYM: (*n.*) directive
ANTONYMS: (*v.*) forbid, ban, outlaw

10. paltry
(pôl' trē)

(*adj.*) trifling, insignificant; mean, despicable; inferior, trashy

The billionaire was so greedy that he contributed only a
_____ sum of money to charity each year.

SYNONYMS: measly, meager, piddling, trivial
ANTONYMS: gigantic, immense, colossal

11. paroxysm
(par' ək siz əm)

(*n.*) a sudden outburst; a spasm, convulsion

The children greeted the clown with a _____ of
laughter when he began making his funny faces.

SYNONYMS: fit, seizure

12. pedantry
(ped' ən trē)

(*n.*) a pretentious display of knowledge; overly rigid attention to
rules and details

The fussy music professor was distinguished more for her
_____ than her true scholarship.

SYNONYMS: nit-picking, hairsplitting, pettifoggery

13. peregrination
(per ə grə nā' shən)

(*n.*) the act of traveling; an excursion, especially on foot or to a
foreign country

After returning from my _____
throughout South America, I began writing a book about
my experiences.

SYNONYMS: journey, wandering, odyssey

14. redolent
(red′ ə lənt)

(*adj.*) fragrant, smelling strongly; tending to arouse memories or create an aura

My grandmother's kitchen was always _____ with the smells of baking.

SYNONYMS: evocative, reminiscent, aromatic
ANTONYMS: unevocative, odorless

15. refulgent
(ri fəl′ jənt)

(*adj.*) shining, radiant, resplendent

The swift-flowing stream beside our house was _____ in the morning light.

SYNONYMS: luminous, splendid
ANTONYMS: dim, dark, obscure, dingy, dull, murky

16. shibboleth
(shib′ ə leth)

(*n.*) a word, expression, or custom that distinguishes a particular group of persons from all others; a commonplace saying or truism

By the time Election Day finally rolls around, most voters are tired of hearing the same old slogans and _____.

SYNONYMS: catchphrase, password, slogan

17. tyro
(tī′ rō)

(*n.*) a beginner, novice; one with little or no background or skill

You cannot expect a mere _____ to perform like a veteran in his first season of major league play.

SYNONYM: neophyte
ANTONYMS: veteran, past master, expert

18. unremitting
(ən ri mit′ iŋ)

(*adj.*) not stopping, maintained steadily, never letting up, relentless

The social laws in Edith Wharton's novels are _____.

SYNONYMS: constant, incessant, unrelenting
ANTONYMS: desultory, intermittent

19. vacillate
(vas′ ə lāt)

(*v.*) to swing indecisively from one idea or course of action to another; to waver weakly in mind or will

Someone who _____ in a crisis should not be in a position of leadership.

SYNONYMS: seesaw, fluctuate, oscillate
ANTONYM: persevere

20. vituperative
(vī tü′ pər ə tiv)

(*adj.*) harshly abusive, severely scolding

That _____ speech in which she blamed others for her own mistakes may have cost her the election.

SYNONYMS: abusive, scurrilous, insulting
ANTONYMS: complimentary, laudatory, flattering

Completing the Sentence

From the words for this unit, choose the one that best completes each of the following sentences. Write the word in the space provided.

1. As we waited through the long night for the arrival of the rescue party, we _____ between hope and despair.

2. However long and hard the struggle, we must be _____ in our efforts to wipe out racism in this country.

3. She may have great musical talents, but she will get nowhere so long as she has the casual attitude of the _____ .

4. The painting shows a restfully _____ scene, with some cows grazing placidly in a meadow as their shepherd dozes under a bush.

5. I had expected a decent tip from the party of six that I waited on early that evening, but all I got was a(n) _____ two bucks!

6. The scene may seem ordinary to you, but I find it _____ with memories of happy summers spent in these woods.

7. Since Lincoln is now considered a great national hero, it is hard to believe that he was bitterly _____ when he was President.

8. The contractor was suspected of having acted in _____ with a state official to fix the bids on certain public works contracts.

9. "The overwhelming victory I have won at the polls," the Governor-elect said, "has given me a clear _____ to carry out my program."

10. As a(n) _____ summer sun sank slowly in the west, the skies were ablaze with color.

11. In a series of searing orations, filled with the most _____ language, Cicero launched the full battery of political invective against the hapless Mark Antony.

12. Every time I sign a new lease on my apartment, my rent goes up, though the _____ are not usually very large.

13. I thought I was unexcitable, but she is as _____ as the granite lions in front of the public library.

14. Even the merest _____ in the use of firearms knows that a gun should never be pointed at another person.

15. Since Lucy had expected no more than polite applause, she was delighted by the _____ she received from the audience.

16. The Pledge of Allegiance is no mere _____ to be recited mechanically and without understanding like some advertising jingle.

17. In my various _____ through that vast metropolis, I ran across many curious old buildings that the ordinary tourist never sees.

18. I have learned from long experience to be extremely _____ about offering advice when it has not been requested.

19. Seized by a(n) _____ of rage, he began to beat the bars of his cell with his bare hands.

20. It is sheer _____ to insist upon applying the rules of formal literary composition to everyday speech and writing.

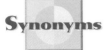 **Synonyms**

*Choose the word from this unit that is **the same** or **most nearly the same** in meaning as the **boldface** word or expression in the given phrase. Write the word on the line provided.*

1. evocative of old memories _____

2. in **cahoots** with the competition _____

3. kept up the **constant** pressure to surrender _____

4. greeted with an overwhelming **ovation** _____

5. bored us with his **hairsplitting** _____

6. overcome by a **fit** of anger _____

7. reluctantly ended her **journeys** _____

8. seesawed in their commitments _____

9. keeps repeating the tired old **catchphrases** _____

10. slandered his rivals at every opportunity _____

11. labeled a mere **trifler** by the experts _____

12. an urgent **directive** from the President _____

13. a **scurrilous** response to the question _____

14. wary of flattery and favor-seekers _____

15. painted a charming **rustic** scene _____

 **Antonyms**

*Choose the word from this unit that is **most nearly opposite** in meaning to the **boldface** word or expression in the given phrase. Write the word on the line provided.*

16. is **excitable** when challenged _____

17. a **colossal** amount of unpaid debts _____

18. reported a steady **loss** in annual sales _____

19. looked up at the **murky** dawn sky _____

20. an **expert** in the art of fencing _____

Choosing the Right Word

Circle the **boldface** word that more satisfactorily completes each of the following sentences.

1. Not satisfied with the slow (**increment, peregrination**) of his savings in a bank account, he turned to speculation in the stock market.

2. Are we to try to make a realistic analysis of our alternatives or let ourselves be distracted by slogans and (**tyros, shibboleths**)?

3. Perhaps he would be less lyrical about the delights of the (**bucolic, redolent**) life if, like me, he had grown up on a farm in Kansas.

4. It has long been known that some twisted and unhappy people derive a kind of satisfaction from (**calumniating, colluding**) others.

5. Once the senator's nomination became a certainty, all opposition to him evaporated, and he was named by (**vituperation, acclamation**).

6. During the course of my (**peregrinations, paroxysms**) through the world of books, I have picked up all kinds of useful information.

7. The phrase "We the people" in the Constitution indicates that the ultimate (**mandate, vacillation**) of our government comes from the popular will.

8. Since she comes from a rural area, she expresses herself in language that is (**redolent, paltry**) of the farm and of country life in general.

9. It is easy to criticize him, but how can we overlook the fact that for 20 years he has worked (**unremittingly, charily**) to help the homeless?

10. Although he has been in this business for 20 years, he still has the sublime innocence of the most helpless (**tyro, shibboleth**).

11. A (**paroxysm, pedantry**) of indignation flashed though the community, and the streets filled with angry people ready to protest the proposal.

12. Clad in the (**refulgent, dilettante**) armor of moral rectitude, he sallied forth to do battle with the forces of evil.

13. How do you have the nerve to offer such a(n) (**paltry, unremitting**) sum for this magnificent "antique" car!

14. Isn't it sheer (**pedantry, refulgence**) on his part to use terms like *Proustian* and *Kafkaesque*, when he knows they mean nothing to his audience?

15. The same difficulties that serve as a challenge to the true professional will be a crushing discouragement to the typical (**mandate, dilettante**).

16. If we (**vacillate, increment**) now at adopting a tough energy policy, we may find ourselves in a desperate situation in the future.

17. I'm not sure if Tom's (**imperturbable, collusive**) spirit is due to toughness or to an inability to understand the dangers of the situation.

18. I am perfectly willing to listen to a reasonable complaint, but I will not put up with that kind of (**bucolic, vituperative**) backbiting.

19. The gambler's predictions of the game scores were so incredibly accurate that we suspected some form of (**acclamation, collusion**).

20. Because my teacher is usually so (**chary, imperturbable**) of giving compliments, I felt especially good when she spoke well of my essay

*Read the following passage, in which some of the words you have studied in this unit appear in **boldface** type. Then complete each statement given below the passage by circling the letter of the item that is **the same** or **almost the same** in meaning as the highlighted word.*

At Home in the Woods

(Line)

A lifelong lover of the outdoors and one of America's most distinguished nature essayists, John Burroughs (1837–1921) was born on a farm near Roxbury, New York, in the **bucolic** Catskill Mountain region. After a **paltry** early education, Burroughs, at 17, became a country schoolteacher in a small Catskill (5) town, and eventually managed to finance some advanced study at the Ashland Collegiate Institute and the Cooperstown Seminary.

In 1860 Burroughs began writing on (10) natural and philosophical subjects for some of the leading periodicals of the day. The young **tyro** learned the essayist's art quickly and became a frequent contributor to the *Atlantic Monthly*, which he later referred to as (15) his "university." While some of his readers appreciated the echoes of Emerson in these early essays, others responded negatively to what they experienced as Burroughs' dry **pedantry**. (20)

In 1863 Burroughs took a job as a clerk in Washington, D.C. While there, he became a close friend of the poet Walt Whitman, and this relationship provided him with material

John Burroughs at home in Roxbury, N.Y., 1910

for his first book: *Notes on Walt Whitman as Poet and Person*. In 1872 Burroughs (25) returned to his native Catskills and began writing more concretely about the wonders he encountered during his **peregrinations** in the local woodlands. His writings from this period show the influence of Whitman's expansive style. **Redolent** of a more leisurely time, his works are still remembered today for their appreciation of the simple. (30)

---

1. Bucolic (line 3) most nearly means
 a. backward
 b. distant
 c. rugged
 d. rustic

2. The meaning of **paltry** (line 3) is
 a. meager
 b. sterling
 c. conventional
 d. boring

3. Tyro (line 13) is best defined as
 a. fighter
 b. neophyte
 c. invalid
 d. scholar

4. The meaning of **pedantry** (line 20) is
 a. style
 b. wit
 c. nit-picking
 d. propaganda

5. Peregrinations (line 27) means
 a. dwellings
 b. speeches
 c. wanderings
 d. writings

6. Redolent (line 29) most nearly means
 a. reminiscent
 b. stinking
 c. composed
 d. proud

Vocabulary for Comprehension

*Read the following passage, in which some of the words you have studied in Units 7–9 appear in **boldface** type. Then answer questions 1–12 on page 106 on the basis of what is stated or implied in the passage and in the introductory statement.*

As this passage shows, the central goal of the League of Women Voters is good citizenship.

(Line)

The League of Women Voters is a citizen advocacy organization that was developed as a result of the women's suffrage movement. It was

(5) founded in 1920 by the suffragist Carrie Chapman Catt, an **unremitting** champion of women's rights and social reform. Its immediate mission was to help inform and empower the

(10) 20 million American women who were enfranchised as a result of the passage in 1920 of the Nineteenth Amendment to the U.S. Constitution.

Over the years, however, the League

(15) has advocated issues less directly related to the women's movement. It has supported programs as diverse as assistance to the **indigent** during the Great Depression, civil rights in the

(20) 1960s, and environmental conservation and campaign finance reform today. Though the League vigorously champions its causes, it sees itself as staunchly nonpartisan. In other words,

(25) the League supports programs and policies but **demurs** when asked to endorse specific parties or candidates. This stance has led critics on both the left and the right to **allege** that the

(30) League is a **coterie** of activists with a hidden agenda concealed behind a banner of nonpartisanship. The

League replies that it is undeniably political but definitely not partisan.

(35) The League also takes great pride in its grassroots style of organization. Policy decisions are not made by a few leaders in the upper **echelons** of the organization, but rather are arrived

(40) at by intense study, debate, and consensus building among the rank-and-file membership at the chapter level. This reflects the League's attitude toward the power of well-

(45) informed citizens in a democracy, who ideally will make choices that will lead to a better life for all.

1. The main purpose of the first paragraph (lines 1–13) is to
   a. show how the League of Women Voters got its name
   b. discuss the origins of the League
   c. highlight the career of Carrie Chapman Catt
   d. analyze the opposition to the Nineteenth Amendment
   e. explain why women had to wait so long for the vote

2. According to the passage, the League's original mission was to
   a. lobby for passage of the Nineteenth Amendment
   b. advise Republican candidates in the 1920 election
   c. inform and empower newly enfranchised women voters
   d. lobby for campaign finance reform
   e. create a grassroots organization of local chapters

3. The meaning of **unremitting** (line 6) is
   a. undefeated
   b. intolerant
   c. unrelenting
   d. incomparable
   e. controversial

4. **Indigent** (line 18) most nearly means
   a. handicapped
   b. despondent
   c. penniless
   d. homeless
   e. oppressed

5. **Demurs** (line 26) is best defined as
   a. objects
   b. rethinks
   c. consents
   d. waffles
   e. debates

6. The meaning of **allege** (line 29) is
   a. imply
   b. dispute
   c. refute
   d. deny
   e. claim

7. **Coterie** (line 30) most nearly means
   a. clique
   b. party
   c. conspiracy
   d. family
   e. gang

8. From the details the author provides in paragraph 2 (lines 14–34), you may reasonably infer that the League has at times been
   a. partisan
   b. inconsistent
   c. unsuccessful
   d. controversial
   e. undemocratic

9. Which of the following best identifies the comparison/contrast the writer makes in paragraph 2?
   a. the Great Depression vs. the Civil Rights movement
   b. Republicans vs. Democrats
   c. national issues vs. local issues
   d. political vs. partisan
   e. critics on the left vs. critics on the right

10. The author identifies all of the following as activities of the League EXCEPT
    a. informing citizens
    b. supporting environmental conservation
    c. advocating campaign finance reform
    d. assisting the indigent
    e. lobbying for tax cuts

11. **Echelons** (line 38) most nearly means
    a. salaries
    b. levels
    c. offices
    d. classes
    e. floors

12. The author's attitude toward the League may best be described as
    a. hostile
    b. skeptical
    c. romantic
    d. admiring
    e. reflective

Grammar in Context

In the sentence "The League of Women Voters is a citizen advocacy organization that was developed as a result of the women's suffrage movement (lines 1–4 on page 105), the relative pronoun *that* has a clear antecedent, the noun *organization*. If a pronoun does not have a clear antecedent, however, ambiguity or confusion may result. Clear writers avoid faulty **pronoun reference and shift**.

Ambiguous pronoun reference occurs when a pronoun can refer to either of two antecedents, as in the sentence "Harriet supported Clare because she was convinced the chapter needed new leadership." *General reference* occurs when a pronoun refers to a general idea rather than to a specific word or phrase, as in the sentence "The League does not endorse individual candidates; this has led to criticism." *Weak reference* occurs when a pronoun refers to an antecedent that has not been expressed, as in the sentence "We attended the candidates' debates but did not endorse a single one." *Indefinite or illogical pronoun shift* occurs when there is an unexpected shift in number or person between a pronoun and its antecedent, as in the sentence "Members of the League study the issues, and you also need patience to educate voters.

On the lines provided, rewrite each of the following sentences, correcting errors in pronoun reference or shift. Write "correct" if the sentence is correct.

1. Carrie Chapman Catt founded the League of Women Voters in 1920. It was a historic action.

_____

_____

2. The League embarked on its immediate mission, which was to inform 20 million women voters.

_____

_____

3. In that magazine article, it describes the League's assistance to the indigent during the Great Depression.

_____

_____

4. The people want good leaders, but many voters do not think that is a strong point of any of the candidates.

_____

_____

5. The rivalry between Caroline and Sandra ended when she was elected chapter president.

_____

_____

6. A grassroots style of organization is where you make decisions among the rank-and-file membership.

_____

_____

Two-Word Completions

Circle the pair of words that best complete the meaning of each of the following passages.

1. Only a thoroughgoing _____ would enjoy castigating other people's behavior in such unremittingly harsh and _____ language.
   a. pedant . . . felicitous
   b. misanthrope . . . vituperative
   c. tyro . . . arrant
   d. dilettante . . . convivial

2. The speed with which the Kaiser issued, then _____, then reissued orders during the crisis was indicative of his essentially weak and _____ personality.
   a. embellished . . . pertinacious
   b. recanted . . . imperturbable
   c. demurred . . . fatuous
   d. countermanded . . . vacillating

3. The _____ rains had so _____ the ground over which we passed that it actually squished and gurgled in protest as we trod on it, and our attack had to be postponed until the sun came out again.
   a. inordinate . . . razed
   b. ephemeral . . . embellished
   c. unremitting . . . saturated
   d. bestial . . . jettisoned

4. At the June 1961 summit meetings in Vienna, President John Kennedy met with his Soviet _____, Nikita Khrushchev, in an effort to deal with sources of friction between the two superpowers and _____ international fears that the so-called cold war was heating up.
   a. counterpart . . . allay
   b. raiment . . . mandate
   c. coterie . . . exacerbate
   d. shibboleth . . . conciliate

5. Though the official is _____ to have been in cahoots with the swindlers, so far no substantive evidence has been brought forward to prove _____.
   a. portended . . . acclamation
   b. demurred . . . peregrination
   c. alleged . . . collusion
   d. calumniated . . . badinage

6. In Chaucer's *Canterbury Tales*, twenty-nine travelers from various _____ of society set out for Canterbury on a pilgrimage to the shrine of Saint Thomas Beckett. At night the _____ of travelers share their stories in order to help time pass.
   a. mandates . . . collusion
   b. litanies . . . raiment
   c. echelons . . . coterie
   d. shibboleths . . . paucity

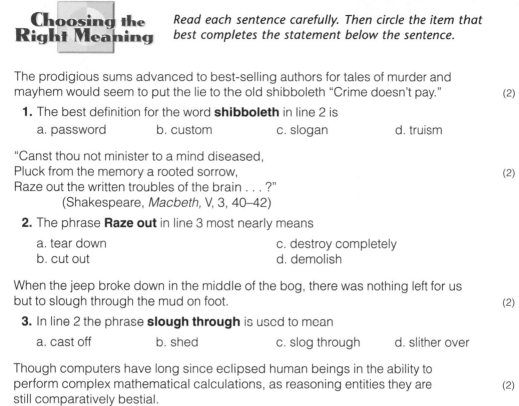

Choosing the Right Meaning

Read each sentence carefully. Then circle the item that best completes the statement below the sentence.

The prodigious sums advanced to best-selling authors for tales of murder and mayhem would seem to put the lie to the old shibboleth "Crime doesn't pay." (2)

1. The best definition for the word **shibboleth** in line 2 is

    a. password   b. custom   c. slogan   d. truism

"Canst thou not minister to a mind diseased,
Pluck from the memory a rooted sorrow, (2)
Raze out the written troubles of the brain . . . ?"
    (Shakespeare, *Macbeth,* V, 3, 40–42)

2. The phrase **Raze out** in line 3 most nearly means

    a. tear down   c. destroy completely
    b. cut out   d. demolish

When the jeep broke down in the middle of the bog, there was nothing left for us but to slough through the mud on foot. (2)

3. In line 2 the phrase **slough through** is used to mean

    a. cast off   b. shed   c. slog through   d. slither over

Though computers have long since eclipsed human beings in the ability to perform complex mathematical calculations, as reasoning entities they are still comparatively bestial. (2)

4. The word **bestial** in line 3 most nearly means

    a. subhuman in intelligence   c. depraved and brutal
    b. beastlike   d. inferior

Antonyms

*In each of the following groups, circle the word or expression that is most nearly the **opposite** of the word in **boldface** type.*

1. ephemeral
a. scheduled
b. infallible
c. perpetual
d. deleterious

2. garish
a. inventive
b. exciting
c. tasteless
d. understated

3. fatuous
a. conceited
b. vapid
c. perceptive
d. surprised

4. calumniate
a. flatter
b. introduce
c. defame
d. debate

5. indigent
a. wealthy
b. ethnic
c. poor
d. segregated

6. irrefutable
a. startling
b. disputable
c. unbiased
d. undeniable

7. badinage
a. persiflage
b. raillery
c. sermon
d. exception

8. convivial
a. grim
b. salutary
c. sociable
d. mysterious

9. furtive
a. open
b. sneaky
c. sorrowful
d. ghostly

11. razed
a. inspected
b. erected
c. destroyed
d. criticized

13. recant
a. reaffirm
b. refute
c. condemn
d. forget

15. felicitous
a. apt
b. witty
c. inappropriate
d. negative

10. acclamation
a. bias
b. cheers
c. jeers
d. departure

12. alleged
a. novice
b. veteran
c. bungling
d. proven

14. jettison
a. eliminate
b. improve
c. retain
d. grasp

16. paucity
a. dearth
b. abundance
c. destruction
d. arrival

A. *On the line provided, write the word you have learned in Units 7–9 that is related to each of the following nouns.*
EXAMPLE: allegation—**allege**

1. portent, portentousness _____

2. bestiality, beast _____

3. saturation, saturator, saturant _____

4. indigence _____

5. exacerbation _____

6. refulgence _____

7. conviviality _____

8. felicity, felicitousness, felicitation _____

9. illusoriness, illusion _____

10. conciliator, conciliation _____

11. vituperation, vituperator _____

12. embellishment, embellisher _____

13. pertinacity _____

14. vacillation, vacillator _____

15. paltriness _____

B. *On the line provided, write the word you have learned in Units 7–9 that is related to each of the following verbs.*
EXAMPLE: acclaim—**acclamation**

16. felicitate _____

17. collude _____

18. perturb _____

19. vituperate _____

20. refute _____

Word Associations

In each of the following groups, circle the word that is best defined or suggested by the given phrase.

1. just a beginner at tennis
   a. counterpart   b. dilettante   c. misanthrope   d. tyro

2. She fills her time with inconsequential work.
   a. picayune   b. saturnine   c. pertinacious   d. unremitting

3. "Why does he have to show off by quoting from Latin poets!"
   a. coterie   b. pedantry   c. badinage   d. paucity

4. laughed until our stomachs hurt
   a. shibboleth   b. acclamation   c. misanthrope   d. paroxysm

5. indications that we may find ourselves in bad trouble
   a. calumniate   b. conciliate   c. saturate   d. portend

6. a brazen request not warranted by circumstances
   a. raiment   b. effrontery   c. badinage   d. paucity

7. kept us laughing with their interchange of jokes and quips
   a. paucity   b. badinage   c. dilettante   d. litany

8. cancel the legislation of the previous commissioner
   a. vacillate   b. slough   c. allege   d. countermand

9. the equivalent of our President in a foreign government
   a. misanthrope   b. shibboleth   c. tyro   d. counterpart

10. a nightly bedtime story that calmed the child's fears
   a. countermand   b. demur   c. allay   d. portend

11. a mirage or a will-o'-the-wisp
   a. illusory   b. chary   c. convivial   d. garish

12. "He seems to do everything in a halfhearted, uninterested way."
   a. refulgent   b. arrant   c. macabre   d. lackadaisical

13. gloomy, serious, and with little to say
   a. convivial   b. saturnine   c. bucolic   d. imperturbable

14. a force of nature as unstoppable as the changing of the seasons
   a. paroxysm   b. litany   c. slough   d. juggernaut

15. "Unfortunately, we had to get rid of him to protect our interests."
   a. jettison   b. demur   c. portend   d. embellish

16. a long list of grievances
   a. collusion   b. badinage   c. litany   d. peregrination

17. look forward to the annual salary increase
   a. collusion   b. increment   c. shibboleth   d. dilettante

18. flowers that emit a strong, sweet smell
   a. refulgent   b. illusory   c. redolent   d. chary

19. a mire
   a. paroxysm   b. acclamation   c. misanthrope   d. slough

20. a car alarm that sounded for what seemed like an eternity
   a. unremitting   b. portending   c. bucolic   d. chary

Building with Classical Roots

clam, claim—to cry out, shout, call

This root appears in **acclamation** (page 98). The literal meaning of acclamation is "shouting at," but it now suggests "applause" or "an overwhelmingly favorable oral vote." Some other words based on the same root are listed below.

acclaim	clamorous	disclaimer	proclamation
claimant	declaim	irreclaimable	reclamation

From the list of words above, choose the one that corresponds to each of the brief definitions below. Write the word in the blank space in the illustrative sentence below the definition.

1. to speak like an orator; to recite in public, make a public speech; to speak bitterly against

The actor would _____ lines from Shakespeare in response to any comment.

2. an official or formal public announcement

The clerk posted the latest mayoral _____ at the entrance to City Hall.

3. a denial or disavowal of responsibility or connection; a formal refusal of one's rights or claims

The manufacturer issued a swift _____ after mediocre reviews of its new product.

4. incapable of being reformed; incapable of being rendered useful

That region of the park is nothing more than _____ swampland.

5. the act of bringing back or restoring to a normal or useful condition (*"to call back"*)

Innovative irrigation techniques have resulted in the _____ of much of the desert.

6. to applaud; to indicate strong approval; noisy and enthusiastic applause

The winning team enjoyed vigorous public _____ in a ticker-tape parade.

7. a person who asserts a right or title

After many years, the estranged son resurfaced as the last _____ to the estate.

8. marked by loud confusion or outcry; noisily insistent (*"crying out"*)

The protesters outside the White House made _____ demands for reform.

From the list of words on page 112, choose the one that best completes each of the following sentences. Write the word in the blank space provided.

1. "By spurning every opportunity to turn away from a life of crime," the judge said to the repeat offender, "you have proven yourself _____."

2. Is there anything in literature to match the eloquence of the funeral speech that William Shakespeare has Mark Antony _____ over the body of Caesar!

3. Throughout the realm, the queen's subjects gathered to hear the _____ announcing the birth of an heir to the throne.

4. For legal purposes, the film carried a brief _____ stating that any resemblance between the characters portrayed and real persons was purely coincidental.

5. The primary objective of our penal system should be the _____ of the great majority of inmates, so that they will have a chance to lead productive lives.

6. Though some people denounced the man as a fraud, others _____ him as a saint.

7. Although he was a legitimate _____ to the throne of France, he lived for years as an exile in poverty and obscurity.

8. A good baby-sitter won't yield to the _____ demands of spoiled children.

*Circle the **boldface** word that more satisfactorily completes each of the following sentences.*

1. The estimated time set aside for completing the lakeshore (**disclaimer, reclamation**) project is between two and three years.

2. Abraham Lincoln issued the Emancipation (**Proclamation, Reclamation**) on January 1, 1863.

3. Following the toxic spill at the chemical plant, civic leaders feared that the land would be (**irreclaimable, clamorous**); but recent environmental tests document a successful cleanup.

4. The special effects are so realistic that audiences may find it hard to believe the (**acclaim, disclaimer**) that no animals were harmed in the making of the adventure film.

5. Firefighters earned widespread (**proclamation, acclaim**) for their many courageous and selfless acts of heroism during the disaster.

6. If you intend to become a (**claimant, declaimer**) in the class-action lawsuit, you must file your legal documents by the end of the month.

7. "What famous speech or poem have you chosen to (**acclaim, declaim**) at Friday's school assembly?" asked the principal.

8. The (**clamorous, irreclaimable**) crowds that line the entire race route are famous for spurring on thousands of weary runners in the annual New York City Marathon.

 **Analogies** *In each of the following, circle the item that best completes the comparison.*

1. furtive is to **overt** as
a. intermittent is to continuous
b. testy is to irascible
c. indigent is to indignant
d. sumptuous is to lavish

2. juggernaut is to **steamroller** as
a. talisman is to record player
b. maelstrom is to washing machine
c. coterie is to hair dryer
d. echelon is to vacuum cleaner

3. tyro is to **neophyte** as
a. dilettante is to cadaver
b. suppliant is to recluse
c. misanthrope is to philanthropist
d. agnostic is to skeptic

4. inane is to **fatuous** as
a. plenary is to limited
b. incumbent is to obligatory
c. convivial is to somber
d. utopian is to practical

5. carping is to **picayune** as
a. sophistry is to irrefutable
b. exigency is to optional
c. verbiage is to inordinate
d. nuance is to egregious

6. nettle is to **conciliate** as
a. raze is to allay
b. exacerbate is to belabor
c. embellish is to portend
d. mandate is to countermand

7. increment is to **more** as
a. deduction is to less
b. debit is to more
c. asset is to less
d. decrease is to more

8. vacillate is to **temporize** as
a. calumniate is to slander
b. eschew is to embrace
c. hallow is to desecrate
d. jettison is to salvage

9. badinage is to **jocular** as
a. acclamation is to pejorative
b. effrontery is to circumspect
c. sarcasm is to mordant
d. sophistry is to felicitous

10. reputed is to **alleged** as
a. articulate is to tongue-tied
b. viscous is to dog-tired
c. myopic is to shortsighted
d. arrant is to old-fashioned

 **Choosing the Right Meaning** *Read each sentence carefully. Then circle the item that best completes the statement below the sentence.*

Bowing to the unbending realities of political deal making, the freshman legislator abandoned his hard-line stance and pronounced himself ready to temporize. (2)

1. The word **temporize** in line 2 most nearly means
a. stall   b. filibuster   c. compromise   d. procrastinate

"Do not embrace me till each circumstance
Of peace, time, fortune, do cohere and jump
That I am Viola. . . ."   (Shakespeare, *Twelfth Night*, V, 1, 256–260) (2)

2. The word **cohere** in line 2 is used to mean
a. stick together
b. make a whole
c. have meaning
d. recognize one another

Behind the facade of a respectable repair shop there hid a fencing operation, and
what passed for customers were in fact petty thieves bringing their furtive goods to   (2)
barter for cash.

3. In line 2 the word **furtive** most nearly means

a. sneaky   b. stealthy   c. shifty   d. stolen

"Still to ourselves in every place consigned,
Our own felicity we make or find,   (2)
With secret course, which no loud storms annoy,
Glides the smooth current of domestic joy."   (4)
      (Samuel Johnson, "Lines Added to Goldsmith's Traveller")

4. The word **felicity** in line 2 is best defined as

a. apposition   b. happiness   c. good taste   d. aptness

Two-Word Completions   *Circle the pair of words that best complete the meaning of each of the following sentences.*

1. As the speaker grew more heated, his address began to turn into an intemperate
_____, chock-full of the most scathing and _____
abuse I have ever been "privileged" to hear.

a. diatribe . . . vituperative   c. encomium . . . taciturn
b. eulogy . . . incendiary   d. indictment . . . halcyon

2. Even though he had been educated by the foremost philosopher of his age, the
emperor Nero possessed the _____ mind and _____
appetites of a monster like Count Dracula or the Marquis de Sade.

a. meretricious . . . refulgent   c. murky . . . abject
b. fecund . . . piquant   d. depraved . . . bestial

3. Any trial that is being conducted by people with absolutely no sense of
_____ can only be considered a _____ of justice.

a. equity . . . travesty   c. concord . . . counterpart
b. propriety . . . figment   d. collusion . . . bastion

4. I realized that my theory about how the crime had been committed was no longer
_____ when I accidentally stumbled across _____
evidence of a quite different scenario.

a. coherent . . . moot   c. ludicrous . . . esoteric
b. tenable . . . irrefutable   d. abject . . . indubitable

5. In my various _____ through the forest that bordered on my
childhood home, I often came quite unexpectedly upon birds, insects, and other
_____ creatures that I had never before encountered.

a. paroxysms . . . bucolic   c. peregrinations . . . sylvan
b. gambits . . . macabre   d. pedantries . . . mundane

Enriching Your Vocabulary

Read the passage below. Then complete the exercise at the bottom of the page.

Abbondanza from Italy

The rousing Broadway show tune "Abbondanza" by Frank Loesser describes the great abundance of food guests will enjoy at a banquet celebrating a bride-to-be. Fortunately, the English language has reaped its own abundant vocabulary from Italy. The word *dilettante* (Unit 9) meaning "amateur, or dabbler in the arts" is borrowed directly from Italian.

Leonardo Ferri throws pizza dough in the air, as chef Claudio Marchesan displays plates of food at Prego restaurant in San Francisco.

One way that English speakers pay homage to Italy is to acknowledge some of its many mouth-watering foods such as *pizza, spaghetti, espresso, salami, pasta, parmesan, macaroni, ravioli,* and *zucchini.* The realm of music also brings the Italian language to the American tongue with such terms as *tempo, soprano, solo, aria, madrigal, piano, duet, opera,* and *trio.* If your school choir presents a piece without instrumental accompaniment, that piece is said to be performed *a cappella.* This phrase derives from the Italian words that mean "in the manner of the chapel," referring to the church, where musical instruments were not originally used. Do you know your school's *motto*—a saying that expresses its goals or ideals? The original Italian meaning of *motto* is "a word."

In Column A below are 8 more words and phrases that come from the Italian heritage. With or without a dictionary, match each word or phrase with its meaning in Column B.

Column A

_____ **1.** cognoscenti
_____ **2.** finale
_____ **3.** imbroglio
_____ **4.** manifesto
_____ **5.** prima donna
_____ **6.** sotto voce
_____ **7.** squadron
_____ **8.** tempo

Column B

a. a public declaration of intentions or principles (from the Italian for "a manifestation")

b. very softly or quietly (from the Italian for "under one's breath")

c. persons of outstanding knowledge or taste, connoisseurs (from the Italian for "those in the know")

d. the lead female singer in an opera; a temperamental person (from the Italian for "first lady")

e. the speed at which a musical composition is played; pace (from the Italian for "time")

f. the end or climax of a theatre piece or other work (from the Italian for "final" or "end")

g. a large military or naval unit; any organized multitude (from the Italian for "a big square" or "formation of troops")

h. a complicated situation (from the Italian for "a tangle")

Definitions

Note carefully the spelling, pronunciation, part(s) of speech, and definition(s) of each of the following words. Then write the word in the blank space(s) in the illustrative sentence(s) following. Finally, study the lists of synonyms and antonyms given at the end of each entry.

1. askance
(ə skans')

(*adv.*) with suspicion, distrust, or disapproval

The English teacher looked _____ at the suggestion that students read compendiums of Dickens's novels.

SYNONYMS: distrustfully, suspiciously, skeptically

2. attenuate
(ə ten' yü āt)

(*v.*) to make thin or slender; to weaken or lessen in force, intensity, or value

After making sure the wound was clean, the doctor took steps to _____ the victim's pain.

SYNONYMS: thin out, dilute, water down
ANTONYMS: thicken, strengthen, bolster

3. benign
(bi nīn')

(*adj.*) gentle, kind; forgiving, understanding; having a favorable or beneficial effect; not malignant

Abraham Lincoln's sensitive stepmother had a _____ influence on the lonely boy who had lost his mother.

SYNONYMS: benevolent, salutary, salubrious, harmless
ANTONYMS: malevolent, deleterious

4. cavil
(kav' əl)

(*v.*) to find fault in a petty way, carp; (*n.*) a trivial objection or criticism

I suggest you do not _____ over small things but instead focus on what is important.

Despite a few _____ I might make, I still find her to be an excellent poet.

SYNONYMS: (*v.*) nitpick, quibble

5. charlatan
(shär' lə tən)

(*n.*) one who feigns knowledge or ability; a pretender, impostor, or quack

The reporter exposed the real estate agent as a _____ who routinely deceived her customers.

SYNONYMS: fraud, mountebank

6. decimate
(des' ə māt)

(*v.*) to kill or destroy a large part of

Again and again, Napoleon was able to _____ the armies of his enemies and lead his men on to further victories.

SYNONYMS: ravage, devastate

7. foible
(foi′ bəl)

(*n.*) a weak point, failing, minor flaw

Backbiting is one human _____ not likely to be eradicated.

SYNONYMS: shortcoming, defect, quirk
ANTONYMS: forte, virtue

8. forgo
(fôr go′)

(*v.*) to do without, abstain from, give up

One of the best, if not the easiest, ways to lose weight is to _____ dessert.

SYNONYMS: refrain from, renounce
ANTONYMS: indulge in, partake of

9. fraught
(frôt)

(*adj.*) full of or loaded with; accompanied by

Even with the most advanced equipment, expeditions to the top of Mt. Everest are still _____ with danger.

SYNONYM: charged with
ANTONYMS: devoid of, lacking, deficient in

10. inure
(in yür′)

(*v.*) to toughen, harden; to render used to something by long subjection or exposure

The Inuit have become _____ to the hardships of the long Arctic winters through years of experience.

SYNONYMS: accustom, acclimate

11. luminous
(lü′ mə nəs)

(*adj.*) emitting or reflecting light, glowing; illuminating

Walking under that _____ night sky induced in me weighty thoughts not often pondered.

SYNONYMS: radiant, bright, refulgent, lustrous
ANTONYMS: dark, opaque, dim, murky

12. obsequious
(əb sē′ kwē əs)

(*adj.*) marked by slavish attentiveness; excessively submissive, often for purely self-interested reasons

Jane Austen ridiculed characters who were _____ to the aristocracy but condescending to their social inferiors.

SYNONYMS: fawning, servile, sycophantic, mealymouthed
ANTONYMS: assertive, bumptious, overbearing, candid, frank, independent

13. obtuse
(äb tüs′)

(*adj.*) blunt, not coming to a point; slow or dull in understanding; measuring between 90° and 180°; not causing a sharp impression

The lieutenant was too _____ to see the danger and led his company right into the hands of the enemy.

SYNONYMS: stupid, dumb, thick, mild, dull-witted
ANTONYMS: acute, perceptive, quick-witted

14. oscillate
(äs′ ə lāt)

(*v.*) to swing back and forth with a steady rhythm; to fluctuate or waver

The terrified narrator in Poe's story *The Pit and the Pendulum* watches the dreaded instrument _____ as it slowly moves toward him.

SYNONYMS: vibrate, vacillate

15. penitent
(pen′ ə tənt)

(*adj.*) regretful for one's sins or mistakes; (*n.*) one who is sorry for wrongdoing

The thief was sincerely _____.

In the Middle Ages, _____ often confessed their sins publicly and were publicly punished.

SYNONYMS: (*adj.*) remorseful, regretful, rueful, sorry
ANTONYMS: (*adj.*) unrepentant, remorseless

16. peremptory
(pə remp′ tə rē)

(*adj.*) having the nature of a command that leaves no opportunity for debate, denial, or refusal; offensively self-assured, dictatorial; determined, resolute

The board members resented the director's _____ tone of voice.

SYNONYMS: high-handed, unconditional
ANTONYMS: irresolute, tentative, mild, unassuming

17. rebuff
(ri bəf′)

(*v.*) to snub; to repel, drive away; (*n.*) a curt rejection, a check

The old man _____ his neighbors by refusing all offers of friendship.

Her _____ of my invitation was quite rude.

SYNONYMS: (*v.*) spurn, repulse, reject; (*n.*) setback
ANTONYMS: (*v.*) accept, welcome

18. reconnoiter
(rē kə noit′ ər)

(*v.*) to engage in reconnaissance; to a make a preliminary inspection

Infantry officers often ask for volunteers to _____ the terrain ahead before ordering their soldiers to advance.

SYNONYM: scout

19. shambles
(sham′ bəlz)

(*n.*) a slaughterhouse; a place of mass bloodshed; a state of complete disorder and confusion, mess

The burglars made a complete _____ of the apartment in their search for money and jewelry.

20. sporadic
(spô rad′ ik)

(*adj.*) occurring at irregular intervals, having no set plan or order

The soldiers heard _____ gunfire from the other side of the river.

SYNONYMS: intermittent, spasmodic
ANTONYMS: constant, steady, continuous, uninterrupted

Completing the Sentence

From the words for this unit, choose the one that best completes each of the following sentences. Write the word in the space provided.

1. Life on the family farm has _____ me to hard physical labor and long hours of unremitting toil.

2. The general sent scouts on ahead of the army to _____ the area for a suitable site to pitch camp.

3. Although there had been some _____ fighting earlier, the real battles of the Civil War did not begin until Bull Run in July, 1861.

4. Unless the title Special Aide to the Assistant Section Manager involves a salary increase, I would just as soon _____ it.

5. The riot converted the quiet streets of that suburban community into a ghastly

_____.

6. Although the moon appears to be a(n) _____ body, the fact is that it only reflects light received from the sun.

7. As all kinds of wild rumors ran rampant through the besieged city, the mood of the populace _____ between hope and despair.

8. Good supervisors know that they can get more cooperation from their staff by making polite requests than by issuing _____ orders.

9. The man's personality was a strange mixture of strengths and weaknesses, fortes and _____.

10. I was totally taken aback when they _____ my kind offers of assistance so rudely and nastily.

11. No doubt he's very sorry he got caught, but that does not mean that he's at all _____ about what he did.

12. Any "investment counselor" who promises to double your money overnight must be regarded as a(n) _____ or a crook.

13. Though my childhood recollections have been _____ by the passage of time, they have not been totally effaced from my memory.

14. In a typical James Bond movie, Agent 007 has a series of adventures that are _____ with tongue-in-cheek peril.

15. His statements have been so uniformly _____ that I get the impression that he is wearing a permanent pair of mental blinders.

16. Though critics _____ at minor faults in the new Broadway show, the general public loved it.

17. I was relieved to learn that the tumor on my arm was _____ and my worst fears groundless.

18. We look _____ at any program that makes it harder for city dwellers to get out and enjoy the beauties of nature.

19. During the 14th century, the Black Death suddenly swept across Europe, _____ the population and paralyzing everyday life.

20. During imperial times, the Roman Senate was little more than a collection of _____ yes-men, intent upon preserving their own lives by gratifying the emperor's every whim.

Synonyms

*Choose the word from this unit that is **the same** or **most nearly the same** in meaning as the **boldface** word or expression in the given phrase. Write the word on the line provided.*

1. quibble over who is at fault _____

2. exposed him as a complete **fraud** _____

3. vacillated between two choices _____

4. looked **skeptically** at their proposals _____

5. accustomed to extremes of temperature _____

6. a storm that **ravaged** the countryside _____

7. an attempt to **scout** the interior _____

8. unwilling to **renounce** her inheritance _____

9. shocked by the **mess** they had created _____

10. a **salutary** effect on consumer confidence _____

11. full of suspense and tension _____

12. willing to overlook its **defects** _____

13. will **spurn** his offer of marriage _____

14. his **high-handed** challenge to our authority _____

15. in the **radiant** circle of the spotlight _____

Antonyms

*Choose the word from this unit that is **most nearly opposite** in meaning to the **boldface** word or expression in the given phrase. Write the word on the line provided.*

16. measures that may **strengthen** the economy _____

17. an entirely **unrepentant** gambler and thief _____

18. her **acute** handling of the issue _____

19. assumed an **overbearing** manner _____

20. his **constant** attention to detail _____

Choosing the Right Word

Circle the **boldface** word that more satisfactorily completes each of the following sentences.

1. We must never allow our passion for justice to be (**inured, attenuated**) to mere halfhearted goodwill.

2. I have learned that (**sporadic, peremptory**) sessions of intense "cramming" can never take the place of a regular study program.

3. Somehow or other, a bull got into the china shop and turned it into a complete (**shambles, foibles**).

4. The (**decimated, penitent**) youths agreed to work without pay until they could make restitution for the damage their carelessness had caused.

5. When I found that people I admired were looking (**askance, sporadic**) at my unconventional clothing, I resolved to remedy the situation.

6. How could you have the heart to (**rebuff, cavil**) those people's piteous appeals for aid?

7. Since he didn't want to give me credit for having done a good job, he took refuge in endless (**foibles, cavils**) about my work.

8. Imagine the general disappointment when the so-called "miracle cure" was exposed as a fraud promoted by a (**charlatan, cavil**).

9. Over the years, her (**luminous, obtuse**) descriptions and scintillating wit have helped her students master the difficult subject she taught.

10. Their relationship has been so (**fraught, benign**) with strife and malice that I don't see how they can ever patch things up.

11. Though I admire the woman's strong points, I find her (**rebuffs, foibles**) comic.

12. All angles are classified as acute, right, (**obtuse, benign**), or straight, according to the number of degrees they contain.

13. Though the small nation was always ready to settle a conflict peacefully, it was not afraid to use (**luminous, peremptory**) force when necessary.

14. At an autocrat's court, free speech is usually replaced by the (**penitent, obsequious**) twaddle of self-serving flunkies and toadies.

15. Do you want to be a ballet dancer badly enough to (**oscillate, forgo**) all other activities?

16. Bank robbers often spend a good deal of time (**reconnoitering, rebuffing**) the neighborhood in which the bank they intend to rob is located.

17. During the Civil War the ranks of both armies were (**decimated, rebuffed**) as much by disease as by enemy action.

18. Even though my experiences in battle have (**inured, caviled**) me to scenes of suffering, I was horrified by the devastation wrought by the tornado.

19. Since he is not guided by firm principles, he (**attenuates, oscillates**) between the rival factions, looking for support from both of them.

20. We believe that classes taught by teachers with specialized training will have a (**sporadic, benign**) effect on the troubled children.

Vocabulary in Context

*Read the following passage, in which some of the words you have studied in this unit appear in **boldface** type. Then complete each statement given below the passage by circling the letter of the item that is **the same** or **almost the same** in meaning as the highlighted word.*

Squirrel It Away!

(Line)

With 260 known species, squirrels are found worldwide. Some are tree-dwelling, others (flying squirrels) glide from tree to tree by means of furry flaps of skin that connect their front and hind legs, and still others (chipmunks) are terrestrial. Most often when we think of squirrels, we envision the gray ones indigenous to North
(5) America that collect nuts from tree to tree, **reconnoitering** the local neighborhoods in search of new sources of food.

Like rats and mice, squirrels are classified in the rodent family. Some might look **askance** at their behavior,
(10) **peremptorily** condemning these creatures who notoriously **decimate** bird feeders and, along with the less comely members of their rodent family, make a **shambles** of garbage
(15) bags left for collection on city streets.

But the squirrel has some **benign** attributes as well, and people have been known to keep them as pets, or feed them in parks and
(20) backyards. It has learned to live with humans in cities, but can also survive in places as rural as the North American tundra. It is an important part of

Like bats, flying squirrels are nocturnal.

the ecosystem, and its digestion of such things as hard shells of nuts, seeds,
(25) and pine cones helps renew soil and scatter seeds. While it may be tempting to allow familiarity to breed contempt, one should consider the fact that squirrels might even be capable of communication. Some infer that the pitch and duration of the shrill sounds they make have meanings, and that even tail gestures are a form of communication. The most common tail gesture is the "flicking," which
(30) means "get away!"

---

1. Reconnoitering (line 5) most nearly means
  a. showing   c. sectioning
  b. recognizing   d. scouting

2. Askance (line 9) most nearly means
  a. curiously   c. seriously
  b. suspiciously   d. fondly

3. Peremptorily (line 10) is best defined as
  a. conditionally   c. unconditionally
  b. angrily   d. sweepingly

4. The meaning of **decimate** (line 11) is
  a. ravage   c. decorate
  b. drop   d. locate

5. Shambles (line 14) most nearly means
  a. mess   c. terrain
  b. vision   d. disruption

6. The meaning of **benign** (line 16) is
  a. benevolent   c. endangered
  b. courageous   d. destructive

Definitions

Note carefully the spelling, pronunciation, part(s) of speech, and definition(s) of each of the following words. Then write the word in the blank space(s) in the illustrative sentence(s) following. Finally, study the lists of synonyms and antonyms given at the end of each entry.

1. abrogate
(ab′ rə gāt)

(*v.*) to repeal, cancel, declare null and void

Often with no legal or moral grounds, the U. S. government would _____ treaties made with Native Americans.

SYNONYMS: annul, revoke
ANTONYMS: reaffirm, renew, ratify

2. ambient
(am′ bē ənt)

(*adj.*) completely surrounding, encompassing

The new filtering system is capable of cleaning and deodorizing the _____ air.

3. asperity
(a sper′ ə tē)

(*n.*) roughness, severity; bitterness or tartness

The _____ of the drama critic's statements undermined the young actor's confidence.

SYNONYMS: rigor, harshness
ANTONYMS: mildness, blandness, softness, lenience

4. burnish
(bər′ nish)

(*v.*) to make smooth or glossy by rubbing, polish; (*n.*) gloss, brightness, luster

The hotel manager ordered the waiters to _____ all the brass candlesticks before the formal banquet.

The _____ on the metal frame had faded with age and neglect.

SYNONYMS: (*v.*) shine, buff
ANTONYMS: (*v.*) tarnish, dull, abrade

5. cabal
(kə bäl′)

(*n.*) a small group working in secret

The members of the _____ met at an unknown location for the purpose of fixing prices and stifling competition.

SYNONYMS: clique, ring, gang, plot, conspiracy

6. delectable
(di lek′ tə bəl)

(*adj.*) delightful, highly enjoyable; deliciously flavored, savory; (*n.*) an appealing or appetizing food or dish

The banquet ended with a truly _____ dessert made of peaches, raspberries, and ice cream.

The eatery attracted customers with a mouth-watering display of _____ in its front window.

SYNONYMS: (*adj.*) delicious, scrumptious
ANTONYMS: (*adj.*) repugnant, repulsive, distasteful

7. deprecate
(dep' rə kāt)

(v.) to express mild disapproval; to belittle

The administration _____ such foolish practices as the hazing of new students but did not ban them outright.

SYNONYMS: deplore, frown upon
ANTONYMS: smile on, countenance, approve

8. detritus
(di trīt' əs)

(n.) loose bits and pieces of material resulting from disintegration or wearing away; fragments that result from any destruction

Pieces of people's homes, furniture, and toys could be seen in the _____ of the landslide.

SYNONYMS: debris, wreckage, ruins, rubble

9. ebullient
(i būl' yənt)

(adj.) overflowing with enthusiasm and excitement; boiling, bubbling

After a string of very favorable reviews, the dance company was in an _____ mood for weeks.

SYNONYMS: exhilarated, elated, exuberant
ANTONYMS: gloomy, morose, sullen, apathetic, blasé

10. eclectic
(e klek' tik)

(adj.) drawn from different sources; (n.) one whose beliefs are drawn from various sources

Stanford White developed an _____ style of architecture that made use of classic and modern elements.

The critics accused the composer of being a mere _____ with no original style of her own.

SYNONYMS: (adj.) selective, synthetic, pick-and-choose
ANTONYMS: (adj.) uniform, monolithic

11. flaccid
(flas' əd)

(adj.) limp, not firm; lacking vigor or effectiveness

Because the injured bodybuilder had not worked out for weeks, his muscles grew _____.

SYNONYMS: soft, flabby
ANTONYMS: hard, firm, solid

12. impecunious
(im pə kyü' nē əs)

(adj.) having little or no money

In my present _____ state, I will not be able to pay for dinner.

SYNONYMS: penniless, impoverished, indigent
ANTONYMS: affluent, wealthy, prosperous, rich

13. inexorable
(in ek' sər ə bəl)

(adj.) inflexible, beyond influence; relentless, unyielding

In the Greek tragedies, nothing could save characters like Oedipus Rex from their _____ fates.

SYNONYMS: inescapable, ineluctable, obdurate
ANTONYMS: avoidable, yielding, pliant

14. moribund
(môr′ ə bənd)

(*adj.*) dying, on the way out

In the age of electronic communication, writing letters by hand seems to be a _____ custom.

SYNONYM: obsolescent
ANTONYMS: flourishing, thriving

15. necromancer
(nek′ rə man sər)

(*n.*) one who claims to reveal or influence the future through magic, especially communication with the dead; in general, a magician or wizard

When the stock market began to tumble, some desperate investors resorted to _____ for financial advice.

SYNONYMS: sorcerer, conjurer

16. onerous
(än′ ər əs)

(*adj.*) burdensome; involving hardship or difficulty

Informing patients of bad news is an _____ duty that every doctor has to perform.

SYNONYMS: oppressive, weighty
ANTONYMS: light, easy, undemanding, untaxing

17. rife
(rīf)

(*adj.*) common, prevalent, widespread, happening often; full, abounding; plentiful, abundant, replete

Since rumors were _____ , the president announced that the company had been bought out by its major competitor.

ANTONYMS: devoid of, lacking

18. rudiments
(rüd′ ə mənts)

(*n. pl.*) the parts of any subject or discipline that are learned first; the earliest stages of anything

At a very young age, the girl learned the _____ of chess from her father, a professional player.

SYNONYMS: fundamentals, basics

19. sequester
(si kwes′ tər)

(*v.*) to set apart, separate for a special purpose; to take possession of and hold in custody

The parties agreed to _____ the disputed funds pending a decision by the court.

SYNONYMS: seclude, segregate, isolate, closet

20. winnow
(win′ ō)

(*v.*) to get rid of something unwanted, delete; to sift through to obtain what is desirable; to remove the chaff from the wheat by blowing air on it; to blow on, fan

Spelling and grammar software programs are designed to help writers _____ inaccuracies from their documents.

SYNONYMS: sift, strain, filter, sort

Completing the Sentence

From the words for this unit, choose the one that best completes each of the following sentences. Write the word in the space provided.

1. I could tell that my boss was really "riled" by the _____ of his tone of voice when he summoned me.

2. I thought the job of revising the manuscript would be a relatively simple matter, but it proved to be a(n) _____ task.

3. She is a very private person who _____ any attempt to honor publicly her great services to humanity.

4. Though monarchies still exist in some parts of the world, they are more or less a(n) _____ form of government.

5. Even before they said a word, I could tell from their _____ expressions that our team had won.

6. In a sense, the man is a(n) _____ philosopher because his ideas have been influenced by many different schools of thought.

7. All the facts and figures point to one _____ conclusion: we are hopelessly outnumbered.

8. As air slowly seeped out through the tiny puncture, the inner tube became more and more _____.

9. Some superstitious Roman emperors consulted _____ and other dabblers in black magic to find out what the future held.

10. It is often difficult to hold a conversation while walking on a busy city street because of the high level of _____ traffic noise.

11. The copper pots had been so highly _____ that I could see my face in them.

12. In order to prevent outside influences from coming into play, a jury is normally _____ until it reaches a decision.

13. Unless you have mastered the _____ of French grammar, you will find it difficult to speak the language fluently.

14. It was then that he began to organize the _____ that would later depose the king.

15. The conversation at dinner tables all over town was _____ with speculation as to the outcome of the big game.

16. We will never allow anyone to curtail or _____ the basic rights and liberties guaranteed to us in the Constitution.

17. The plot of the novel centers on a(n) _____ adventurer who attempts to remedy his financial embarrassment by marrying into money.

18. One of Darwin's theories suggests that nature ensures the survival of a species by slowly _____ out the less fit members.

19. Late that night, we began the heartbreaking task of sifting through the _____ of our ravaged home.

20. There is nothing more _____ on a hot day than to stretch out in a hammock with a good book and pitcher of icy lemonade!

Synonyms

*Choose the word from this unit that is **the same** or **most nearly the same** in meaning as the **boldface** word or expression in the given phrase. Write the word on the line provided.*

1. sort the good ideas from the bad _____

2. taught us the **fundamentals** of physics _____

3. the **encompassing** sound of the drums _____

4. cleaned up the **debris** from the parade _____

5. fooled by a **sorcerer's** tricks _____

6. secluded on a remote country estate _____

7. a ruthless **clique** of gangsters _____

8. could not miss the **harshness** in his tone _____

9. the **inescapable** consequences of her actions _____

10. rebelled against the **oppressive** taxation _____

11. weeds that were **widespread** in the area _____

12. tempted me with **delicious** treats _____

13. a **varied** collection of opinions _____

14. the **exuberant** cheerleading squad _____

15. sheltered the **penniless** immigrants _____

Antonyms

*Choose the word from this unit that is **most nearly opposite** in meaning to the **boldface** word or expression in the given phrase. Write the word on the line provided.*

16. tarnish the silver _____

17. noticed her **firm** handshake _____

18. the **flourishing** downtown area _____

19. will **reaffirm** his oath to the king _____

20. countenanced our peaceful protest _____

Choosing the Right Word

*Circle the **boldface** word that more satisfactorily completes each of the following sentences.*

1. "The (**inexorable, moribund**) march of the years," said the aged speaker, "decrees that this is the last time I will address you."

2. Writing that is so full of soggy clichés, gummy sentence structure, and excessive wordiness can best be described as (**inexorable, flaccid**).

3. What appeared to be an informal study group was in a reality a highly organized (**detritus, cabal**) determined to overthrow the establishment.

4. (**Asperity, Necromancy**) and other forms of witchcraft were punishable by death during the Middle Ages.

5. The investigating committee spent long hours trying to (**burnish, winnow**) fact from fiction in the witnesses' testimony.

6. Though she entered this country as a(n) (**impecunious, rife**) child, she eventually made a fortune in the garment industry.

7. Anyone who has the slightest acquaintance with the (**rudiments, cabals**) of economic theory understands that we cannot solve our financial problems simply by borrowing more and more money.

8. (**Eclectic, Ambient**) schools of art are typical of a period when there is little original inspiration or bold experimentation.

9. Though the presidency confers great powers on the person who holds the office, it also saddles that person with (**onerous, eclectic**) responsibilities.

10. Since archaeologists spend a lot of time rummaging through the (**detritus, asperity**) of vanished civilizations, they bear a striking resemblance to junk collectors and ragpickers.

11. As we sat in the locker room after our heartbreaking loss, the (**ambient, impecunious**) gloom was so thick you could almost cut it.

12. It is one thing to (**burnish, deprecate**) human follies and pretensions; it is quite another to correct them.

13. Though skeptics insist that patriotism is (**onerous, moribund**) in America, I believe that it is alive and well in the hearts of the people.

14. The old adage that "one man's meat is another man's poison" simply means that what is considered (**delectable, onerous**) is often quite subjective.

15. Any political party that is (**rife, ebullient**) with petty jealousies and backbiting can never hope to present a united front in an election.

16. The (**moribund, burnished**) helmets and breastplates of the warriors gleamed and twinkled in the morning sunlight.

17. As one veteran aptly observed, a soldier had to be hardy to cope with the (**asperities, cabals**) of life in the trenches during World War I.

18. The charm of this musical comedy lies in its slam-bang pacing, its sprightly music, and its generally (**onerous, ebullient**) good cheer.

19. Oliver Wendell Holmes, Jr., once observed that he did not wish to lead a(n) (**sequestered, abrogated**) life far from the conflicts of his times.

20. No one, however powerful or dominant, can (**abrogate, sequester**) the basic moral laws on which civilization rests.

Read the following passage, in which some of the words you have studied in this unit appear in **boldface** type. Then complete each statement given below the passage by circling the letter of the item that is **the same** or **almost the same** in meaning as the highlighted word.

Merlin the Magician

(Line)

The legend of Camelot has carried cultural resonance throughout the centuries. Modern writers have reinvented the tale, and directors have made films about it. It is a dynamic legend that changes in order to reflect the mores of the times. The one thing that has not changed, however, is the mysterious nature of Merlin, at once a fearsome **necromancer**, and at the same time, (5) a kindly protector and advisor to King Arthur.

The Merlin character is **eclectic**, drawn partly from historical sources, but mostly constructed from early Celtic legends. The kernel of history that can be **winnowed** from (10) the chaff of legend relates Merlin to a wanderer with the gift of prophecy, who roamed through the forests of southern Scotland around 575 A.D. A similar figure with powers to divine the future, called Myrddin, (15) appeared in early Welsh poetry. In the twelfth century, Geoffrey of Monmouth combined the **rudiments** of the wandering prophet stories and the Myrddin legends with his own newly invented material to create the character he (20) called Merlin. Writing in Latin for a Norman French audience, Geoffrey divulged that Merlin was responsible for engineering the secret conception of Arthur by King Uther Pendragon, **sequestering** the royal offspring during his boyhood, and later giving Arthur the magical power to pull the sword from the stone and secure his kingship. (25)

A famous wizard from American popular culture, The Wizard of Oz (1939).

Merlin's luster was further **burnished** by later medieval writers, who added new elements to his character, making him the inspiration for Arthur's foundation of the idealistic institution of the Round Table.

---

1. Necromancer (line 5) most nearly means
a. explorer   c. sorcerer
b. storyteller   d. emperor

2. Eclectic (line 7) is best defined as
a. mysterious   c. famous
b. powerful   d. synthetic

3. The meaning of **winnowed** (line 10) is
a. sifted   c. dropped
b. learned   d. made

4. The meaning of **rudiments** (line 18) is
a. riches   c. features
b. basics   d. rules

5. Sequestering (line 23) most nearly means
a. educating   c. misleading
b. endangering   d. secluding

6. Burnished (line 26) most nearly means
a. tainted   c. polished
b. betrayed   d. clouded

Definitions

Note carefully the spelling, pronunciation, part(s) of speech, and definition(s) of each of the following words. Then write the word in the blank space(s) in the illustrative sentence(s) following. Finally, study the lists of synonyms and antonyms given at the end of each entry.

1. aesthetic
(es thet′ ik)

(*adj.*) pertaining to beauty; sensitive or responsive to beauty

Since the structure had no practical purpose, keeping it in place could only be justified on _____ grounds.

SYNONYM: artistic

2. defunct
(di fəŋkt′)

(*adj.*) no longer in existence or functioning, dead

I could find no forwarding address or phone number for the _____ organization.

SYNONYMS: extinct, nonexistent
ANTONYMS: alive, extant

3. discomfit
(dis kəm′ fit)

(*v.*) to frustrate, thwart, or defeat; to confuse, perplex, or embarrass

The general tried to _____ his enemies by repeatedly beginning an advance and then pulling back.

SYNONYMS: nonplus, disconcert, foil

4. espouse
(es paŭz′)

(*v.*) to take up and support; to become attached to, adopt; to marry

To appeal to the large number of dissatisfied voters, the candidate _____ a strong program of reform.

SYNONYMS: embrace, wed
ANTONYMS: repudiate, disavow, renounce

5. fetish
(fet′ ish)

(*n.*) an object believed to have magical powers; an object of unreasoning devotion or reverence

The rabbit's foot, once a very popular _____, seems to have lost its hold on the public imagination.

SYNONYMS: charm, talisman, obsession

6. gregarious
(grə gār′ ē əs)

(*adj.*) living together in a herd or group; sociable, seeking the company of others

I would expect the recreation director of a cruise ship to be a _____ person.

SYNONYMS: outgoing, extroverted
ANTONYMS: aloof, introverted, reclusive

7. hapless
(hap' lis)

(*adj.*) marked by a persistent absence of good luck

Once again, my younger brother has become the
_____ victim of a silly practical joke.

SYNONYMS: unlucky, ill-starred, unfortunate
ANTONYMS: lucky, charmed, fortunate

8. impeccable
(im pek' ə bəl)

(*adj.*) faultless, beyond criticism or blame

We always consulted my grandmother about what to wear
because she had _____ taste in
clothing.

SYNONYMS: flawless, spotless, immaculate
ANTONYMS: grimy, soiled, spotted, sullied

9. importune
(im pôr tyün')

(*v.*) to trouble with demands; to beg for insistently

My bankrupt uncle _____ my
father for a loan.

SYNONYMS: implore, entreat, dun, tax

10. interpolate
(in tər' pə lāt)

(*v.*) to insert between other parts or things; to present as an
addition or correction

At the director's request, the screenwriter
_____ some new lines into the script.

SYNONYMS: inject, interpose, introduce

11. irreparable
(i rep' ər ə bəl)

(*adj.*) incapable of being repaired or rectified

The husband believed that the surgeon did
_____ harm to his wife and sued
the doctor and the hospital.

SYNONYM: irremediable
ANTONYMS: remediable, fixable, reversible

12. laconic
(lə kän' ik)

(*adj.*) concise, using few words

The senator issued a _____
statement declaring her innocence after the accusations of
fraud were made public.

SYNONYMS: terse, succinct, pithy, compact
ANTONYMS: garrulous, prolix, loquacious, verbose

13. languish
(laŋ' gwish)

(*v.*) to become weak, feeble, or dull; to droop; to be depressed
or dispirited; to suffer neglect

Without the Constitutional guarantee of a speedy trial, the
accused could _____ in jail for years.

SYNONYMS: flag, wilt, fade, pine

14. mendacious
(men dā 'shəs)

(*adj.*) given to lying or deception; untrue

The deputy gave a _____ account of his employer's actions on the day of the alleged crime.

SYNONYMS: untruthful, false
ANTONYMS: truthful, veracious

15. nadir
(nā' dər)

(*n.*) the lowest point

At the _____ of his popularity, the prime minister decided to resign his office and call for new elections.

SYNONYMS: rock bottom
ANTONYMS: apex, pinnacle, zenith

16. omnipresent
(äm ni pre' zənt)

(*adj.*) present in all places at all times

They believed in an _____ deity that existed in all things.

SYNONYMS: ubiquitous, ever-present

17. perfunctory
(per fəŋk' tə rē)

(*adj.*) done in a superficial or halfhearted manner; without interest or enthusiasm

The police made a _____ search for the missing handbag, but they really did not expect to find it.

SYNONYMS: slapdash, cursory, shallow
ANTONYMS: thorough, assiduous, diligent, meticulous

18. plaintive
(plān' tiv)

(*adj.*) expressive of sorrow or woe, melancholy

The recently widowed man spoke of his loneliness in a _____ tone of voice.

SYNONYMS: sad, doleful, lugubrious
ANTONYMS: cheerful, blithe, joyous, merry

19. requite
(ri kwīt')

(*v.*) to make suitable repayment, as for a kindness, service, or favor; to make retaliation, as for an injury or wrong; to reciprocate

We made sure to _____ the neighbors for looking after our house while we were away.

SYNONYMS: reimburse, recompense, avenge

20. tantamount
(tan' tə maunt)

(*adj.*) equivalent, having the same meaning, value, or effect

The armed invasion of their territory was _____ to a declaration of war.

SYNONYM: indistinguishable from

Completing the Sentence

From the words for this unit, choose the one that best completes each of the following sentences. Write the word in the space provided.

1. No matter where candidates for high political office go these days, the _____ eye of the TV camera seems focused on them.

2. As his irrepressible flow of reminiscences continued without a letup, I tried in vain to _____ a few observations of my own.

3. To say that he is _____ does not even begin to convey just how alienated he is from any regard for the truth.

4. One wall of the museum was filled with charms and _____ designed to ward off everything from a hangnail to the evil eye.

5. They claim to have made a thorough search of the premises, but I suspect that their efforts were no more than _____.

6 Last night, Central High's Netnicks captured the basketball championship by _____ the South High Slammers, 61 to 44.

7. I thought our state legislators would consider the proposal at the earliest opportunity, but they let it _____ in committee for months.

8. Responding to the melancholy note in the song of the nightingale, Keats wrote of its "_____ anthem."

9. Suddenly I was surrounded by a mob of street urchins loudly _____ me for a handout.

10. I was greatly relieved to learn that the accident I had with my car last week didn't do any _____ damage to the motor.

11. The _____ creature had somehow gotten its foot caught in the grate and could not extricate it without help.

12. When asked what terms he would offer the Confederate army, General Grant made the _____ reply, "Unconditional surrender!"

13. I felt a little foolish when the librarian told me that I was asking for the current issue of a magazine that had long been _____.

14. Every general seems to have one defeat that marks the _____ of his military fortunes—for example, Lee at Gettysburg, or Grant at Cold Harbor.

15. It's easy enough to back a popular program, but it takes real courage to _____ a cause that most people oppose.

16. Since extroverts are _____ by nature, they usually prefer not to live alone.

17. Never once has the least whiff of a scandal or impropriety tainted the man's _____ reputation as an upstanding member of this agency.

18. "Don't you think it's a little foolish to pursue the young lady when your warm feelings for her are clearly not _____?" I asked.

19. From a(n) _____ point of view, the painting didn't appeal to me, but I kept it because it was a memento of my childhood.

20. When you get more experience on the job, you will learn that a "request" from your employer is _____ to an order.

Synonyms

*Choose the word from this unit that is **the same** or **most nearly the same** in meaning as the **boldface** word or expression in the given phrase. Write the word on the line provided.*

1. **recompensed** them for their hospitality _____

2. **entreated** the governor for a pardon _____

3. clinging to a **talisman** _____

4. **disconcerted** the conservative audience _____

5. kept repeating that **doleful** melody _____

6. tried to **interject** a different opinion _____

7. **wilt** under the hot sun _____

8. the **ubiquitous** sound of cell phone chatter _____

9. no more than a **cursory** note of apology _____

10. the **unfortunate** recipient of bad advice _____

11. **embraced** the values of democracy _____

12. expressed some **artistic** objections _____

13. **equivalent** to betraying a friend _____

14. an **irremediable** act of perfidy _____

15. known for his **outgoing** personality _____

Antonyms

*Choose the word from this unit that is **most nearly opposite** in meaning to the **boldface** word or expression in the given phrase. Write the word on the line provided.*

16. an **extant** species of sea turtles _____

17. the **apex** of her fame _____

18. a **truthful** account of the events _____

19. gave a **verbose** tribute to his partner _____

20. a **sullied** reputation _____

Choosing the Right Word

*Circle the **boldface** word that more satisfactorily completes each of the following sentences.*

1. Though I left the house feeling "as fit as a fiddle," my spirits began to (**requite, languish**) after only five minutes in that withering heat.

2. Though few of us today stand on ceremony to quite the extent that our ancestors did, common courtesy is by no means (**plaintive, defunct**).

3. It is one thing to be concerned about discipline; it is quite another to make a (**perfunctory, fetish**) of it.

4. A diplomat must always proceed on the assumption that no rupture between nations, no matter how serious, is (**irreparable, perfunctory**).

5. Although fate has decreed that he make his living as a stockbroker, his main interests and talents are definitely (**irreparable, aesthetic**).

6. Prehistoric peoples banded together into tribes, not only for protection, but also to satisfy their (**gregarious, mendacious**) instincts.

7. The sternness of my boss's expression so (**discomfited, languished**) me that at first I had difficulty responding to the question.

8. In our desire to improve the quality of life in America, we should not be too quick to (**importune, espouse**) an idea simply because it is new.

9. The (**omnipresent, gregarious**) threat of a nuclear holocaust that characterized the Cold War era changed many people's attitudes toward war in profound ways.

10. When the scandal broke, the man found himself the (**hapless, impeccable**) victim of other people's misdeeds.

11. One of the best-known figures of American folklore is the lean, tough, (**laconic, hapless**) cowboy.

12. Perhaps we should be overjoyed that the great man condescended to give us a(n) (**aesthetic, perfunctory**) nod as we passed by.

13. I don't know which is more painful—to have to ask someone for a favor, or to have some unfortunate (**importune, discomfit**) one for help.

14. Her sense of tact is so (**hapless, impeccable**) and unerring that she can handle the most trying situation as if it were mere child's play.

15. Fortunately, our lawyer was able to produce documents that disproved the (**mendacious, omnipresent**) assertions of our former partner.

16. I hope to (**espouse, requite**) my parents for all the care they have shown me.

17. The legal adage "Silence implies consent" means that not objecting to an action that concerns you is (**perfunctory, tantamount**) to approving to it.

18. One of the comforting things about reaching the (**fetish, nadir**) of one's career is that the only place to go from there is up.

19. She sang a (**laconic, plaintive**) little ditty about a man who yearns wistfully for the girl he left behind many years before.

20. Many scholars believe that Beaumont or Fletcher (**interpolated, requited**) a scene or two into the present text of Shakespeare's *Macbeth*.

*Read the following passage, in which some of the words you have studied in this unit appear in **boldface** type. Then complete each statement given below the passage by circling the letter of the item that is **the same** or **almost the same** in meaning as the highlighted word.*

The Lost Generation

(Line)

Not only did World War I (1914–1918) have profound economic and political effects on the United States, but it also changed the social and moral outlook of the generation that lived through it. American youth lost its innocence on the bloody battlefields of Europe, and when the survivors returned home, they were
(5) **discomfited** by the very values they had gone off to war to defend. In their war-weary eyes, self-sacrificing patriotism and unquestioning respect for authority were **defunct**, even dangerous, ideals. They had seen the bravery of too many young men **requited** with a violent death or a
(10) gruesome maiming, and the psychic wounds inflicted by the war seemed as **irreparable** as the physical ones.

The American novelist Ernest Hemingway (1899–1961) has become a
(15) symbol of this post-World War I generation. Wounded in Italy in 1918 while serving as an ambulance driver for the Red Cross, Hemingway returned from the war disillusioned and restless.
(20) No longer able to **espouse** the values he had grown up with, Hemingway went to Paris in 1921 in search of a new moral and **aesthetic** code by which he could

Ernest Hemingway sits at his typewriter and reads his writings during his World War II work as a war correspondent.

live and work. There he met other artists and writers engaged in a similar search. In
(25) fact, it was one of these fellow expatriates, the American writer Gertrude Stein, who applied the phrase "the lost generation" to Hemingway and his contemporaries.

In Paris, Hemingway found the new values he was looking for and created a new type of hero and prose style to express what he had discovered. The Hemingway protagonist in novels like *The Sun Also Rises* and *A Farewell to Arms* finds
(30) meaning in a shattered world by constructing a personal code of honor and remaining faithful to it against all odds.

---

1. Discomfited (line 5) most nearly means
  a. shocked   c. excited
  b. disconcerted   d. comforted

2. The meaning of **defunct** (line 7) is
  a. noble   c. dead
  b. unrealistic   d. childish

3. Requited (line 9) is best defined as
  a. recompensed   c. erased
  b. equated   d. condemned

4. The meaning of **irreparable** (line 12) is
  a. deep   c. irremediable
  b. deadly   d. invisible

5. Espouse (line 20) most nearly means
  a. reject   c. proclaim
  b. ignore   d. embrace

6. Aesthetic (line 23) most nearly means
  a. artistic   c. superior
  b. personal   d. unbreakable

Vocabulary for Comprehension

Read the following passage, in which some of the words you have studied in Units 10–12 appear in **boldface** *type. Then answer questions 1–11 on page 139 on the basis of what is* <u>stated</u> *or* <u>implied</u> *in the passage and in the introductory statement.*

This passage focuses on the brief but remarkable era of silent films.

(Line)

It may be tempting for modern viewers to **deprecate** silent films. After all, they are technically primitive compared with today's movies. Much

(5) of the acting is exaggerated and overwrought, and the plots are often melodramatic or sentimental. Also, there is no dialogue except for some **laconic** titles that appear on the

(10) screen from time to time. Yet in their day, audiences flocked to see these movies, marveling at the **luminous** images on the flickering screen. To these enthusiastic new moviegoers,

(15) there was nothing as exciting as moving pictures!

Two men, Louis Lumiere and Thomas Alva Edison, one French and one American, are usually credited

(20) with the invention of the motion picture camera. In 1895 Louis Lumiere invented what he called the *cinematographe.* This compact, versatile instrument was **tantamount**

(25) to a camera, film-processing unit, and projector all in one. Because Edison's camera was bulkier and less portable than Lumiere's, the Europeans took an early lead in the development of

(30) motion pictures. The Americans soon caught up, however, and Hollywood eventually became the capital of a vastly profitable international film industry, which began in the 1910s

(35) with the production of silent movies.

Many contemporary viewers have overlooked the masterpieces of the silent era because they find the adjustments they must make to watch

(40) these films **onerous**. Without knowing it, however, they are depriving themselves of some unparalleled pleasures. These include the brilliant physical comedy of Buster Keaton,

(45) the visual expressiveness of Charlie Chaplin, and the landmark editing, camera work, and set designs of the great pioneer filmmakers D. W. Griffith, Sergei Eisenstein, F. R.

(50) Murnau, and Fritz Lang.

1. In the first paragraph (lines 1–16), the writer's main focus is on
a. contrasting the drawbacks of silent films with the excitement they inspired in audiences of the day
b. describing the landmark camera work of some silent filmmakers
c. discussing the invention of the motion picture camera
d. comparing Keaton and Chaplin
e. introducing some of the writer's favorite silent films

2. The meaning of **deprecate** (line 2) is
a. underestimate
b. belittle
c. ignore
d. misunderstand
e. overpraise

3. In paragraph 1, the author mentions all of the following as drawbacks of silent films EXCEPT
a. overwrought acting
b. laconic captions
c. melodramatic plots
d. primitive technical achievements
e. unattractive set designs

4. **Laconic** (line 9) most nearly means
a. obscure
b. humorous
c. succinct
d. brilliant
e. redundant

5. **Luminous** (line 12) is best defined as
a. bright
b. shocking
c. blurred
d. lifelike
e. timeless

6. From the details given in paragraph 2 (lines 17–35), one may reasonably infer that the Americans caught up with the Europeans because
a. the Americans made more films
b. technical refinements made film equipment less bulky and more portable

c. most of the leading actors and filmmakers were American
d. the climate of Hollywood was appealing
e. Louis Lumiere's equipment often broke down

7. **Tantamount** (line 24) most nearly means
a. opposed
b. compared
c. similar
d. supplementary
e. equivalent

8. According to the passage, the international film industry began in
a. the 1880s
b. the 1890s
c. the 1910s
d. the 1920s
e. the 1930s

9. In paragraph 3 (lines 36–50), the writer most likely includes so many examples in order to
a. display a high level of expertise
b. persuade the reader of the claims made for silent films in the passage
c. bolster the claim that silent moves are primitive compared with today's films
d. prove that directors were more skilled than actors in the silent film era
e. trace the ways in which silent film stars influenced one another

10. **Onerous** (line 40) most nearly means
a. silly
b. impossible
c. burdensome
d. easy
e. annoying

11. The writer's attitude toward silent films might best be described as
a. enthusiastic
b. respectful
c. neutral
d. skeptical
e. dismissive

Grammar in Context

In the sentence "Yet in their day, audiences flocked to see these movies, marveling at the luminous images on the flickering screen" (lines 10–14 on page 138), the participial phrase "marveling at the luminous images" clearly modifies "audiences." However, this connection would have been lost if the author of the passage had written "Marveling at the luminous images on the flickering screen, these movies were flocked to by audiences." A participial phrase that does not sensibly modify any word or group of words in a sentence is called a **dangling participle**.

You can use these techniques to correct a dangling participle: (1) Add a word or words that the phrase can logically modify. (2) Add words to the phrase so that its meaning is clear. (3) Reword the entire sentence.

On the lines provided, rewrite each of the following sentences, correcting dangling participles. Write "correct" if the sentence is correct.

1. Listening to my great-uncle's stories, it was interesting to hear him describe the silent film era.

_____

_____

2. Tightly constructed, all my uncle's contemporaries enjoyed silents.

_____

_____

3. When evaluating a silent film, a number of criteria should be employed.

_____

_____

4. While discussing silents with some friends, the topic of titles came up.

_____

_____

5. After searching in several catalogs, *City Lights* with Charlie Chaplin was located.

_____

_____

6. Contrasting the comedy of Charlie Chaplin and Buster Keaton, the lecturer enthralled the audience.

_____

_____

7. Sitting on the edge of their seats, the films of Fritz Lang and D. W. Griffith delighted audiences.

_____

_____

8. Beginning in the late 1920s, however, silents were eclipsed in popularity by talkies.

_____

_____

Two-Word Completions

Circle the pair of words that best complete the meaning of each of the following passages.

1. As soon as I heard its _____ cries for help, I knew that the
_____ animal had once again got its paw caught in the grillwork
on the front porch.
a. obsequious . . . moribund   c. onerous . . . defunct
b. laconic . . . impeccable   d. plaintive . . . hapless

2. Though Seneca embraced the tenets of Stoicism in their entirety, Cicero
_____ no one school of Greek philosophy but, like a true
_____, chose what he thought best from each and ignored the rest.
a. discomfited . . . penitent   c. espoused . . . eclectic
b. abrogated . . . aesthetic   d. deprecated . . . foible

3. Although many of the pioneers found it difficult at first to cope with the
_____ of frontier life, they were a hardy race who quickly
became _____ such rough-and-tumble living.
a. rudiments . . . importuned by   c. detritus . . . decimated by
b. asperities . . . inured to   d. shambles . . . discomfited by

4. In *Of Human Bondage,* W. Somerset Maugham's main character Philip Carey is
_____ by external adversity as well as his own self-consciousness
because at birth he was the _____ recipient of a club foot.
a. rebuffed . . . sporadic   c. decimated . . . laconic
b. requited . . . benign   d. discomfited . . . hapless

5. The "truth-in-advertising" laws that many states have recently passed were in part
designed to discourage crooks and _____ from making
_____ claims about the products they offer to the unsuspecting public.
a. charlatans . . . mendacious   c. fetishes . . . laconic
b. necromancers . . . sporadic   d. cabals . . . eclectic

6. Though the man appeared to be the most _____ pauper on the
face of the earth, he had actually _____ large sums of money in
various hiding places in the hovel he called home.
a. flaccid . . . burnished   c. ambient . . . interpolated
b. impecunious . . . sequestered   d. benign . . . decimated

Choosing the Right Meaning

Read each sentence carefully. Then circle the item that best completes the statement below the sentence.

The infamous Hatfield-McCoy feud began in earnest when, in 1882, the Hatfields requited the slaying of Ellison Hatfield by executing three McCoy brothers. (2)

1. In line 2 the word **requited** is used to mean

a. avenged　　b. recompensed　　c. reimbursed　　d. witnessed

The deep hush was broken when a gust of wind billowed through the parlor window and winnowed the pages of the book that lay open on the table. (2)

2. The word **winnowed** in line 2 most nearly means

a. deleted　　b. sorted out　　c. tore　　d. fanned

By 1864 Southern war-making resources were so depleted that Confederate commanders could deal only temporary rebuffs to the Union juggernaut. (2)

3. In line 2 the word **rebuffs** is best defined as

a. curt rejections　　b. cease-fires　　c. snubs　　d. setbacks

"When from our better selves we have too long
Been parted by the hurrying world, and droop (2)
Sick of its business, of its pleasures tired,
How gracious, how benign, is Solitude," (Wordsworth, *The Prelude*) (4)

4. In line 4 the word **benign** is used to mean

a. forgiving　　b. salutary　　c. benevolent　　d. lonely

The mad scientist, a stock character of Hollywood B movies, is often found in a dark laboratory, surrounded by a sinister array of beakers of ebullient potions. (2)

5. The best definition for the word **ebullient** in line 2 is

a. boiling　　b. enthusiastic　　c. delicious　　d. poisoned

Antonyms

*In each of the following groups, circle the word or expression that is most nearly the **opposite** of the word in **boldface** type.*

1. forgo
a. indulge
b. concoct
c. refrain from
d. serve

2. espouse
a. devise
b. select
c. repudiate
d. support

3. abrogate
a. renew
b. debate
c. nullify
d. reveal

4. rebuff
a. spurn
b. expect
c. welcome
d. question

5. delectable
a. delicious
b. powerful
c. traditional
d. repulsive

6. impecunious
a. impoverished
b. close
c. wealthy
d. kindly

7. burnish
a. tarnish
b. melt
c. polish
d. steal

8. laconic
a. humorous
b. verbose
c. concise
d. sarcastic

9. mendacious
a. deceitful
b. convincing
c. unwilling
d. truthful

11. onerous
a. burdensome
b. easy
c. supplementary
d. obligatory

13. sporadic
a. fitful
b. continuous
c. bloody
d. mock

15. irreparable
a. fatal
b. instant
c. unforeseen
d. reversible

10. eclectic
a. selective
b. weird
c. creative
d. uniform

12. deprecate
a. approve
b. describe
c. contrive
d. condemn

14. moribund
a. dying
b. depressed
c. flourishing
d. controversial

16. flaccid
a. weak
b. firm
c. new
d. elected

Word Families

A. *On the line provided, write the word you have learned in Units 10–12 that is related to each of the following nouns.*
EXAMPLE: attenuation—**attenuate**

1. deprecation, deprecator _____

2. gregariousness _____

3. oscillation, oscillator _____

4. mendacity, mendaciousness _____

5. omnipresence _____

6. abrogation _____

7. plaintiveness _____

8. ebullience, ebullition _____

9. requital _____

10. espousal, espouser _____

11. inexorability, inexorableness _____

12. discomfiture _____

13. decimation _____

14. interpolation, interpolator _____

15. sequestration _____

16. obtuseness _____

17. impeccability _____

B. *On the line provided, write the word you have learned in Units 10–12 that is related to each of the following verbs.*
EXAMPLE: fetishize—**fetish**

18. repent _____

19. repair _____

20. illuminate _____

Word Associations

In each of the following groups, circle the word that is best defined or suggested by the given phrase.

1. humbling himself in an effort to be accepted
   a. sporadic   b. obsequious   c. peremptory   d. mendacious

2. never happy unless she has a lot of people around her
   a. peremptory   b. irreparable   c. moribund   d. gregarious

3. suffering an unbroken string of bad breaks and disappointments
   a. delectable   b. benign   c. obtuse   d. hapless

4. regard his suggestions with deep suspicion
   a. defunct   b. askance   c. plaintive   d. laconic

5. laden with
   a. sporadic   b. fraught   c. tantamount   d. impeccable

6. a small group that plotted to oust me from the club presidency
   a. necromancer   b. cabal   c. cavil   d. charlatan

7. getting used to cold weather before going on the camping trip
   a. inure   b. espouse   c. winnow   d. attenuate

8. a minor, often humorous failing
   a. cavil   b. foible   c. rebuff   d. detritus

9. "At that moment, life seemed more hopeless that it ever had before or since."
   a. detritus   b. cabal   c. nadir   d. shambles

10. pine away
   a. sequester   b. decimate   c. languish   d. inure

11. given to trivial and frivolous objections
   a. attenuate   b. forgo   c. reconnoiter   d. cavil

12. lessen the impact of the economic recession
   a. oscillate   b. winnow   c. rebuff   d. attenuate

13. how fate may sometimes be characterized
   a. inexorable   b. charlatan   c. perfunctory   d. ambient

14. will never undertake anything without his "lucky coin" with him
   a. fetish   b. burnish   c. detritus   d. nadir

15. a type of wizard or warlock
   a. penitent   b. charlatan   c. necromancer   d. cabal

16. genuinely sorry for one's mistakes
   a. obsequious   b. ebullient   c. moribund   d. penitent

17. exposed as an utter fraud
   a. shambles   b. charlatan   c. cavil   d. detritus

18. learning the basic strokes, moves, and tactics of tennis
   a. rudiments   b. fetishes   c. foibles   d. eclectics

19. an artillery barrage that took a heavy toll of life and limb
   a. abrogate   b. decimate   c. sequester   d. importune

20. wreckage
   a. detritus   b. fetish   c. shambles   d. nadir

rog—to ask, beg, call

This root appears in **abrogate** (page 124), meaning "to cancel, to abolish by authoritative action." Some other words based on the same root are listed below.

abrogation	**derogation**	**interrogative**	**supererogatory**
arrogance	**interrogation**	**prorogue**	**surrogate**

From the list of words above, choose the one that corresponds to each of the brief definitions below. Write the word in the blank space in the illustrative sentence below the definition.

1. exaggerated self-importance, haughty pride

The king was corrupted by power and, over time, exchanged his humility for

_____ .

2. an act or expression that detracts from reputation, value, power, etc. (*"to call down"*)

The aid workers deeply resented any _____ of their motives.

3. a substitute, deputy; a judge in charge of the probate of wills, administration of estates, and appointment of guardians

While my parents were on vacation, my aunt served as a _____ guardian.

4. an act of formal or systematic questioning

The detective asked question after question during the _____ of the prime suspect.

5. a cancellation; the act of repealing or annulling (*"calling off"*)

Unfavorable evidence has emerged, forcing the _____ of the agreement between the two parties.

6. to discontinue a session of a legislative body; to defer, postpone

The prime minister was determined to _____ the legislative assembly until all members were present.

7. asking a question; having the form or character of a question; a word or sentence that asks a question

In Spanish class, we are learning how to phrase _____ sentences.

8. performed or observed beyond the degree required; demanded, or expected; unnecessary; superfluous

"We could do with fewer _____ remarks," the teacher observed.

From the list of words on page 145, choose the one that best completes each of the following sentences. Write the word in the space provided.

1. The suspect was led into a small _____ room, where two police officers questioned him until the wee hours of the morning.

2. It was kind of the gas station attendant to give me directions to the next town, but to give me a map, along with written directions, was clearly _____.

3. Her colossal _____ led her to dismiss the feelings and concerns of her "inferiors" as scarcely worth noting.

4. "Do-gooder" is occasionally used as a term of _____, in which the meaning of the word is inverted; it actually denotes someone who performs benevolent acts, but for dubious or attention-seeking reasons.

5. It is up to the _____ court to ensure that the estate is given to the appropriate parties.

6. Though her comment about cleaning the room was _____ in form, it was clear that she was issuing an order, not asking a question.

7. Our society may need improvement, but the answer does not lie in the _____ of the ideals, rules, and institutions we have inherited from the past.

8. The kings of England would often abruptly _____ Parliament to prevent the passage of measures unwelcome to the throne.

---

*Circle the **boldface** word that more satisfactorily completes each of the following sentences.*

1. Remember to use the proper end punctuation to distinguish (**interrogative, supererogatory**) sentences from exclamatory statements.

2. My Great-Aunt Sylvia was like a (**derogation, surrogate**) grandmother to me.

3. Legislators worked as quickly as possible to complete the bill before the session could be (**interrogated, prorogued**).

4. Since the (**abrogation, interrogative**) of the international trade agreement, debts owed to the World Bank have increased.

5. The experienced trial lawyer instructed her client to stay calm during what might prove to be a grueling (**interrogation, surrogate**).

6. Jonathan Swift hurled (**arrogances, derogations**) against the British for not doing more to aid the impoverished in Ireland.

7. My father always regarded it as a mark of utter (**arrogance, abrogation**) to attempt to solve the devilishly difficult Sunday crossword puzzle using a pen.

8. After a delicious pear tart, cinnamon ice cream, and hot cider, we simply had no room for the (**surrogate, supererogatory**) chocolates the waiter brought to our table.

Analogies   *In each of the following, circle the item that best completes the comparison.*

1. surveillance is to **monitor** as
a. espionage is to overlook
b. vigilance is to sleep
c. sabotage is to pacify
d. reconnaissance is to reconnoiter

2. carp is to **cavil** as
a. decry is to deprecate
b. conciliate is to nettle
c. hallow is to travesty
d. espouse is to eschew

3. omnipresent is to **ubiquitous** as
a. moribund is to obsolescent
b. laconic is to garrulous
c. extant is to extinct
d. eclectic is to monolithic

4. pendulum is to **oscillate** as
a. clock is to temporize
b. scale is to portend
c. wave is to undulate
d. wheel is to disarray

5. hypocrite is to **dissemble** as
a. charlatan is to feign
b. suppliant is to sham
c. derelict is to simulate
d. counterpart is to conceal

6. sporadic is to **intermittent** as
a. brackish is to fresh
b. ephemeral is to transitory
c. fraught is to devoid
d. utopian is to feasible

7. indigent is to **impecunious** as
a. furtive is to overt
b. halcyon is to turbulent
c. hapless is to unfortunate
d. felicitous is to awkward

8. acuity is to **obtuse** as
a. perspicacity is to myopic
b. equity is to impartial
c. credence is to gullible
d. asperity is to harsh

9. luminous is to **refulgent** as
a. ebullient is to saturnine
b. murky is to lucid
c. verdant is to arid
d. redolent is to aromatic

10. miser is to **sequester** as
a. misanthrope is to invest
b. neophyte is to filch
c. agnostic is to embezzle
d. spendthrift is to squander

Choosing the Right Meaning   *Read each sentence carefully. Then circle the item that best completes the statement below the sentence.*

I am at a loss to judge whether her self-deprecating manner bespeaks genuine humility or false modesty.   (2)

1. The word **self-deprecating** in line 1 is best defined as
   a. self-belittling   b. self-satisfied   c. self-assured   d. self-serving

"Such smiling rogues as these,
Like rats, oft bite the holy cords a-twain   (2)
Which are too intrise t'unloose; smooth every passion . . .
Renege, affirm, and turn their halcyon beaks   (4)
With every gale, and vary of their masters,
Knowing nought, like digs, but following."   (6)
        (Shakespeare, King Lear, II, 2, 79–81, 84–86)

2. In line 4 the word **halcyon** is used to mean
   a. peaceful   b. kingfisher   c. prosperous   d. happy

A blockbuster movie or a best-selling novel often spawns a host of usually paltry imitations cranked out by those opportunist hacks whose eyes are ever fixed on the dollar. (2)

3. The best definition for the word **paltry** in line 1 is

a. despicable   b. mean   c. measly   d. inferior

Physicists employ gigantic devices called particle accelerators to smash atoms together at tremendous velocities in order to investigate the primordial nature of matter. (2)

4. The word **primordial** in line 2 most nearly means

a. earliest   b. fundamental   c. primeval   d. original

The movie is cracked up to be a scathing indictment of the fashion industry, but I could detect very little sting in it at all. On the contrary, its effect, to my mind, was rather obtuse. (2)

5. In line 3 the word **obtuse** is used to mean

a. blunt   b. thick   c. dumb   d. mild

Two-Word Completions

Circle the pair of words that best complete the meaning of each of the following sentences.

1. The poor man had been _____ in the Bastille and left to _____ there without hope of reprieve for over twenty years.

a. mandated . . . demur
b. incarcerated . . . languish
c. inured . . . exacerbate
d. garnered . . . vacillate

2. The _____ antics of the troupe of clowns convulsed the audience. _____ of laughter repeatedly shook the hall like salvos of musketry.

a. fatuous . . . Gambits
b. ludicrous . . . Paroxysms
c. feckless . . . Bastions
d. inane . . . Litanies

3. After the bulldozers and wrecking balls had completed the lengthy task of _____ the building, a convoy of dump trucks began the job of carting off the resultant _____ .

a. embellishing . . . flotsam
b. belaboring . . . murk
c. razing . . . detritus
d. exhuming . . . largesse

4. For two solid hours, our artillery kept up an _____ barrage of cannon fire. It _____ the enemy's ranks with such deadly accuracy that barely one man in ten was left standing after it was over.

a. unremitting . . . decimated
b. intermittent . . . winnowed
c. inexorable . . . atrophied
d. illusory . . . enervated

5. Since all the members of my little _____ of friends truly enjoy each other's company, our weekly get-togethers are remarkably _____ affairs.

a. echelon . . . vituperative
b. cabal . . . laconic
c. shambles . . . gregarious
d. coterie . . . convivial

Enriching Your Vocabulary

Read the passage below. Then complete the exercise at the bottom of the page.

Borrowings from Arabic

In 1095, Pope Urban II appealed to the Christian knights and lords of Western Europe to undertake the First Crusade. He wanted to liberate the Holy Land from Arab Moslems, who had been living there since the 7th century. Subsequently, and for more than a century, additional crusades were launched. These expeditions brought Europeans into contact with Arabic civilization. As a result of these and other encounters, some Arabic words were eventually incorporated into the English language. One such word is *nadir* (Unit 12), meaning the lowest point.

Prior to the Crusades, Moslem armies had conquered most of the lands that comprise the Iberian Peninsula. Europeans and Arabs met and mingled in thriving commercial and artistic centers like Cordova and Granada. Some English words borrowed from Arabic at this time include: *caraway, jasmine, lilac, lime, orange, saffron,* and *tamarind.* Europeans also learned to understand the *salaam,* or respectful salutation that involves a deep bow and placement of the right hand on the forehead. This formal Arabic greeting is literally a wish for peace.

Marrakech street fairs serve as a mecca for cultural exchange between Europeans, Americans, Asians, and Africans.

In Column A below are 7 more words and phrases that have entered English from the Arabic. With or without a dictionary, match each word or phrase with its meaning in Column B.

Column A

_____ **1.** alcove
_____ **2.** algebra
_____ **3.** cipher
_____ **4.** sherbet
_____ **5.** sofa
_____ **6.** tariff
_____ **7.** zenith

Column B

a. a long upholstered piece of furniture designed to seat several people at once (from the Arabic for "divan")

b. a sweet kind of ice cream made from water or milk and egg white, fruit juice, or gelatin (from the Arabic for "a drink")

c. a person or thing without value or influence; a kind of code; a coded message (from the Arabic for "zero")

d. the highest point above the horizon attained by a celestial body; any summit (from the Arabic for "road over head")

e. a partly enclosed recess forming part of a room or garden (from the Arabic for "the vault")

f. a duty on imported or exported goods; a system of such duties (from the Arabic for "information")

g. the branch of mathematics dealing with the properties of quantities (from the Arabic for "the science of calculating")

 **Definitions**

Note carefully the spelling, pronunciation, part(s) of speech, and definition(s) of each of the following words. Then write the word in the blank space(s) in the illustrative sentence(s) following. Finally, study the lists of synonyms and antonyms given at the end of each entry.

1. abstruse
(ab strüs')

(*adj.*) extremely difficult to understand

The physicist tried to explain her _____ research in the field of quantum mechanics.

SYNONYMS: esoteric, arcane, recondite, occult
ANTONYMS: simple, straightforward

2. affront
(ə frənt')

(*n.*) an open or intentional insult; a slight; (*v.*) to insult to one's face; to face in defiance, confront

The prisoner felt that being referred to by number rather than by name was an _____ to her dignity.

In the nineteenth century, Irish immigrants to the United States were _____ by signs reading: No Irish Need Apply.

SYNONYMS: (*n.*) offense; (*v.*) offend
ANTONYMS: (*n., v.*) compliment, praise

3. canard
(kə närd')

(*n.*) a false rumor, fabricated story

The tabloid journalist was responsible for spreading the _____ about the candidate's mental health.

SYNONYM: hoax

4. captious
(kap' shəs)

(*adj.*) excessively ready to find fault; given to petty criticism; intended to trap, confuse, or show up

She is an invariably _____ critic.

SYNONYMS: faultfinding, nit-picking, carping
ANTONYM: uncritical

5. cognizant
(käg' ni zənt)

(*adj.*) aware, knowledgeable, informed; having jurisdiction

Police officers must make sure that crime suspects are made _____ of their rights before they are questioned.

SYNONYMS: conscious, acquainted
ANTONYMS: unaware, unconscious, oblivious

6. contrite
(kən trīt')

(*adj.*) regretful for some misdeed or sin; plagued by a sense of guilt; thoroughly penitent

The convicted felon had the look of someone who was truly _____ and ready to pay for his crimes.

SYNONYMS: remorseful, rueful
ANTONYMS: unrepentant, unapologetic, impenitent

7. cynosure
(sī′ nə shür)

(*n.*) the center of attraction, attention, or interest; something that serves to guide or direct

For over a century, the Statue of Liberty has been the
_____ for millions of immigrants entering New York Harbor.

SYNONYM: focus

8. decorous
(dek′ ər əs)

(*adj.*) well behaved, dignified, socially proper

On formal occasions, like weddings and graduations, participants are expected to behave in a
_____ manner.

SYNONYMS: seemly, becoming, tasteful
ANTONYMS: unseemly, unbecoming, improper, tasteless

9. deign
(dān)

(*v.*) to think it appropriate or suitable to one's dignity to do something; to condescend

The enlisted men were surprised that the four-star general
_____ to speak to them as he toured the camp.

SYNONYMS: deem, stoop

10. desiccated
(des′ ə kā tid)

(*adj., part.*) thoroughly dried out; divested of spirit or vitality; arid and uninteresting

The cornfield was _____ by the scorching sun after the long, hot summer without rain.

SYNONYMS: dehydrated, shriveled, parched
ANTONYMS: sodden, soggy, waterlogged, drenched

11. efficacy
(ef′ ə kə sē)

(*n.*) the power to produce a desired result

The pharmaceutical company has done extensive research to prove the _____ of the new drug they are marketing.

SYNONYMS: effectiveness, potency, reliability
ANTONYMS: ineffectiveness, impotence

12. engender
(in jen′ dər)

(*v.*) to bring into existence, give rise to, produce; to come into existence, assume form

The university has made an appealing videotape in order to _____ student interest in studying abroad.

SYNONYMS: beget, generate, cause, form
ANTONYMS: stop, deter

13. ethereal
(i thēr′ ē əl)

(*adj.*) light, airy, delicate; highly refined; suggesting what is heavenly (rather than earthbound)

The Renaissance painter Fra Angelico captured the
_____ beauty of angels in his
famous frescoes.
SYNONYMS: heavenly, celestial, gossamer
ANTONYMS: infernal, hellish, thick, heavy

14. facade
(fə säd′)

(n.) the front or face of a building; a surface appearance (as opposed to what may lie behind)

After years of neglect, the sooty _____
of the cathedral is finally getting a much needed cleaning.
SYNONYMS: exterior, surface, mask, pretense
ANTONYM: interior

15. ghoulish
(gül′ ish)

(adj.) revolting in an unnatural or morbid way; suggestive of someone who robs graves or otherwise preys on the dead

The _____ practice of grave robbing is
sometimes motivated by the desire to find and sell valuables.
SYNONYMS: fiendish, barbarous, monstrous

16. incongruous
(in kän′ grü əs)

(adj.) not in keeping, unsuitable, incompatible

Abraham Lincoln, the backwoods lawyer, and Mary Todd,
the rich socialite, seemed an _____ couple.
SYNONYMS: discordant, jarring
ANTONYMS: compatible, harmonious, consistent

17. machination
(mak ə nā′ shən)

(n.) a crafty, scheming, or underhanded action designed to accomplish some (usually evil) end

Shakespeare's Othello was the victim not only of Iago's evil
_____ but also of his own jealous nature.
SYNONYMS: plot, scheme, maneuver

18. mesmerize
(mez′ mə rīz)

(v.) to hypnotize, entrance; to fascinate, enthrall, bewitch

The magician was able to _____ the
audience with his fast-moving hands and distracting chatter.

19. opprobrium
(ə prō′ brē əm)

(n.) disgrace arising from shameful conduct; contempt, reproach

Despite the passage of centuries, _____
is still attached to the name of the traitor Benedict Arnold.
SYNONYMS: infamy, dishonor, odium, shame
ANTONYMS: acclaim, honor, glory, renown

20. putative
(pyü′ tə tiv)

(adj.) generally regarded as such; reputed; hypothesized, inferred

Ancient Celtic rituals and ceremonies are the
_____ origins of some of our
modern Halloween customs.
SYNONYMS: supposed, presumed
ANTONYMS: known, corroborated, confirmed

Completing the Sentence

From the words for this unit, choose the one that best completes each of the following sentences. Write the word in the space provided.

1. The longer I study this country's history, the more _____ I become of my rich heritage of freedom.

2. Some historians question whether Benedict Arnold really deserves all the _____ he has been accorded as America's arch-traitor.

3. At the risk of appearing a trifle _____, I would like to raise a few small objections to the wording of this proposal.

4. After the battle, camp followers began the _____ process of stripping the dead of whatever valuables they possessed.

5. Some teachers are able to present the most _____ subjects in terms that are crystal-clear to even the dullest of students.

6. The _____ of the unscrupulous wheeler-dealers involved in that unsavory scandal boggle the imagination.

7. I didn't really believe that he was sorry for what he had done until I saw the _____ expression on his sad little face.

8. The pages of the old book were so _____ that they began to crumble as soon as we touched them.

9. There is not a vast body of evidence that supports the idea that poverty tends to _____ crime.

10. To be the _____ of all eyes could be the joyous fulfillment of a dream or the unhappy realization of a nightmare.

11. The only surefire way to establish the _____ of a new drug in treating a disease is to test it "in the field."

12. For more than five minutes she stared at the telegram containing the bad news, as if she were _____.

13. His fantastic stories about his academic, athletic, financial, and romantic achievements are a(n) _____ to common sense.

14. Am I supposed to feel honored simply because that arrogant lout sometimes _____ to nod vaguely in my direction?

15. Except for a balcony built during the Truman administration, the _____ of the White House has remained virtually unchanged since it was constructed.

16. What could be more _____ than the 6-foot, 7-inch center on the basketball team dolled up in a baby clothes for the class play!

17. No one knows for sure who really wrote the scene, but Shakespeare is generally regarded as its _____ author.

18. Only a thoroughly naive and gullible person would actually believe every preposterous _____ that circulates in this school.

19. The child's conduct during the ceremony may not have been appropriately _____, but it wasn't horrendous either.

20. The cherubic faces and _____ voices of the choristers almost made me believe that the music they were singing was coming from heaven.

Synonyms

*Choose the word from this unit that is **the same** or **most nearly the same** in meaning as the **boldface** word or expression in the given phrase. Write the word on the line provided.*

1. a **fiendish** interest in death _____

2. exposed as a total **hoax** _____

3. **bewitched** by the speaker's soothing voice _____

4. **esoteric** concepts developed by experts _____

5. **stooped** to give a few interviews _____

6. the **focus** of a dazzled audience _____

7. **conscious** of our mutual responsibilities _____

8. disliked for his **nit-picking** tendencies _____

9. an **offense** to an entire group of people _____

10. the **jarring** reunion of longtime rivals _____

11. foiled the **schemes** of the villain _____

12. **begets** distrust by covering up mistakes _____

13. paintings of women with **heavenly** qualities _____

14. showed a mere **pretence** of gratitude _____

15. brought **shame** on the whole family _____

Antonyms

*Choose the word from this unit that is **most nearly opposite** in meaning to the **boldface** word or expression in the given phrase. Write the word on the line provided.*

16. the **known** whereabouts of the fugitive _____

17. the **ineffectiveness** of our foreign policy _____

18. the **unrepentant** ringleaders of the riot _____

19. looked over the **soggy** farmland _____

20. the **unseemly** appearance of the judge _____

Choosing the Right Word

Circle the **boldface** word that more satisfactorily completes each of the following sentences.

1. If you had listened to my warnings in the first place, there would be no need for you to feel (**contrite, desiccated**) now.

2. A government that fails to bring about peaceful reform (**engenders, deigns**) the kind of social unrest that makes violent revolution inevitable.

3. "Do we have sufficient evidence at hand," I asked, "to judge the (**efficacy, cognizance**) of the new method of teaching reading?"

4. In my youthful folly, I inadvertently (**affronted, engendered**) the very people whose aid I was attempting to enlist.

5. The (**efficacy, opprobrium**) of history forever attaches itself to the name of Lee Harvey Oswald, the assassin of President Kennedy.

6. For any actor, it is a unique thrill to know that when you are alone on stage, you are the (**facade, cynosure**) of hundreds of pairs of eyes.

7. He tried to conceal his lack of scholarship and intellectual depth by using unnecessarily (**efficacious, abstruse**) language.

8. The book describes in great detail the odious (**machinations, facades**) involved in Adolf Hitler's rise to power in Germany.

9. The President must always be on his toes because a careless answer to a (**contrite, captious**) question could land him in political hot water.

10. The candidate's "shocking revelation" about his opponent was later shown to be nothing more than a malicious (**canard, cynosure**).

11. I resent your nasty question about whether or not I will "(**deign, affront**) to speak to ordinary students" after I'm elected class president.

12. The audience was so quiet after the curtain fell that I couldn't tell whether they were bored or (**deigned, mesmerized**) by her artistry.

13. Like many people who are completely wrapped up in themselves, she simply isn't (**cognizant, decorous**) of the larger world around her.

14. His unmistakable interest in the gruesome details of the tragedy revealed that he possessed the sensibilities of a (**canard, ghoul**).

15. The play is so peopled with spirits and other incorporeal beings that it has the (**ethereal, captious**) quality of a dream.

16. Her quiet speech, subdued clothes, and (**decorous, desiccated**) manner made it hard to believe that she was a famous rock star.

17. He acts like someone whose vital juices have long since dried up, leaving only a drab and (**desiccated, contrite**) shell behind.

18. It has been said that humor is essentially the yoking of (**incongruous, ethereal**) elements within a familiar or recognizable framework.

19. Philologists believe that many Western languages can be traced back to a (**putative, decorous**) parent tongue known as Indo-European.

20. It wasn't at all hard of recognize signs of extreme uneasiness beneath her (**canard, facade**) of buoyant optimism.

*Read the following passage, in which some of the words you have studied in this unit appear in **boldface** type. Then complete each statement given below the passage by circling the letter of the item that is **the same** or **almost the same** in meaning as the highlighted word.*

Portrait of a Lady

(Line)

At the Louvre, the famous art museum in Paris, the **cynosure** for many is the *Mona Lisa*. This portrait was painted in the early sixteenth century by the Renaissance genius Leonardo da Vinci, and it has been fascinating viewers ever since.

The subject is an aristocratic woman with a **mesmerizing** gaze and the tantalizing hint of a smile. Contrary to popular opinion, the word "Mona" is not (5) part of the woman's name but a title of respect similar to "madam" or "my lady." The identity of Leonardo's sitter is not absolutely certain, but she is generally believed to be Lisa di Antonio Maria Gherardini, the wife of a (10) prominent Florentine named Francesco del Giocondo. It is on the basis of this **putative** identification that the painting is sometimes referred to as *La Gioconda*. Whoever the lady was, Leonardo placed her amidst an amazing (15) landscape of rocks, roads, water, and trees that were more a product of his imagination than a realistic depiction of the Tuscan countryside near where he was born and spent most of his life. (20)

Why this painting has **engendered** so much public and professional interest over the centuries is hard to pinpoint. The sitter is not beautiful by most conventional standards, and yet she exerts a powerful allure. Perhaps it is (25) the contrast between her **decorous** posture and her direct, almost challenging, gaze that so captivates. Or maybe it is the way her mysterious smile suggests both the **ethereal** and earthly dimensions of feminine attractiveness. But whatever the allure, the *Mona Lisa* is certain to captivate for years to come. (30)

The Mona Lisa, on display at the Louvre in Paris, is painted with such subtle brush strokes that they are almost invisible to the naked eye.

---

1. Cynosure (line 1) most nearly means
  a. confusion
  b. focus
  c. excitement
  d. assurance

2. The meaning of **mesmerizing** (line 4) is
  a. entrancing
  b. myopic
  c. deadly
  d. inspiring

3. Putative (line 12) is best defined as
  a. careful
  b. positive
  c. shameful
  d. presumed

4. The meaning of **engendered** (line 21) is
  a. produced
  b. devoured
  c. satisfied
  d. disappointed

5. Decorous (line 26) most nearly means
  a. careless
  b. casual
  c. dignified
  d. slack

6. Ethereal (line 28) most nearly means
  a. excellent
  b. formal
  c. sensitive
  d. heavenly

Definitions

Note carefully the spelling, pronunciation, part(s) of speech, and definition(s) of each of the following words. Then write the word in the blank space(s) in the illustrative sentence(s) following. Finally, study the lists of synonyms and antonyms given at the end of each entry.

1. beatific
(bē ə tif′ ik)

(*adj.*) blissful; rendering or making blessed

During the awards ceremony, the Gold Medal winner had a positively _____ expression on her face.

SYNONYMS: rapturous, ecstatic, transcendent
ANTONYMS: disconsolate, dejected, doleful

2. behemoth
(bi hē′ məth)

(*n.*) a creature of enormous size, power, or appearance

The Loch Ness monster is a famous _____.

SYNONYMS: mammoth, whale, elephant, colossus
ANTONYMS: dwarf, pygmy, midget

3. blandishment
(blan′ dish mənt)

(*n., often pl.*) anything designed to flatter or coax; sweet talk, apple-polishing

The king was often influenced by subtle _____.

SYNONYMS: allurement, enticement, cajolery
ANTONYMS: threat, intimidation

4. cacophonous
(kə käf′ ə nəs)

(*adj.*) harsh-sounding, raucous, discordant, dissonant

The scene opened with _____ laughter coming from three witches gathered around a steaming cauldron.

ANTONYMS: harmonious, melodious, mellifluous

5. chicanery
(shi kā′ nə rē)

(*n.*) trickery, deceptive practices or tactics, double-dealing

The accountants used legal _____ to cover up the company's shaky financial position.

ANTONYM: fair dealing

6. consign
(kən sīn′)

(*v.*) to give over to another's care, charge, or control; to entrust, deliver; to set apart for a special use

The ship's captain _____ many duties to her trusted first mate.

SYNONYMS: transfer, remit, convey

7. coup
(kü)

(*n.*) a highly successful stroke, masterstroke, tour de force, act, plan, or stratagem; a sudden takeover of power or leadership

The surprise _____ by high-ranking military officers toppled the weak government in a matter of hours.

ANTONYMS: blunder, faux pas, gaffe

8. euphemism
(yü' fə miz əm)

(*n.*) a mild or inoffensive expression used in place of a harsh or unpleasant one; a substitute

Common _____ for *die* include the expressions *pass away* and *go to the other side.*

9. febrile
(feb' ril)

(*adj.*) feverish; pertaining to or marked by fever; frenetic

The journalist wrote with _____ intensity.

ANTONYMS: leisurely, relaxed

10. gainsay
(gān' sā)

(*v.*) to deny, contradict, controvert; to dispute, oppose

Some wished to _____ the conclusions of the US Supreme Court in the matter of the 2000 Presidential election.

ANTONYMS: confirm, corroborate, support, admit

11. imminent
(im' ə nənt)

(*adj.*) about to happen, threatening

An _____ hurricane forced the islanders back to the mainland.

SYNONYMS: impending, looming
ANTONYMS: distant, remote, faraway

12. innate
(i nāt')

(*adj.*) natural, inborn, inherent; built-in

Musical excellence often comes from _____ ability.

SYNONYMS: intrinsic, congenital
ANTONYMS: learned, acquired, extrinsic, accidental

13. loath
(lōth)

(*adj.*) unwilling, reluctant, disinclined

My hard-working grandfather was _____ to retire.

SYNONYMS: averse, indisposed
ANTONYMS: willing, eager, inclined

14. manifest
(man' ə fest)

(*adj.*) clear, evident to the eyes or mind; (*v.*) to show plainly, exhibit, evince; (*n.*) a list of cargo and/or passengers

It was _____ to many nineteenth-century Americans that the nation was destined to extend to the Pacific Ocean.

When the man began to _____ signs of hearing loss, he went to a specialist.

The passenger _____ helps investigators find out who is on board a plane.

SYNONYMS: (*adj.*) apparent; (*v.*) reveal, disclose
ANTONYMS: (*adj.*) unrevealed, hidden; (*v.*) hide, conceal

15. minutiae
(mə nü' shē ə)

(*pl. n.*) small or trivial details, trifling matters

Because the researcher was too concerned with

_____, she was unlikely to make an original discovery.

SYNONYMS: trivia, trifles
ANTONYM: essentials

16. moratorium
(môr ə tōr' ē əm)

(*n.*) a suspension of activity; an official waiting period; an authorized period of delay

The conference was held to try to negotiate a

_____ on arms sales to both sides of the conflict.

SYNONYMS: postponement, stoppage
ANTONYMS: acceleration, escalation

17. nostrum
(näs' trəm)

(*n.*) an alleged cure-all; a remedy or scheme of questionable effectiveness

The federal Food and Drug Administration was created in part to keep unsavory characters from peddling

_____ to the public.

SYNONYMS: panacea, elixir

18. pariah
(par ī' ə)

(*n.*) one who is rejected by a social group or organization

In most of the world today, those who are suffering from the disease of leprosy are no longer treated as

_____.

SYNONYMS: outcast, untouchable, persona non grata

19. visionary
(vizh' ə ner ē)

(*adj.*) not practical, lacking in realism; having the nature of a fantasy or dream; (*n.*) one given to far-fetched ideas; a dreamer or seer characterized by vision or foresight

Ideas that once were considered _____ often become widely accepted over time.

The Reverend Martin Luther King, Jr., was a

_____ whose dreams inspired the American civil rights movement.

SYNONYMS: (*adj.*) utopian, idealistic, impractical
ANTONYMS: (*adj.*) realistic, practical

20. wizened
(wiz' ənd)

(*adj., part.*) dry, shrunken, and wrinkled (often as the result of aging)

The _____ old woman walked with the aid of a cane.

SYNONYMS: withered, shriveled
ANTONYMS: bloated, distended

*From the words for this unit, choose the one that best
completes each of the following sentences. Write the
word in the space provided.*

1. However much I may dispute your views, I will never _____ your
right to hold them.

2. Just when it seemed that defeat was inevitable, she pulled off a dazzling
_____ that totally discomfited her opponent.

3. When it became clear just how shamelessly he had treated his brother, he
became a virtual _____ in his own family.

4. In a touching ceremony, the soldiers _____ the body of their
fallen leader to the grave and his memory to their hearts.

5. On the first play, our diminutive quarterback was "sacked" by a veritable
_____ of a linebacker, ominously nicknamed "Bone Crusher."

6. When the swollen river threatened to overflow its banks, a devastating flood
seemed _____ .

7. Since I was brought up in a sleepy country town, I found it very hard to adjust to
the _____ pace of big-city life.

8. You may be, as you say, "_____ to leave such a fascinating
book," but I'm telling you right now to take out the garbage!

9. If you spend all your time on _____ , you won't have any left for
really important matters.

10. The nation's economic ills call for a variety of remedies; they cannot be cured by
any single, miraculous _____ .

11. Suddenly I was overcome by such a feeling of _____ peace that
I began to wonder whether I was on earth or in heaven.

12. One way to bring relief to small farmers who cannot meet their mortgage
payments is to declare a temporary _____ on foreclosures.

13. Before you dismiss him as just another impractical _____ , think
of how many great inventors were once regarded as mere "cranks."

14. Though the ability to paint is probably a(n) _____ gift, it can
certainly be improved by training and practice.

15. Some Civil War generals weren't professional soldiers and got their jobs through
wire-pulling and other forms of political _____ .

16. Though her body had become bent and _____ with age, her
mind was as alert and active as ever.

17. No matter what _____ you use to describe his conduct, you
can't disguise the fact he betrayed his best friend.

18. Some people enjoy the type of atonal music written by such composers as Arnold Schoenberg; others find it _____.

19. We were all surprised that someone with the reputation of a frivolous playboy could _____ such courage and determination.

20. Only a fool would have succumbed to the cloying _____ of that smooth-talking rascal!

Synonyms

*Choose the word from this unit that is **the same** or **most nearly the same** in meaning as the **boldface** word or expression in the given phrase. Write the word on the line provided.*

1. a **substitute** for the word *fired* _____

2. considered an **outcast** by her neighbors _____

3. delivered a well-timed **masterstroke** _____

4. fooled by a worthless **panacea** _____

5. when **mammoths** roamed the Earth _____

6. accused of outright **double-dealing** _____

7. an **intrinsic** capacity for learning _____

8. dared to **controvert** the scientific evidence _____

9. without the **withered** look of advanced age _____

10. fascinated by the **trivia** of celebrity gossip _____

11. **transcendent** vision of another world _____

12. the **raucous** roar from the trading floor _____

13. **transferred** to an underground facility _____

14. warned of an **impending** investigation _____

15. open to the **enticement** of lobbyists _____

Antonyms

*Choose the word from this unit that is **most nearly opposite** in meaning to the **boldface** word or expression in the given phrase. Write the word on the line provided.*

16. a **realistic** blueprint for change _____

17. proceeded at a **relaxed** pace _____

18. was **willing** to make a compromise _____

19. demanded an immediate **acceleration** _____

20. the **hidden** cause of the problem _____

Choosing the Right Word

*Circle the **boldface** word that more satisfactorily completes each of the following sentences.*

1. Although I play a fair hand of bridge, I'm not capable of the brilliant (**coups, manifests**) that mark a true master of the game.

2. Only when we tried to implement the plan did its (**innate, imminent**) defects become clear to us.

3. The (**wizened, febrile**) tempo of the symphony's opening movement gives way to a placid and stately largo in the next.

4. Accidents at nuclear power plants have prompted some people to agitate for a (**moratorium, nostrum**) on the construction of such facilities.

5. When he took his first bite of Mother's famous coconut custard pie, a look of (**visionary, beatific**) joy spread over his face.

6. The plan is certainly ingenious, but it strikes me as far too (**visionary, imminent**) to serve as the basis for practical legislation.

7. It is a rare leader indeed who can tell the public unpleasant truths without evasions or (**pariahs, blandishments**).

8. Someone who "can't see the forest for the trees" is usually too concerned with (**minutiae, nostrums**) to be aware of the overall picture.

9. "As soon as we received the order," I said, "we crated the equipment and (**gainsaid, consigned**) it to the buyer in Atlanta."

10. The kind of financial (**minutiae, chicanery**) involved in bringing off that deal may not have been illegal, but it was certainly unethical.

11. No one who knows the facts would venture to (**gainsay, consign**) your claim to have done your utmost to improve this community.

12. The solution to our problems is to be found in long-term programs of social planning, not in easy (**pariahs, nostrums**).

13. Although I am (**febrile, loath**) to boast, I must acknowledge my superior qualities as a student, athlete, financier, and all-round social luminary.

14. "How much of a chance do you suppose a 98-pound weakling like me actually stands against that 320-pound (**coup, behemoth**)?" I asked incredulously.

15. After it had been left to rot in the sun for a few days, the plump little apple began to take on the (**visionary, wizened**) appearance of a prune.

16. (**Imminent, Loath**) disaster stared us in the face when we were thrown for a loss and then fumbled the ball on our own five-yard line.

17. After he killed Alexander Hamilton in a duel, Aaron Burr found himself no longer a respected statesman, but a social and political (**coup, pariah**).

18. The (**cacophony, moratorium**) that suddenly greeted my ears made me suspect that a fox had somehow gotten into the henhouse.

19. "The evidence that we will present in this trial," the prosecutor told the jury, "will make the defendant's guilt abundantly (**beatific, manifest**)."

20. It didn't make me any happier to learn that my firing was being referred to (**euphemistically, cacophonously**) as a "termination."

Vocabulary in Context

*Read the following passage, in which some of the words you have studied in this unit appear in **boldface** type. Then complete each statement given below the passage by circling the letter of the item that is **the same** or **almost the same** in meaning as the highlighted word.*

Meet the Maestro

(Line)

Few will **gainsay** the fact that Arturo Toscanini was one of the great conductors of the twentieth century, a **manifest** musical genius of extraordinary temperament, aspiration, and energy. Born in Parma, Italy in 1867, Toscanini began his musical career as a cellist but soon moved to

(5) conducting, making his debut in a performance of Verdi's opera *Aida* in Rio de Janeiro in 1886. After returning to Italy, he premiered Puccini's *La Boheme*.

His first major assignment was as the

(10) musical director of La Scala, the great opera house in Milan. Here Toscanini launched a **visionary** program to purify and ennoble the operatic art, which had degenerated into a social entertainment for

(15) Italian society. Toscanini was determined to restore seriousness to the opera, and he largely succeeded, but not without gaining a reputation as a single-minded purist. His admirers, perhaps **euphemistically**, called

(20) him uncompromising. His detractors took the more blatant road, describing him as

The exacting maestro conducting the NBC Symphony Orchestra in New York

dictatorial. Once, the maestro even stopped conducting a performance because he could not rid the audience of their annoying (to him) habit of breaking into lengthy and **cacophonous** demands for encores.

(25) The last twenty-five years of Toscanini's great career were spent mostly in New York City. He was principal conductor of the combined Philharmonic and Symphony orchestras, where he performed with great clarity, precision, and intensity. Then in 1937, he took the reins of the newly formed orchestra of the National Broadcasting Company, where he conducted and recorded in his

(30) characteristically **febrile** style until his death in 1954.

---

1. Gainsay (line 1) most nearly means
  a. detract
  b. examine
  c. confirm
  d. deny

2. The meaning of **manifest** (line 2) is
  a. exceptional
  b. latent
  c. evident
  d. possible

3. Visionary (line 12) is best defined as
  a. intangible
  b. idealistic
  c. mundane
  d. hypothetical

4. The meaning of **euphemistically** (line 19) is
  a. without knowledge
  b. with respect
  c. with a substitute
  d. with hostility

5. Cacophonous (line 24) means
  a. colossal
  b. discordant
  c. unsightly
  d. harmonious

6. Febrile (line 30) most nearly means
  a. frenetic
  b. dominating
  c. placid
  d. impending

Definitions

Note carefully the spelling, pronunciation, part(s) of speech, and definition(s) of each of the following words. Then write the word in the blank space(s) in the illustrative sentence(s) following. Finally, study the lists of synonyms and antonyms given at the end of each entry.

1. amenity
(ə men′ ə tē)

(*n.*) that which is pleasant or agreeable; (*pl.*) attractive features, customs, etc.

When I backpack there are certain basic _____, such as clean sheets and a dry tent, that I will not go without.

ANTONYMS: unpleasantness, disagreeableness

2. aperture
(ap′ ər chər)

(*n.*) an opening, gap, hole; orifice

After the earthquake, rain and cold came through the _____ in the wall of the damaged house.

ANTONYMS: closure, blockage, occlusion

3. dissidence
(dis′ ə dəns)

(*n.*) a difference of opinion; discontent

When the commanding officer announced that all leave was cancelled, there was widespread _____ in the ranks.

SYNONYMS: disagreement, dissent, disaffection
ANTONYMS: agreement, harmony, concord

4. epicurean
(ep ə kyü′ rē ən)

(*adj.*) devoted to the pursuit of pleasure; fond of good food, comfort, and ease; with discriminating tastes; (*n.*) a person with discriminating tastes

The chef took an _____ delight in presenting the most delicious dishes to his demanding clientele.

Even the most fervent _____ should not expect fine dining in a poor, war-torn country.

SYNONYMS: (*adj.*) hedonistic, sybaritic, discriminating
ANTONYMS: (*adj.*) ascetic, self-denying, abstemious

5. improvident
(im präv′ ə dənt)

(*adj.*) not thrifty; failing to plan ahead

Some people are so _____ that despite high incomes they struggle to make ends meet.

SYNONYMS: prodigal, spendthrift, extravagant
ANTONYMS: thrifty, frugal, economical, cautious

6. iniquity
(i nik′ wə tē)

(*n.*) wickedness, sin; a grossly immoral act

English Puritans looked upon the court that surrounded King Charles I as a den of _____.

SYNONYMS: evil, crime
ANTONYMS: probity, rectitude, uprightness

7. inviolable
(in vī' ə lə bəl)

(*adj.*) sacred; of such a character that it must not be broken, injured, or profaned

Safeguarding the retirement income of millions of Americans is an _____ trust of the federal government.

SYNONYMS: sacrosanct, unassailable
ANTONYMS: vulnerable, assailable

8. mutable
(myü' tə bəl)

(*adj.*) open to or capable of change, fickle

Most people would agree that one's principles and moral values should not be as _____ as fashion.

SYNONYMS: changeable, variable
ANTONYMS: changeless, steadfast, constant

9. nascent
(nā' sənt)

(*adj.*) just beginning to exist or develop; having just come into existence

Recent public opinion polls registered _____ opposition to the proposed tax increase.

SYNONYMS: budding, incipient, embryonic
ANTONYMS: dying, moribund, senescent

10. obeisance
(ō bē' səns)

(*n.*) a deep bow or other body movement indicating respect or submission; deference, homage

Upon entering the throne room, each courtier made a respectful _____ before the king and queen.

SYNONYMS: respect, honor
ANTONYMS: disrespect, irreverence, disregard

11. panegyric
(pan ə ji' rik)

(*n.*) formal or elaborate praise; a tribute

The speaker delivered a _____ in honor of the award-winning author.

SYNONYMS: tribute, encomium, testimonial
ANTONYMS: diatribe, tirade, philippic

12. pillory
(pil' ə rē)

(*n.*) a device for publicly punishing offenders; a means for exposing one to public contempt or ridicule; (*v.*) to expose to public contempt or ridicule

The _____ was placed in the center of town so that everyone could view the outlaws and their shame.

The candidate tried to _____ her political opponent by suggesting that he had ties to organized crime.

ANTONYMS: (*v.*) praise, extol, laud, acclaim

13. pittance
(pit′ əns)

(*n.*) a woefully meager allowance, wage, or portion

In comparison to the overwhelming need for food and medicine, the shipment was a mere _____.

SYNONYMS: modicum, trifle
ANTONYM: fortune

14. presage
(pres′ ij)

(*v.*) to foreshadow or point to a future event; to predict; (*n.*) a warning or indication of the future

The skirmishes at the border _____ a war.

The fall in stock prices and retail sales may be a _____ of hard economic times to come.

SYNONYMS: (*v.*) augur, portend, foretell

15. progeny
(präj′ ə nē)

(*n.*) descendants, offspring, children, followers, disciples

The Bill of Rights guarantees certain civil rights and protections to ourselves and our _____.

SYNONYMS: issue, posterity
ANTONYMS: ancestors, forebears, antecedents

16. promulgate
(präm′ əl gāt)

(*v.*) to proclaim or issue officially; to make known far and wide

The School Board _____ a new approach to education that emphasized phonics.

SYNONYM: announce
ANTONYMS: withdraw, retract, abrogate, nullify

17. rectitude
(rek′ tə tüd)

(*n.*) uprightness, righteousness; correctness

The mayor is a person of unquestionable _____.

SYNONYMS: probity, integrity
ANTONYMS: iniquity, heinousness

18. restive
(res′ tiv)

(*adj.*) restless, hard to manage, balky

The _____ horse had not been taken out of the stable for five days.

SYNONYMS: uneasy, fidgety, recalcitrant
ANTONYMS: serene, unruffled, docile

19. seraphic
(sə raf′ ik)

(*adj.*) angelic, heavenly, celestial

The artist painted the children with _____ smiles to suggest their innocence.

SYNONYM: cherubic
ANTONYMS: devilish, impish

20. subsist
(səb sist′)

(*v.*) to have existence; to remain alive, manage to make a living or maintain life; to persist or continue

Peasants in nineteenth-century Ireland were able to _____ almost exclusively on potatoes.

SYNONYMS: last, survive, sustain

Completing the Sentence

From the words for this unit, choose the one that best completes each of the following sentences. Write the word in the space provided.

1. We are sure that their vow is _____ because their sense of moral obligation will prevent them from ever breaking it.

2. Conscientious parents will do everything they can to foster and develop the _____ intellectual curiosity of a small child.

3. Imagine someone with my _____ tastes having to live for a week on that watery mush!

4. The biography is a pretty evenhanded appraisal of the man's strengths and weaknesses, not just another _____ to a great hero.

5. I see no reason to question the _____ of her dealings with us since I know her to be "as honest as the day is long."

6. He inveighs against the sins of society with all the stridency of an Old Testament prophet castigating the _____ of the ungodly.

7. The wranglers suspected that there were wolves or mountain lions nearby when the herd suddenly grew nervous and _____.

8. The Bible tells us that visitors to the court of Solomon, the great Hebrew king, willingly paid him _____.

9. For many ancient peoples, the appearance of a comet was a fearful omen that _____ great social upheaval.

10. After a few days in which everything went my way, I suddenly learned just how _____ Lady Luck can be.

11. Am I to be _____ before the entire student body because I made a few minor mistakes as a member of the Student Council?

12. The liberties that we have inherited from our forefathers are a sacred trust that we must pass on undiminished to our _____.

13. Authoritarian governments often resort to violence and coercion in their efforts to repress political _____.

14. Our financial situations are so different that what she considers a mere _____ seems a fortune to me.

15. It was the _____ of its natural setting on those rolling hills that led the architect to dub the estate "Mount Pleasant."

16. The President has _____ a policy that commits the nation to curbing pollution.

17. "I'm afraid that the child's _____ countenance belies the devilry in his heart," I observed sadly.

18. The _____ on most cameras can be adjusted to admit more or less light, as required.

19. Nutritionists say that most of us could _____ on a great deal less food than we actually consume.

20. Though I'm by no means _____ with my money, I don't hoard it either.

Synonyms

*Choose the word from this unit that is **the same** or **most nearly the same** in meaning as the **boldface** word or expression in the given phrase. Write the word on the line provided.*

1. tried to **survive** in a desert   _____

2. dark clouds **portending** rain   _____

3. the **angelic** tones of the choir   _____

4. challenged the **integrity** of the judge   _____

5. a **hedonistic** display of luxury   _____

6. stuffed the **orifice** with old newspapers   _____

7. showed a **budding** interest in politics   _____

8. paid **respect** to those who came before her   _____

9. the **pleasantness** of a quiet garden   _____

10. the **sacrosanct** principle of equality   _____

11. will be punished for their **crimes**   _____

12. repaid a mere **modicum** of what is owed   _____

13. **announced** by the public health authorities   _____

14. **fidgety** after the caffeine   _____

15. a **fickle** disposition   _____

Antonyms

*Choose the word from this unit that is **most nearly opposite** in meaning to the **boldface** word or expression in the given phrase. Write the word on the line provided.*

16. insulted the king's **ancestors**   _____

17. always **praises** those in authority   _____

18. gave a long **diatribe** on the military   _____

19. widespread political **agreement**   _____

20. a **thrifty** manager   _____

Choosing the Right Word

*Circle the **boldface** word that more satisfactorily completes each of the following sentences.*

1. Religious (**obeisance, dissidence**) was one of the motives that led many people to leave their homes and found colonies in North America.

2. Writers often regard their works as their (**dissidence, progeny**) in much the same way as other people regard their pets as family members.

3. The resounding victory we scored at the polls is an eloquent tribute to the (**rectitude, dissidence**) of her approach as campaign manager.

4. As the speaker's remarks became more inflammatory, the crowd grew more sullen and (**nascent, restive**).

5. The novel centers on a(n) (**improvident, seraphic**) young man who squanders his inheritance on riotous living and dies in the poorhouse.

6. I realize the official made a serious mistake, but that is no reason to (**pillory, subsist**) him so unmercifully in the press.

7. We would like to believe that the intensifying fear of ecological catastrophe (**subsists, presages**) an era of environmental harmony in the near future.

8. The cost of living has risen so sharply that a salary that was adequate a decade ago is now no more than a mere (**panegyric, pittance**).

9. The new "gourmet" deli features delicacies that are bound to delight even the most exacting of (**epicurean, nascent**) palates.

10. No matter how well defended, no boundary is (**inviolable, restive**) unless the people on either side of it respect each other.

11. "Angelica" is indeed an apt name for one whose (**mutable, seraphic**) beauty is complemented by such sweetness of temper and gentleness of spirit.

12. One cannot expect a(n) (**epicurean, nascent**) democracy to go through its early years without experiencing serious growing pains.

13. Recently, the Principal (**promulgated, presaged**) a new dress code that abolished some of the unnecessary strictness of the old rules.

14. Liberty (**subsists, presages**) only so long as people have the intelligence to know their rights and the courage to defend them.

15. There was a loophole in the law, and through this (**aperture, obeisance**) the defendant escaped the legal consequences of his crime.

16. Instead of being so concerned with the (**iniquities, apertures**) of others, they would do well to concentrate on correcting their own shortcomings.

17. The study of government shows us that many political institutions thought to be unchanging are in fact highly (**inviolable, mutable**).

18. Specific customs vary widely in different lands, but the basic (**affectations, amenities**) of civilized living are much the same everywhere.

19. Like so many others of his generation, he paid unquestioning (**iniquity, obeisance**) to the accepted symbols of material success.

20. Instead of mouthing empty (**panegyrics, apertures**) to the Bill of Rights, let's strive to make this great document a reality in our lives.

Vocabulary in Context

*Read the following passage, in which some of the words you have studied in this unit appear in **boldface** type. Then complete each statement given below the passage by circling the letter of the item that is **the same** or **almost the same** in meaning as the highlighted word.*

The Scarlet Woman

(Line)

One of the most vivid female characters in American fiction is Hester Prynne, the protagonist of Nathaniel Hawthorne's *The Scarlet Letter*. Published in 1850, the novel is set in Puritan New England in the mid-seventeenth century and deals with two major Puritan preoccupations: sin and redemption.

The particular **iniquity** of which Hester is (5) guilty is adultery. She has broken what her Puritan neighbors view as the **inviolable** bond of matrimony, and, therefore, must be publicly exposed and punished for her sin. To that end, she is forced to wear a scarlet (10) *A* for adultery on the bodice of her dress, and to stand **pilloried** in the town square with her illegitimate **progeny** Pearl in her arms. Hester is a strong-willed woman, however, and although she acknowledges (15) her own guilt and accepts her punishment, she will not cooperate in punishing others. Repeatedly, she refuses to reveal the identity of the father of her child, choosing to leave her former lover, the young minister (20) Arthur Dimmesdale, to wrestle with his own conscience. And wrestle he does. A model

Old-fashioned pillory in Colonial Williamsburg

of apparent **rectitude**, the Reverend Dimmesdale is torn between his inner sense of guilt and the fear of losing his good name in the community.

After years of self-defeating struggle, Dimmesdale finally confesses and dies (25) in Hester's arms, **presaging** the fate of those who hide away their guilt and fail to acknowledge their wrongdoings. Hester alone forgives herself and others, and she alone goes on, with renewed strength, to live and love generously.

---

1. Iniquity (line 5) most nearly means
a. misstatement   c. evil
b. prejudice   d. disturbance

2. The meaning of **inviolable** (line 7) is
a. loving   c. fragile
b. sacrosanct   d. eternal

3. Pilloried (line 12) is best defined as
a. exposed   c. compelled
b. protected   d. exonerated

4. The meaning of **progeny** (line 13) is
a. ancestry   c. name
b. issue   d. gains

5. Rectitude (line 23) most nearly means
a. selflessness   c. courage
b. gentleness   d. integrity

6. Presaging (line 26) most nearly means
a. mocking   c. defying
b. confusing   d. foretelling

Vocabulary for Comprehension

Read the following passage, in which some of the words you have studied in Units 13–15 appear in **boldface** *type. Then answer questions 1–12 on page 172 on the basis of what is* stated *or* implied *in the passage and in the introductory statement.*

This passage focuses on one of the most famous American novelists of the twentieth century, F. Scott Fitzgerald.

(Line)

Few writers have been as identified with an age as F. Scott Fitzgerald (1896–1940). Not only is his best fiction set in the 1920s, but he helped
(5) define that era as the Jazz Age, an **epicurean** decade of fevered pleasure-seeking, **improvident** spending, and gaudy excess.

Born in St. Paul, Minnesota,
(10) Francis Scott Key Fitzgerald (named after his famous ancestor) was a restless young man full of romantic dreams. In 1917 he left Princeton University before receiving
(15) his degree, to train as an Army officer, but he never made it overseas. While stationed at Camp Sheridan near Montgomery, Alabama, Fitzgerald fell for a local southern
(20) beauty, Zelda Sayre. By dint of sheer charm and persistence, Fitzgerald got Zelda to agree to marry him, but she was too **cognizant** of his poverty to succumb
(25) permanently to his **blandishments**. When the novel he was writing was rejected for a second time, she broke off the engagement.

Scott, however, was not deterred.
(30) He went back to St. Paul and rewrote the novel again. Upon its third submission to the Scribners publishing house, the manuscript was

accepted. It was published in 1920
(35) as *This Side of Paradise* and became an instant success. Scott and Zelda were married within a week. Like the characters in Fitzgerald's Jazz Age novels, the couple spent the next
(40) decade shuttling between New York and Europe, living the high life and spending lavishly. Behind the frothy **facade**, however, lay a darker reality that Fitzgerald depicted in his most
(45) famous novel, *The Great Gatsby* (1925). In *Gatsby*, Fitzgerald examines the moral decadence **engendered** by the American dream of wealth and success. When
(50) Fitzgerald died of a heart attack at the age of 44 (Zelda died in a fire only a few years later), his works that chronicled such a discrete period of American history seemed on their
(55) way to obscurity. In the 1950s, however, critics revived such classics as *Gatsby* and *Tender Is the Night* (1934), securing a place for him in the canon of American writers.

1. According to the author, which era did Fitzgerald help to define?
   a. the Age of Discovery
   b. the Jazz Age
   c. the Great Depression
   d. the Civil Rights era
   e. the Information Age

2. The meaning of **epicurean** (line 6) is
   a. impoverished
   b. turbulent
   c. idyllic
   d. uneventful
   e. hedonistic

3. **Improvident** (line 7) most nearly means
   a. prudent
   b. extravagant
   c. intermittent
   d. frugal
   e. impressive

4. In paragraph 2 (lines 9–28), it may be inferred that when Scott was courting Zelda, her values were
   a. idealistic
   b. literary
   c. patriotic
   d. materialistic
   e. romantic

5. **Cognizant** (line 24) is best defined as
   a. proud
   b. ashamed
   c. aware
   d. scornful
   e. oblivious

6. The meaning of **blandishments** (line 25) is
   a. enticements
   b. threats
   c. fantasies
   d. apologies
   e. tantrums

7. You can reasonably infer that an important factor responsible for Scott and Zelda's marriage was
   a. his repeated pleas to her
   b. the instant success of *This Side of Paradise*
   c. the intervention of Zelda's parents

d. the couple's admiring European friends
   e. Scott's promise to leave New York for Europe

8. According to the author, the main focus in the novel *The Great Gatsby* is on which of the following?
   a. the complex rhythms of jazz
   b. the moral decadence flowing from the American dream
   c. contrasts between American and European society
   d. the pitfalls of romance
   e. the corruption of American politics

9. **Facade** (line 43) most nearly means
   a. costume
   b. mask
   c. attitude
   d. lifestyle
   e. celebration

10. **Engendered** (line 48) most nearly means
    a. generated
    b. baffled
    c. offended
    d. deterred
    e. enraged

11. The primary purpose of the passage is to
    a. analyze contrasts between Fitzgerald's early novels and his later works
    b. show how the Fitzgeralds epitomized the Jazz Age lifestyle
    c. survey the highlights of Fitzgerald's life and literary career
    d. support the claim that *The Great Gatsby* is Fitzgerald's masterpiece
    e. emphasize the irony in Fitzgerald's handling of the theme of illusion vs. reality

12. For the most part, what organizational scheme does the author use in the passage?
    a. order of importance
    b. spatial order
    c. order of impression
    d. chronological order
    e. comparison and contrast

Grammar in Context

In the sentence "When the novel he was writing was rejected for the second time, she broke off the engagement" (lines 26–28 on page 171), the independent clause "she broke off the engagement" expresses the main idea. However, if the author had written "Before she broke off the engagement, the novel he was writing was rejected for the second time," the independent clause would have misleadingly stressed a subordinate idea, rather than the main idea. This error is known as **faulty subordination**.

To avoid faulty subordination, review your sentences for logical emphasis and balance of ideas. For example, make sure that your sentences reflect the relative importance of ideas. Do not use a coordinating conjunction to join ideas of unequal importance. Be careful to link ideas clearly and accurately. Be sure to express cause and effect logically.

On the lines provided, rewrite each of the following sentences to correct faulty subordination. Write "correct" if the sentence is correct.

1. F. Scott Fitzgerald was born in St. Paul, Minnesota, and he is identified with a particular era in American history.

_____

_____

2. Fitzgerald's fiction is set in the 1920s, but he helped define that era as the Jazz Age.

_____

_____

3. Fitzgerald was a restless young man full of romantic dreams, and he studied for a while at Princeton University.

_____

_____

4. Fitzgerald trained as an army officer, but he never made it overseas in World War I.

_____

_____

5. He was stationed at an army camp in Alabama, yet he fell for a local southern beauty, Zelda Sayre.

_____

_____

6. The couple lived the high life in New York and Europe, but they spent lavishly.

_____

_____

7. Fitzgerald's works seemed on their way to obscurity after he died at the age of 44.

_____

_____

Two-Word Completions

Circle the pair of words that best complete the meaning of each of the following passages.

1. Disgruntled army officers and other _____ elements in the society engineered the bloody _____ that toppled the duly elected government a few months after it had taken office.
  a. contrite . . . nostrum
  b. restive . . . moratorium
  c. visionary . . . pittance
  d. dissident . . . coup

2. Behind the courtier's outward _____ of decorous sloth there lurked the _____ imagination of an inveterate opportunist, eager to capitalize on any windfall that came his way.
  a. aperture . . . incongruous
  b. facade . . . febrile
  c. cynosure . . . nascent
  d. chicanery . . . improvident

3. Any official who is genuinely concerned about the _____ of his or her behavior while in public office will think twice before engaging in the kinds of political _____ and backroom shenanigans that sometimes go on when a juicy government contract is up for grabs.
  a. rectitude . . . chicanery
  b. imminence . . . blandishments
  c. progeny . . . machinations
  d. iniquity . . . cognizance

4. Once the news broke, the public heaped so much _____ on the head of the hapless city official that he soon found himself a veritable political _____, even in his own party.
  a. euphemism . . . canard
  b. dissidence . . . amenity
  c. opprobrium . . . pariah
  d. efficacy . . . ghoul

5. As soon as the famous movie star walked into my shop, she became the _____ of all eyes. Customers stopped what they were doing to stare at her as if _____ by the spell of her celebrity.
  a. aperture . . . engendered
  b. cynosure . . . mesmerized
  c. moratorium . . . subsisted
  d. pillory . . . promulgated

6. The characters in Jane Austen novels display _____ manners, obeying the _____ of social conventions that range from how many consecutive waltzes a couple may dance to the type of tea that should be served to guests.
  a. abstruse . . . canards
  b. ethereal . . .pariahs
  c. decorous . . . minutiae
  d. beatific . . . recriminations

Choosing the Right Meaning

Read each sentence carefully. Then circle the item that best completes the statement below the sentence.

The bill sparked controversy when it was introduced. There was even a tug-of-war between chairpersons over which congressional committee was properly cognizant. (2)

1. The word **cognizant** in line 2 is used to mean

a. knowledgeable   b. informed   c. having jurisdiction   d. aware

Only a historian of great imaginative power could extract from the desiccated figures of dusty old ledger books the drama of a great family's decline. (2)

2. In line 1 the word **desiccated** most nearly means

a. complicated   b. shriveled   c. dried out   d. uninteresting

Ralph Waldo Emerson, the guiding light of American transcendentalism, counted among his progeny such distinguished contemporaries as Henry Thoreau and Margaret Fuller. (2)

3. The word **progeny** in line 2 is used to mean

a. children   b. disciples   c. offspring   d. descendants

"But would the honest patriot, in the full tide of successful experiment, abandon a government which has so far kept us free and firm, on the theoretic and visionary (2) fear that this government, the world's best hope, may by possibility want energy to preserve itself?" (Thomas Jefferson, "First Inaugural Address") (4)

4. In line 2 the word **visionary** is best defined as

a. utopian   b. fantastic   c. idealistic   d. predictable

In *The Autocrat of the Breakfast-Table*, Oliver Wendell Holmes paraphrases Plutarch's "Epicurean paradox" this way: "Give us the luxuries of life, and we will dispense with (2) its necessaries."

5. The best definition for the word **Epicurean** in line 2 is

a. pursuing pleasure   b. discriminating   c. insoluble   d. ancient

Antonyms

*In each of the following groups, circle the word or expression that is most nearly the **opposite** of the word in **boldface** type.*

1. inviolable
a. honest
b. fundamental
c. vulnerable
d. sound

2. engender
a. deter
b. beget
c. aggravate
d. exploit

3. loath
a. unwilling
b. eager
c. afraid
d. unable

4. epicurean
a. hedonistic
b. ascetic
c. refined
d. predictable

5. cacophonous
a. modern
b. harmonious
c. dissonant
d. classical

6. promulgate
a. enforce
b. formulate
c. issue
d. withdraw

7. abstruse
a. poetic
b. foreign
c. straightforward
d. fallacious

8. pilloried
a. ridiculed
b. caricatured
c. censored
d. extolled

9. dissidence
a. agreement
b. opposition
c. debt
d. intrigue

11. imminent
a. looming
b. distant
c. sudden
d. destructive

13. desiccated
a. parched
b. polluted
c. sodden
d. hardened

15. improvident
a. incompetent
b. inexperienced
c. shortsighted
d. cautious

10. panegyric
a. obituary
b. tribute
c. introduction
d. diatribe

12. contrite
a. apologetic
b. unrepentant
c. repeat
d. accused

14. incongruous
a. complex
b. compatible
c. jarring
d. vivid

16. iniquity
a. daring
b. wickedness
c. rectitude
d. skill

A. *On the line provided, write the word you have learned in Units 13–15 that is related to each of the following nouns.*
EXAMPLE: manifestation—**manifest**

1. cacophony

2. subsistence, subsister

3. consignment, consigner, consignation

4. desiccation, desiccant

5. mesmerism, mesmerizer

6. imminence, imminency

7. promulgation, promulgator

8. incongruence, incongruity, incongruousness

9. cognizance

10. ghoul, ghoulishness

11. contrition, contriteness

12. decorousness, decorum

13. mutability

14. improvidence

B. *On the line provided, write the word you have learned in Units 13–15 that is related to each of the following verbs.*
EXAMPLE: dissent—**dissidence**

15. provide

16. mutate

17. wizen

18. machinate

19. envision

20. violate

Word Associations

In each of the following groups, circle the word that is best defined or suggested by the given phrase.

1. someone who is the center of attention
a. machination   b. cynosure   c. presage   d. coup

2. pulled some strings to get a contract
a. pillory   b. panegyric   c. chicanery   d. canard

3. an air-conditioned room with color TV and private bath
a. amenities   b. facades   c. efficacies   d. pittance

4. a charming person who behaves with outstanding propriety
a. captious   b. decorous   c. abstruse   d. mutable

5. a remark made deliberately to cause offense
a. blandishment   b. minutiae   c. iniquity   d. affront

6. an attitude of respect and awe upon meeting a world-famous writer
a. affront   b. efficacy   c. obeisance   d. coup

7. "I rise to dispute the accuracy of the statements made by the last speaker."
a. gainsay   b. affront   c. manifest   d. engender

8. barely enough to make ends meet
a. canard   b. pittance   c. amenity   d. coup

9. how you might characterize an instinct
a. epicurean   b. ghoulish   c. innate   d. captious

10. shipped the equipment to the buyer by parcel post
a. consign   b. presage   c. subsist   d. engender

11. "underprivileged" instead of "poor"
a. pariah   b. euphemism   c. canard   d. facade

12. "Flattery will get you nowhere!"
a. manifests   b. canards   c. facades   d. blandishments

13. a brilliant oratorical style that left the audience spellbound
a. engender   b. mesmerize   c. subsist   d. pillory

14. relies on chicken soup as a remedy for all disorders of body and mind
a. nostrum   b. aperture   c. coup   d. visionary

15. unshakable moral integrity
a. efficacy   b. rectitude   c. nostrum   d. opprobrium

16. obvious enough to be readily perceived by all
a. manifest   b. incongruous   c. cognizant   d. beatific

17. the first faint stirrings of an idea
a. desiccated   b. nascent   c. wizened   d. ethereal

18. "The weird story about me has absolutely no basis in fact."
a. amenity   b. panegyric   c. canard   d. moratorium

19. an "untouchable" in the caste system
a. pariah   b. recrimination   c. obeisance   d. facade

20. a battleship next to a rowboat
a. manifest   b. pariah   c. pillory   d. behemoth

Building with Classical Roots

vid, vis—to look, see

This root appears in **visionary** (page 159), which means "lacking in practicality" or, as a noun, "a dreamer or seer." Some other words based on this same root are listed below.

advisement	providence	proviso	visitation
envisage	provident	visage	vista

From the list of words above, choose the one that corresponds to each of the brief definitions below. Write the word in the blank space in the illustrative sentence below the definition.

1. a face, countenance, appearance, look, aspect (*"that which is seen"*)

The links of chains he carried, which signified his sins, gave Jacob Marley a frightening _____.

2. divine guidance or care; a manifestation of such guidance

Despite hard times, or perhaps especially during hard times, people of faith put their trust in _____.

3. a distinct view or prospect through an opening; an extensive mental view

As we rounded the bend, we suddenly beheld the most breathtaking _____ of our trip.

4. a conditional stipulation; an article or clause in a contract that introduces a condition (*"that which is foreseen"*)

They agreed to sign the deal, with the _____ that we serve as witnesses.

5. a visit for the purpose of making an official inspection; an act of visiting; a severe punishment or affliction

Health specialists are meeting to discuss the possibility of a new _____ of tuberculosis.

6. to picture to oneself (*"see into"*); conceive of, especially as a future possibility

It is hard to _____ a modern America made up entirely of small farmers.

7. providing for future needs or contingencies; thrifty, economical

It is our agency's mission to explore the most _____ use of our natural resources.

8. a careful consideration (*"act of seeing to"*)

The committee has agreed to take your most recent request under _____.

From the list of words on page 178, choose the one that best completes each of the following sentences. Write the word in the blank space provided.

1. From the summit of the mountain, a dramatic _____ of lush pastures and rolling hills spreads out in every direction as far as the eye can see.

2. An old maxim says that luck is merely a nickname for _____.

3. Is it possible for you to _____ a world free of poverty, famine, hatred, and war?

4. She agreed to chair this year's prom committee with the _____ that six other class members act as her assistants.

5. The scholarship committee has the application under _____ and has promised a decision by the end of the week.

6. It was only after I saw his gaunt eyes and haggard _____ that I began to realize just how intense an ordeal he had experienced.

7. That old mansion is reputedly inhabited by some fiendish spirit, whose nocturnal _____ have frightened away anyone who has tried to live in the place.

8. "If you'd learn to be a bit more _____ with your allowance," he scolded, "you wouldn't constantly need to borrow money from others."

---

*Circle the **boldface** word that more satisfactorily completes each of the following sentences.*

1. A good education can expose open-minded people to new (**vistas, advisements**) for the future.

2. We had few prospects of obtaining a legal remedy for our problem until a new attorney agreed to take our case under (**advisement, vista**).

3. The normal (**providence, visitation**) hours at the hospital are 2:00 PM to 8:00 PM, except for patients who are in the intensive-care unit.

4. We tried to (**advise, envisage**) the creation of the Hoover Dam by studying detailed architectural drawings chronicling its erection.

5. It must have been an act of (**providence, visage**) that the boy was rescued from the well.

6. Photographic portraits of Abraham Lincoln provide the first modern record of the deteriorating effects of constant political stress on the presidential (**visage, proviso**).

7. Our agreement with the cable company includes a (**visage, proviso**) that we must return the converter box when we move, or we will lose our security deposit.

8. It was thanks to the (**provident, envisaged**) planning of frugal pioneer women that many homesteading families were able to endure some of their unexpected hardships.

Analogies

In each of the following, circle the item that best completes the comparison.

1. pariah is to **opprobrium** as
a. aesthete is to ignominy
b. celebrity is to acclamation
c. victor is to animadversion
d. saint is to improvident

2. penitent is to **contrite** as
a. unwonted is to nefarious
b. sumptuous is to depraved
c. visionary is to utopian
d. pecuniary is to cacophonous

3. desiccate is to **heat** as
a. saturate is to liquid
b. mesmerize is to air
c. rebuff is to wax
d. burnish is to fire

4. captious is to **cavil** as
a. disgruntled is to grouse
b. avid is to demur
c. febrile is to importune
d. chary is to allege

5. loath is to **reluctance** as
a. insatiable is to boredom
b. blasé is to concern
c. avid is to enthusiasm
d. fervent is to apathy

6. stratagem is to **crafty** as
a. chicanery is to overt
b. peregrination is to coherent
c. juggernaut is to picayune
d. machination is to devious

7. encomium is to **panegyric** as
a. diatribe is to harangue
b. facade is to cynosure
c. canard is to verity
d. eulogy is to philippic

8. amenity is to **asperity** as
a. complicity is to collusion
b. rectitude is to iniquity
c. aesthetic is to euphemism
d. moratorium is to hiatus

9. myopic is to **discernment** as
a. pertinacious is to determination
b. imperturbable is to composure
c. improvident is to foresight
d. cognizant is to awareness

10. misanthrope is to **gregarious** as
a. pickpocket is to furtive
b. liar is to mendacious
c. lackey is to obsequious
d. hero is to pusillanimous

Choosing the Right Meaning

Read each sentence carefully. Then circle the item that best completes the statement below the sentence.

"All the choir of heaven and furniture of earth . . . have not subsistence without a mind."   (Bishop Berkeley, *Principles of Human Knowledge*)   (2)

1. In line 1 the word **subsistence** most nearly means
a. persistence   b. sustenance   c. existence   d. continuance

Archaeologists could only wonder that objects so ethereal had survived intact the rude treatment of the grave robbers.   (2)

2. The best definition for the word **ethereal** in line 1 is
a. heavenly   b. airy   c. celestial   d. delicate

Of all the celestial bodies that crowd the night sky none is a more faithful and steadfast cynosure to the navigator than the North Star.   (2)

3. In line 2 the word **cynosure** is used to mean
a. center of attraction
b. guiding light
c. object of beauty
d. focal point

"The sumptuous feast the careworn king consumes,
Though served on gold or plate or china fine, (2)
Ofttimes tastes not so wholesome or so sweet
As lowly cotter's porridge, set out plain (4)
In sylvan trencher carved by his own hand
Of mighty oak or aspen quaking or tall pine." (6)
      (A. E. Glug, "Runes," 6–11)

4. The word **sylvan** in line 5 most nearly means
a. made of wood
b. pertaining to woods
c. living in the forest
d. mythical

Two-Word Completions

Circle the pair of words that best complete the meaning of each of the following sentences.

1. A century ago it may have been possible to _____ on pennies a day, but I don't see how you expect a person to live on the mere _____ you are proposing to pay me.
a. calumniate . . . nostrum
b. accost . . . talisman
c. subsist . . . pittance
d. deign . . . figment

2. The straitlaced Victorians, who were concerned about the _____ of a person's behavior, would have looked _____ at the casualness of modern social conventions.
a. propinquity . . . summarily
b. celerity . . . reputedly
c. propriety . . . askance
d. sophistry . . . indubitably

3. If the government provides only _____ quick-fixes to complicated international problems, it runs the risk of _____ rather than solving them.
a. ephemeral . . . exacerbating
b. unwonted . . . countermanding
c. tenable . . . engendering
d. peremptory . . . requiting

4. A _____ should stick to the _____ of a sport and leave its finer points to the experts.
a. pedant . . . exigencies
b. neophyte . . . rudiments
c. dilettante . . . idiosyncrasies
d. tyro . . . minutiae

5. As soon as they received the appropriate order from the court, the local cemetery workers began the somewhat _____ business of _____ the victim's body and delivering it to the coroner for reexamination.
a. nefarious . . . interpolating
b. macabre . . . interpolating
c. abject . . . promulgating
d. ghoulish . . . exhuming

Enriching Your Vocabulary

Read the passage below. Then complete the exercise at the bottom of the page.

A Linguistic Rendezvous with the French

In 1066 William the Conqueror, a powerful invader from Normandy (in what is now France), overtook King Harold II and his English forces at the Battle of Hastings. From that moment onward, the sound of the English language changed forever. Norman French supplanted English in the court and in the church. For at least the next hundred years, the kings of England and the English elite spoke French rather than English! French words flooded English. Over time, their spellings and pronunciations evolved to the point where some words of French origin, such as *coupon, fanfare, iodine, liter,* and *velour,* sound like they might always have had English roots.

Modern English has embraced an extensive store of words and phrases that have been borrowed more or less unchanged from the French. One such word, *coup* (Unit 14), a highly successful plan, act, or stratagem, is pronounced as the French would pronounce it: kü. The ordinary English pronunciation of the words and phrases that follow generally observe the rules of French diction.

Baguettes, a word and food borrowed from the French, are long, thin loaves of bread.

In Column A below are 8 more words and phrases that come from the French. With or without a dictionary, match each word or phrase with its meaning in Column B.

Column A

_____ **1.** avant-garde
_____ **2.** communiqué
_____ **3.** de rigueur
_____ **4.** ensemble
_____ **5.** joie de vivre
_____ **6.** nom de plume
_____ **7.** tête-à-tête
_____ **8.** vis-à-vis

Column B

a. something private, between two persons only; a private conversation between two persons (from the French for "head-to-head")

b. a group composed of complementary elements or parts that contribute to a single effect ("together")

c. face-to-face with; in relation to; as compared with

d. a pseudonym used by an author ("pen name")

e. a bulletin; an official announcement

f. a group that develops experimental or innovative techniques; an intelligentsia ("vanguard")

g. required by the prevailing fashion or custom; socially obligatory ("indispensable")

h. a keen or carefree enjoyment of life ("joy of living")

Selecting Word Meanings

*In each of the following groups, circle the word or expression that is **most nearly the same** in meaning as the word in **boldface** type in the given phrase.*

1. the **nadir** of my fortunes
   - a. twist
   - b. bottom
   - c. irony
   - d. pinnacle

2. a **moratorium** on the sale of arms
   - a. emphasis
   - b. suspension
   - c. penalty
   - d. symposium

3. **countermand** the decision
   - a. elucidate
   - b. exonerate
   - c. inundate
   - d. repudiate

4. **cognizant of** the facts
   - a. informed of
   - b. ignorant of
   - c. indifferent to
   - d. indignant about

5. drew water from a **brackish** stream
   - a. muddy
   - b. salty
   - c. fast-moving
   - d. quiet

6. **raze** the tenements
   - a. renovate
   - b. appraise
   - c. demolish
   - d. condemn

7. **avid** advocates of democracy
   - a. cynical
   - b. lukewarm
   - c. enthusiastic
   - d. famous

8. the **asperities** of life
   - a. rewards
   - b. severities
   - c. uncertainties
   - d. pastimes

9. resented their **mordant** remarks
   - a. harsh
   - b. offhand
   - c. contemptuous
   - d. irrelevant

10. the **flotsam** of a big city
    - a. skyscrapers
    - b. frenzy
    - c. debris
    - d. exploiters

11. cleared up the **discrepancy**
    - a. motive
    - b. negligence
    - c. inconsistency
    - d. mess

12. yielded **paltry** results
    - a. overwhelming
    - b. insignificant
    - c. ruinous
    - d. beneficial

13. composed the **eulogy**
    - a. critique
    - b. tribute
    - c. concerto
    - d. satire

14. the only member to **demur**
    - a. accept
    - b. volunteer
    - c. object
    - d. applaud

15. rule by **fiat**
    - a. consent
    - b. democracy
    - c. whim
    - d. decree

16. disappointed by their **myopic** outlook
    - a. nasty
    - b. insincere
    - c. pessimistic
    - d. shortsighted

17. an **abject** beggar
    - a. carefree
    - b. fearless
    - c. wretched
    - d. wandering

18. **substantiate** a statement
    - a. reveal
    - b. verify
    - c. deny
    - d. amplify

19. had the **effrontery** to laugh
    - a. desire
    - b. gall
    - c. sense
    - d. humor

20. their **picayune** criticisms
   a. trifling   b. humorous   c. irrelevant   d. vicious

21. portend a life-or-death struggle
   a. overcome   b. prevent   c. foreshadow   d. decide

22. delivered a **panegyric**
   a. explanation   b. rebuke   c. apology   d. encomium

23. the **mandate** of the people
   a. betrayal   b. objection   c. folly   d. authorization

24. deign to acknowledge my presence
   a. seem   b. stoop   c. refuse   d. attempt

25. deprecate such behavior
   a. approve   b. deplore   c. analyze   d. improve

Word Pairs

In the space before each of the following pairs of words write:

S—if the words are synonyms or near-synonyms;
O—if the words are antonyms or near-antonyms;
N—if the words are unrelated in meaning.

26. _____ saturnine—morose

27. _____ arrogate—renounce

28. _____ moot—indisputable

29. _____ fecund—fatuous

30. _____ feckless—effective

31. _____ laconic—terse

32. _____ chicanery—flaccid

33. _____ shortcoming—foible

34. _____ ubiquitous—omnipresent

35. _____ moribund—thriving

36. _____ ambient—pejorative

37. _____ detritus—gambit

38. _____ frenetic—calm

39. _____ flatter—calumniate

40. _____ relentless—inexorable

Words That Describe People

In the space before each word in Column A, write the letter of the item in Column B that best defines it.

Column A	Column B
_____ **41.** agnostic	a. one who hates all people
_____ **42.** penitent	b. a person given to impractical schemes
_____ **43.** charlatan	c. an extremely patriotic person
_____ **44.** visionary	d. a rank beginner
_____ **45.** incumbent	e. a faker
_____ **46.** suppliant	f. a sorcerer
_____ **47.** misanthrope	g. one who implores
_____ **48.** necromancer	h. a current officeholder
_____ **49.** tyro	i. a homeless wanderer
_____ **50.** derelict	j. a religious skeptic
	k. one who regrets misdeeds

Words That Describe Physical Qualities

Some words that describe physical qualities are listed below. In the space before each word in Column A, write the letter of the item in Column B that best defines it.

	Column A	Column B
_____	**51.** oscillate	a. dried out
_____	**52.** desiccated	b. unpleasant to the ear
_____	**53.** refulgent	c. a delicate gradation
_____	**54.** piquant	d. shining brightly
_____	**55.** viscous	e. to raise to a greater height
_____	**56.** congeal	f. lacking clarity
_____	**57.** nuance	g. thick and gluey
_____	**58.** propinquity	h. having a sharp, savory taste
_____	**59.** cacophonous	i. blocking out light
_____	**60.** murky	j. nearness
		k. to swing back and forth
		l. to thicken or coagulate

Words of Evaluation

Some words that indicate favorable or unfavorable evaluations are listed below. They may apply to people, things, language, etc. Write the appropriate word on the line next to each of the following descriptive sentences.

Group A

acquisitive	ethereal	overweening	pedantry
dilettante	garish	sylvan	sacrilege
decorous	carping	felicitous	ebullient
banal	perspicacity	wizened	pariah

61. Even in casual conversation, his language seems to provide exactly the right words for any purpose or situation. _____

62. She is a brilliant executive because she sees through surface appearances and gets right down to the heart of a problem. _____

63. The plot of the soap opera was so familiar, stale, and predictable that we soon stopped watching it. _____

64. She is terribly overdressed—too many jewels, too many bright colors, too many fancy frills. _____

65. Her unfailingly lively and high-spirited personality makes her delightful company. _____

66. Because he has an exaggerated idea of his own importance, he assumes an arrogant attitude in dealing with other people. _____

67. Don't you realize that you will discourage and antagonize people with that constant, petty criticism? _____

68. Her poetry seems to carry beyond the gross substance of this world into the realm of pure spirit. _____

69. He keeps bringing literary allusions into his conversation even though he knows most people won't understand them. _____

70. He has considerable talent as a painter, but since he is unwilling to work at that profession seriously, he will never accomplish much. _____

Group B

lackadaisical	bestial	benign	pusillanimous
redolent	incendiary	sophistry	taciturn
pertinacious	mundane	inane	mendacious
vituperative	incongruous	mutable	ephemeral

71. His greatest weakness is that he does everything in a half-hearted way, without drive or enthusiasm. _____

72. I tried at great length to elicit an opinion from the child, but to no avail. _____

73. Telling lies is not just an occasional thing with him but a way of life. _____

74. The arguments presented in the editorial look good at first, but they are full of deceptive half-truths and clever fallacies. _____

75. Their behavior was so devoid of all moral standards that it seemed subhuman. _____

76. Once Tom begins something, he sticks to it until it's completed. _____

77. His remarks seemed calculated to ignite the heated feelings of his audience. _____

78. Don't you think that a high-rise office tower would look out of place in that residential neighborhood? _____

79. In their efforts to be amusing, they succeed only in being silly and vapid. _____

80. Their policy of "peace at any price" was denounced by the opposition as craven appeasement. _____

Word Associations

*In each of the following, circle the word or expression that best completes the meaning of the sentence or answers the question, with particular reference to the meaning of the word in **boldface** type.*

81. An example of a **euphemism** is
a. "old man" for "father"
b. "boob tube" for "television"
c. "liberate" for "steal"
d. "indeterminate" for "unsettled"

82. An **agnostic** will likely say
a. "I believe."
b. "I don't know."
c. "I'm running late."
d. "My socks are always missing."

83. Typical **amenities** of urban life might include
a. air pollution and litter
b. muggings on the street
c. traffic jams
d. museums and concerts

84. one's **progeny** might include
a. trophies and awards
b. fame and fortune
c. sons and daughters
d. assets and liabilities

85. Which advice would be most suitable for a person who is **recumbent**?
a. "Keep your eye on the ball."
b. "Rise and shine!"
c. "Turn left at the first light."
d. "Grin and bear it."

86. A **figment** usually develops in
a. a factory
b. an orchard
c. the human mind
d. the wild blue yonder

87. A taxi driver who takes you to your destination by a **devious** route may be
a. trying to build up the fare
b. getting rid of you quickly
c. showing off his driving skill
d. saving you money

88. If you **temporize** when a decision is called for, you are
a. acting decisively
b. stalling for time
c. misjudging the situation
d. losing your temper

89. The **motif** of a play refers to its
a. financial backing
b. adaptation for television
c. basic theme
d. cast of characters

90. Which would be a **coup** for a diplomat?
a. arranging an advantageous treaty
b. being sent home
c. taking a vacation
d. retiring after 40 years of service

91. The wisest course of action when confronted by a **juggernaut** is to
a. get out of its way
b. take its picture
c. stand your ground
d. make up your mind

92. **Histrionic** behavior is best suited to
a. the stage
b. the laboratory
c. the classroom
d. the museum

93. A remark you might expect to hear from someone who is **impecunious** is
a. "Let me pay for it."
b. "Keep the change."
c. "Can you change a fifty?"
d. "Why am I always broke?"

94. One generally hopes to **espouse**
   a. accidents
   b. charlatans
   c. specious reasoning
   d. good ideas

95. Primordial times occurred
   a. in Ancient Greece
   b. first
   c. as a result of negligence
   d. during WWII

96. To **allege** that someone is guilty of a crime means that
   a. the person is clearly guilty
   b. the charge remains to be proved
   c. the charge is malicious
   d. an indictment will be handed down

97. Which of the following can be **abrogated**?
   a. mother and child
   b. tonsils and adenoids
   c. the ups and downs of life
   d. contracts and treaties

98. In a **convivial** atmosphere, people may be expected to
   a. suffer from boredom
   b. enjoy themselves
   c. go into shock
   d. show off their erudition

99. You would be well advised not to give **credence** to
   a. your friends
   b. your creditors
   c. a reliable witness
   d. a habitual liar

100. Plaintive tones may issue from you if you
   a. get a good night's sleep
   b. receive a compliment
   c. do well on this Final Mastery Test
   d. do poorly on this Final Mastery Test

The following tabulation lists all the basic words taught in the various units of this book, as well as those introduced in the *Vocabulary of Vocabulary, Working with Analogies, Building with Classical Roots,* and *Enriching Your Vocabulary* sections. Words taught in the units are printed in **boldface** type. The number following each entry indicates the page on which the word is first introduced. Exercises and review materials in which the word also appears are not cited.